ENVIRONMENTAL SCIENCE
IN PERSPECTIVE

Environmental Science in Perspective

by THOMAS G. SPIRO

Professor, Department of Chemistry,
Princeton University

and WILLIAM M. STIGLIANI

Research Associate,
Atmospheric Sciences Research Center,
State University of New York at Albany

State University of New York Press | *Albany*

Grateful acknowledgement is made to the American Chemical Society for permission to reprint illustrative material in this volume.

Published by
State University of New York Press, Albany

© 1980 State University of New York

For information, address State University of New York
Press, State University Plaza, Albany, N.Y., 12246

Library of Congress Cataloging in Publication Data
Spiro, Thomas G   1935–
    Environmental science in perspective.

    Includes bibliographies and index.

    1. Environmental protection—United States.
2. Environmental policy—United States. 3.
Environmental chemistry—United States. I.
Stigliani, William M., joint author. Title.
TD171.S68   363.7   80–24710
ISBN 0-87395-428-9

To our families—

Helen, Michael, and Peter Spiro
Sarah, Anthony, and Nicholas Stigliani

CONTENTS

Preface   ix

Part I. ENERGY   1

   1. Introduction   1
   2. Natural Energy Flows   1
   3. Carbon Cycle   3
   4. Human Energy Consumption   4
   5. Petroleum   6
   6. Survey of Alternative Energy Sources   10
   7. Coal   13
   8. Nuclear Fission   19
   9. Nuclear Power   24
      Pressurized light water reactor   24
      Breeder reactor   24
  10. Weapons Proliferation   26
  11. Radioactivity   28
  12. Fusion Power   33
  13. Solar Energy   37
  14. Energy Storage   42
  15. Thermal Pollution   48
  16. Energy Consumption and Conservation   51
  17. Summary   58
      Problem Set   59
      Suggestions for Further Reading   61

Part II: ATMOSPHERE   67

   1. Earth's Radiation Balance   67
   2. Greenhouse Effect   71
   3. Atmospheric Structure   80
   4. Ozone Chemistry   86
   5. Nitrogen Oxides   87
   6. Chlorofluoromethanes   91
   7. Oxide Chemistry   93
   8. Air Pollution   97
      Carbon monoxide   98
      Nitrogen oxides and hydrocarbons   101

9. Automotive Emissions   107
10. Sulfur Dioxide   113
11. Primary Particles   116
12. Summary   118
Problem Set   119
Suggestions for Further Reading   121

Part III: HYDROSPHERE   125

1. Water Resources   125
2. Acidity   127
3. Hardness   133
4. Eutrophication   137
5. The Oceans   144
6. Sewage Treatment   147
Domestic sewage treatment   148
Industrial wastewater treatment   155
7. Drinking Water Supplies   158
8. Agricultural Pollution   159
9. Summary   161
Problem Set   162
Suggestions for Further Reading   164

Part IV: BIOSPHERE   167

1. Nitrogen and Food Production   167
2. Nutrition   175
3. Insecticides   180
4. Inadvertent Contamination by Toxic Organic Chemicals   190
5. Contamination by Toxic Metals   197
Lead   198
Mercury   203
Cadmium   207
6. Cancer   208
7. Conclusion   214
Problem Set   215
Suggestions for Further Reading   217

Appendix   223
Index   227

PREFACE

Several years have elapsed since a wave of concern for environmental causes swept across the United States, culminating in the celebration of Earth Day in 1970. The enthusiasm of the moment has ebbed, but environmental issues have not gone away and there is no prospect that they will disappear in the foreseeable future. The debates over what to do about these issues have steadily grown, in volume and in complexity, as hard choices are faced. This is also true in other countries where the initial wave of environmental concern was less pronounced or absent. The environment is now ineradicably lodged in our consciousness, even if our perceptions of it change with time, as indeed they must.

The aim of this book is to make sense of the environmental debates by examining the natural cycles that human activities may be upsetting. The issues involved are very difficult. Should the plutonium breeder reactor be developed? Do fluorocarbon aerosol cans pose a serious threat to the atmosphere's ozone layer? Are streams fouled with detergent phosphates? Is saccharin a dangerous food additive? None of these questions has an easy answer, but in following the arguments pro and con, it helps to understand the natural balances that are threatened.

At a deeper level, it is highly satisfying to understand the world we inhabit in terms that are relevant to our age. To an important extent these terms are chemical in nature. Plutonium, fluorocarbons, phosphates, and saccharin are all chemical substances. We live in a chemical age, not only in the narrow sense that industrial society produces new chemicals in abundance, but also in the broader sense that we have come to a general understanding of the molecular relationships that underlie and determine natural phenomena. There are still innumerable gaps in our knowledge, but the chemical context of the natural world is reasonably coherent and provides the unifying principle of this book.

Chemistry is not, of course, the only perspective on environmental issues. Ecological, social, political, and economic questions are all vitally bound up in them, and some of these necessarily enter into any description of environmental issues. No attempt has been made to keep them out of the present discussion, even though the primary emphasis is on chemistry.

This book is structured in four sections: energy, atmosphere, hydrosphere, and biosphere. These divisions are for our convenience; environmental problems do not fall into neat categories, and we can expect them to pop up in more than one place in the book, as in real life.

PART I | ENERGY

1 | Introduction

The question of energy use underlies virtually all environmental issues. We are coming to realize that supplies of energy that we have taken for granted will be exhausted before long. At the same time there is a heightened awareness of adverse impacts on the environment that stem from increased energy consumption, such as air and water pollution, the spread of toxic materials, and the scarring of land by strip mining. Increasingly, there seems to be a clash between those who place greatest emphasis on maintaining an expanding supply of cheap energy, and those who are more concerned with the environmental costs of such expansion. In this part of the book, we will explore the background of energy production and energy consumption. We will see that protecting the environment and meeting the energy needs of society are not necessarily incompatible, and that there are avenues for resolving the apparent conflict.

2 | Natural Energy Flows

It is instructive to view our energy problems against a backdrop of the continual and massive daily flow of energy that occurs at the surface of the earth. This flow is diagrammed in Figure 1.1. In the figure, the magnitudes of the energy fluxes are given in calories per year. A calorie is the amount of energy needed to raise the temperature of 1 g of water by $1°$ C (see the Appendix for a comprehensive listing of the common forms and units of energy). The sun radiates a nearly unimaginable number of calories every year—28×10^{32}.

A very small fraction of the total, 13×10^{23} calories per year, is intercepted by the earth, which is 93 million miles from the sun. Of this quantity, about 34% is reflected or scattered back into space. This fraction is called the *albedo,* and it determines the total energy balance of the earth. The figure of 34% is an average value; it is difficult to estimate accurately because the reflectivity of the earth varies a great deal from place to place. The ocean reflects very little of the light, about

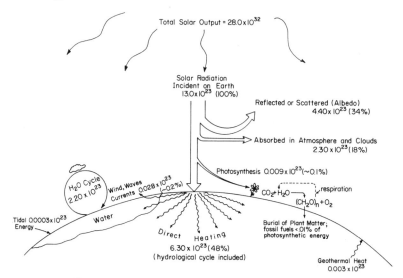

Figure 1.1   Yearly Energy Fluxes on Earth (in calories)

6%, whereas areas covered with snow reflect a large fraction, 80-90%; land areas an amount somewhere in between, depending on their covering, such as vegetation or sand. The extent of cloudiness is also an important determinant of the albedo.

The rest of the light is absorbed by the earth or its atmosphere, and its energy is used to drive a number of natural processes. About 48% is converted directly into heat. More than one-third of this is used to drive the hydrologic cycle—the massive evaporation and precipitation of water, upon which we depend for our freshwater supplies. While it takes 1 calorie to heat a gram of water 1° C, 540 calories is required to convert that same gram of water to vapor. This is called the *latent heat* of water. The same 540 calories of heat is released when a gram of water vapor condenses into rain; this is the reason that rainfall is associated with storms. A huge amount of energy is released by even a modest rainfall. The estimate of the total amount of energy involved in the hydrologic cycle is based on the heat released by the known amount of rainfall plus the energy required to raise the water up into the atmosphere. We use the energy available from falling water through dams and hydroelectric projects, which constitute an indirect tapping of the daily solar energy flow.

A small fraction, about 0.2%, of the incident sunlight is converted into the energy of wind and water currents and waves. An even smaller fraction, 0.1%, is used by green plants and algae in photosynthesis, which is vital for our food supply. A tiny part of the earth's energy comes from nonsolar sources: tidal energy, which arises from the gravitational attraction between the moon and the earth, and geothermal heat, which emanates from the earth's molten core.

3 | Carbon Cycle

The fraction of the sunlight that is used by plants in photosynthesis is converted to chemical energy. It is stored in the form of carbohydrates such as glucose, surose, and starch. They contain two atoms of hydrogen and one of oxygen for every atom of carbon. The carbohydrates are formed by the reduction of carbon dioxide, and at the same time, water is oxidized to form molecular oxygen. The reduced carbon is reoxidized to carbon dioxide in the process of respiration, which provides the energy needs of biological organisms. Plants themselves use up about 20% of their carbohydrates for their own energy needs. The remainder, which represents stored photochemical energy, is called *net primary productivity*.

The processes of photosynthesis and respiration are balanced closely, and the cycling of carbon between the carbon dioxide of the atmosphere and the reduced organic compounds of biological organisms is essentially a closed loop. A very small fraction of plant and animal matter, however, estimated at less than 1 part in 10,000, is buried in the earth and removed from contact with atmospheric oxygen. Over the millennia this small fraction adds up to a large amount of reduced carbon compounds, and it is generally felt that essentially all the oxygen in the atmosphere has been produced by this process. The original atmosphere of the earth is thought to have been devoid of oxygen. It was the evolution of green plants, some 600 million years ago, that led to the accumulation of oxygen through photosynthesis and the burial of organic matter.

Some of the buried carbon compounds accumulated in deposits and were subjected to high temperatures and pressures in the earth's crust. They became coal, oil, and gas, which we now use to fuel our industrial civilization. We are, therefore, living off the store of solar energy of past ages.

Since the burial of organic compounds is thought to have been responsible for the evolution of atmospheric oxygen, you might wonder whether we are in danger of using up our oxygen supply if these same compounds are now being mined and burned as fuel. Evidently only a small fraction of the buried carbon is available in recoverable deposits of fuel; the rest is presumably widely dispersed in the earth's crust. The total energy that is estimated to be available in recoverable fossil fuels is about 0.7×10^{23} calories. This is about 100 times the annual net primary productivity. Burning all this fuel would consume about 1.6% of the oxygen in the atmosphere. While the percentage decrease in oxygen would be small enough to be scarcely noticeable, the increase in carbon dioxide would be very significant. The concentration of carbon dioxide in the atmosphere is very much lower than that of oxygen. Converting 1.6% of the oxygen to carbon dioxide would increase its concentration by a factor of nearly ten. This has serious implications for warming up the earth's surface through the greenhouse effect, as we will see in the next part of the book.

4 | Human Energy Consumption

Table 1.1 shows some of the quantities that have been discussed. It also shows that the total energy consumed by the burning of fossil fuels amounted to 6.0 × 10^{19} calories in 1975. This is about one-twelfth of the net primary productivity. The energy content of the food consumed by human beings in the same year was only 3.2 × 10^{18} calories. This is 2.2 million calories per person per day, which is close to the minimum estimated to be required for the daily energy needs of humans. Some people consume much more than this, while a large fraction of the world's population has an inadequate diet. (It should be noted that measurements of nutritionists are usually in Calories with a capital C, which are 1,000 ordinary calories. The average human diet is usually given as 2,200 Calories. This notation can be a source of confusion.)

Table 1.1 also shows that the total external energy consumed in the United States was about 30% of the worldwide energy consumption in 1975, although the United States had only 5% of the total population. The growth curves for both U.S. and world energy consumptions are given in Figure 1.2. World energy consumption has been increasing at a faster rate than that of the United States, but so has the population in the rest of the world. Both curves in the figure show nearly exponential growth, which means that consumption is increasing at a rate that is proportional to the amount already present; there is a constant percentage increase from year to year. The curves in Figure 1.2 show that this type of growth is not reasonable for the long term. Something that increases at a rate of 4% a year takes only 18 years to double, and then another 18 years to double again. Nothing in the natural world can grow through too many doubling periods before it runs into some constraint. Eventually all exponential growth curves have to level off, and the growth of energy consumption is no exception. In the long run,

Table 1.1   Global Energy Fluxes

Energy Transfer	Rate (calories/year)
Energy radiated by the sun into space	2.8 × 10^{33}
Solar energy incident on earth	1.3 × 10^{24}
Solar energy affecting earth's climate and biosphere	8.6 × 10^{23}
Energy used to evaporate water	2.2 × 10^{23}
Solar energy used in photosynthesis	9.4 × 10^{20}
Energy used in net primary productivity	7.2 × 10^{20}
Energy conducted from earth's interior to its surface	3.0 × 10^{20}
Total energy consumed externally by humans, 1975	6.0 × 10^{19}
Energy content of food consumed by humans, 1975	3.2 × 10^{18}
Total energy consumed in the United States, 1975	1.8 × 10^{19}
Electrical energy produced in the United States, 1975	1.7 × 10^{18}

Source: Adapted from J. Harte and R. H. Socolow, *Patient Earth* (New York: Holt, Rinehart and Winston, Inc., 1971), p. 277; 1975 values from "World Energy Supplies, 1971–1975," U.N. Statistical Papers, Series J, No. 20 (New York: United Nations, 1977).

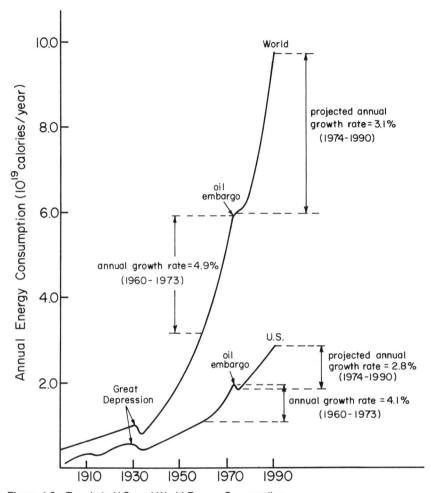

Figure 1.2   Trends in U.S. and World Energy Consumption

Source: Data up to 1970 taken from J. Harte and R. H. Socolow, *Patient Earth* (New York: Holt, Rinehart and Winston, Inc., 1971), p. 285. Data from 1971 to 1975 from "World Energy Supplies, 1971–1975," U.N. Statistical Papers, Series J, No. 20 (New York: United Nations, 1977). Projected U.S. values from "National Energy Outlook, Executive Summary, 1976," Federal Energy Administration (Washington, D.C.: U.S. Government Printing Office, 1976). Projected world values estimated from "Energy Facts II," Subcommittee on Energy Research, Development and Demonstration, U. S. House of Representatives, 94th Congress, Library of Congress, Serial H, August 1975, p. 44.

energy inputs and outputs for human society must be in a steady state, just as they are for the earth as a whole. The present era of rapid energy use represents a transition to a new level of energy consumption. There remains considerable debate, however, about what that level will be and at what rate it is to be attained. Already the immediate projections for the next decade or so are for lower annual growth rates for both U.S. and world energy consumption.

5 | Petroleum

The most immediate constraint on energy growth is the availability of petroleum and natural gas. The Industrial Revolution was initially fueled by coal, but we have increasingly switched to oil and gas, which are cleaner fuels and are transported more easily. Figure 1.3 illustrates that coal displaced fuel wood as an energy source in the late 1800s, but since the early part of this century it has been losing ground to gas and oil, which now account for nearly 80% of total energy consumption in the United States.

Oil is a complex mixture of hydrocarbons, which are molecules that contain only carbon and hydrogen. Figure 1.4 shows a diagram of an oil refinery, in which the various fractions of petroleum are separated by distillation. The table at the bottom of the figure gives the range of molecular sizes for the different fractions. The lightest liquid fraction is used for gasoline, the heaviest for lubricating oil.

We have become very dependent on petroleum and gas, but the rate of increase

Figure 1.3 U.S. Energy Consumption Patterns

Source: "Historical Statistics of the United States Bureau of the Census," U.S. Bureau of Mines (Washington, D.C., 1974).

Chemical Composition

fraction	carbon atoms	molecular weight	boiling range, °C
gaseous	1 – 4	16 – 58	-126 – 0
gasoline	5 – 12	72 – 170	0 – 204
kerosene	10 – 16	156 – 226	180 – 274
gas oil	15 – 22	212 – 294	260 – 371
lube oil	19 – 35	268 – 492	338 – 468
residue	36 – 90	492 – 1262	468 +

Figure 1.4   Crude Oil Refining

in production has begun to fall off, at least for U.S. reserves. Figure 1.5 shows past consumption and production curves, and projects two different estimates for future domestic production. There is some controversy about the total size of the reserves, which are represented by the area under the production curves in Figure 1.5. The lower curve is projected from a continuation of present trends, which

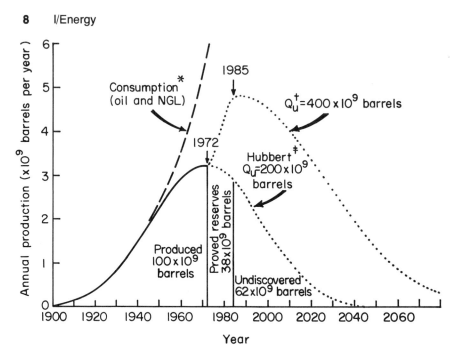

Figure 1.5 History and Trends for U.S. Oil Production

*Consumption curve includes crude oil and natural gas liquids (NGL), the latter accounting for about 15 percent of consumption.

†Q_u refers to the total quantity of produced oil—proved reserves plus potentially undiscovered reserves.

‡Hubbert estimate of Q_u from M. K. Hubbert, *Am. Assoc. Petrol. Geol. Bull.* 51 (1967):2207.

Source: R. R. Berg, J. C. Calhoun, and R. L. Whiting, *Science* 184 (1974):332. Copyright 1974 by the American Association for the Advancement of Science.

show a decrease in the rate of productive drilling in the United States. It is possible that drilling rates are influenced to some extent by the availability of less expensive foreign oil, however, and the upper curve represents a more optimistic assessment of total U.S. reserves based on a different set of assumptions. In any case, the amount of oil available is clearly inadequate to meet the ever-increasing demand.

The prognosis for worldwide petroleum reserves is similar. As shown in Figure 1.6 world production has increased more than fivefold from 1950 to 1976, when it amounted to 22×10^9 barrels. Table 1.2 lists the petroleum reserves for various areas of the world, as well as the production and consumption patterns. The total estimate of easily recoverable petroleum, perhaps 800×10^9 barrels, is only 36 times the amount produced in 1976. Among the four largest consumers, the United States, Western Europe, the communist countries, and Japan, only the

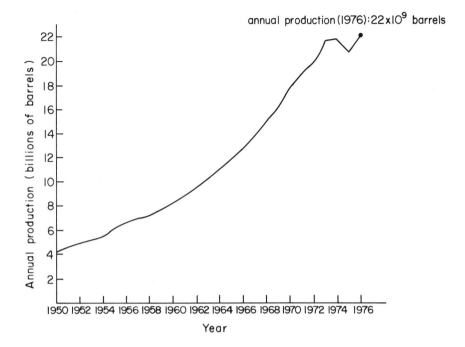

annual production (1976): 22×10⁹ barrels

Figure 1.6   Trends in Worldwide Oil Production, 1950–1976*

*Includes crude petroleum and natural gas liquids.
Source: From data compiled in "World Energy Supplies, 1971–1975," U.N. Statistical Papers, Series J, No. 20 (New York: United Nations, 1977), Table I.

communist countries produce enough petroleum to supply their present needs. The United States, Western Europe, and especially Japan must continue to depend on the surplus oil of other areas, the Middle East in particular, to supplement their internal supplies. A large oil deposit has recently been found in Mexico, and similar discoveries may occur in China and other unexplored regions, and these will extend the world's oil supplies somewhat. Nevertheless, the surpluses are dwindling and will certainly be depleted sometime in the next century.

The energy crisis, then, really boils down to the question of how to respond to this fairly imminent exhaustion of our most versatile and convenient fuel. While there are many conceivable alternatives, as we shall see, the choices to be made are difficult and complex because of the massiveness of the energy supply system, which undergirds so many of our activities, and the long lead times needed to produce any significant change in this system.

Table 1.2   Worldwide Petroleum Resources

Distribution of Easily Extractable Reserves	
Area	Reserve (barrels)
Middle East	326.3×10^9
Communist countries*	101.1×10^9
Africa	60.6×10^9
Mexico†	$50{-}200 \times 10^9$
United States	31.3×10^9
Other countries in Western Hemisphere	35.8×10^9
Western Europe	24.5×10^9
Far East and Oceania	19.4×10^9
Japan	Negligible
Estimated total	$\overline{649{-}799 \times 10^9}$

Distribution of Consumption and Production, 1975		
Area	Consumption (barrels)	Production (barrels)
United States	5.3×10^9	3.6×10^9
Western Europe	4.1×10^9	0.3×10^9 (1976)
Communist countries	3.7×10^9	4.5×10^9
Japan	1.5×10^9	Negligible
All other areas	3.5×10^9	12.6×10^9

*China may have significant untapped reserves.
†A new large reserve has recently been discovered; its size is presently uncertain. [See *Science* 202 (1978): 1261.]
Source: Top table: U.S. Department of the Interior, press release, *New York Times,* July 31, 1977. Bottom table: "World Energy Supplies, 1971–1975," U.N. Statistical Papers, Series J, No. 20 (New York: United Nations, 1977), Tables I and II.

6 | Survey of Alternative Energy Sources

Table 1.3 is a survey of the energy sources potentially or actually available to the United States. There are two kinds of sources: depletable and renewable. The former, tabulated in the first part, includes all the fossil fuel deposits, including coal, petroleum, and natural gas, as well as oil shales, which are rocky deposits impregnated with oil. Depletable resources also include nuclear fuel, uranium, and possibly deuterium for the fusion reaction. Renewable sources, shown in the second part of Table 1.3, include sunlight and various indirect forms of solar energy such as hydropower, wind power, the energy stored in photosynthesis, and tidal energy. The estimates of the amounts of energy available are expressed in units of the national energy consumption in 1975. Thus the numbers in the columns are equivalent to the number of years the resource would last if all our energy came from that source alone, and if consumption remained at the 1975 level. In the first part, the numbers in the middle column show the relative amounts of depletable resources that are available at current energy prices in the United States. Coal is much more abundant than petroleum and natural gas, and could last for many decades even at present energy prices. The amount of energy available in uranium deposits is relatively small, comparable to that stored in the oil and gas reserves, unless the breeder reactor comes into use; this question will be examined shortly. Geothermal energy is listed as a depletable energy source because, although energy flows continuously from the interior of the earth, it can be extracted practically only from concentrated deposits where it has been stored in hot rocks and water. At present prices, this appears to be a fairly small resource.

The right-hand column lists the resources that are potentially available at greater expense. These figures are much less certain than those in the middle column. Fuel deposits come in a wide range of concentrations, and the amount that is economically recoverable obviously depends on what price it makes sense to pay. The eventual limit is a concentration so low that it takes more energy to obtain the fuel than is recovered from it. This depends, however, on the efficiency of the extraction technology, which can change with time. Oil shale is a good example of this uncertainty. Very large amounts of hydrocarbons are trapped in oil shale, but at the moment extracting them requires that the shale be crushed and heated to quite high temperatures, thus limiting the attractiveness of the process from both an economic and an energy utilization point of view. This situation is changing as more effective means are found to extract the hydrocarbons from the rock. The amounts of energy that are potentially available from the fusion reaction dwarfs any of the other figures, if this technology can be made to work.

The numbers for the renewable sources in the second part of Table 1.3 represent the amounts of energy available per year. The annual solar flux is much larger than the total energy consumption. The main problem in harnessing the sun's rays is that they are widely dispersed over the surface of the land and are easily obstructed by clouds. Also, the sun shines during only 12 hours a day on the average, and much less than this in the winter at high latitudes.

Wind power represents a smaller, but still significant, resource. The technology for extracting the energy from wind is available now and may soon be practical. Again, the main problem is the intermittent nature of wind. A comparable resource is the ocean thermal gradients. The sun heats the surface of the ocean, producing a thermal gradient with respect to the underlying waters. In the tropical oceans the temperature difference is 20° C between the surface and the waters 1,000 m below. A large amount of energy is stored in this gradient, which is available on a continuous basis. The temperature difference is rather small,

Table 1.3   Estimates of Sources of Energy in the United States*

	Depletable Sources†	
Resource	Known and Economically Recoverable Reserves	Potential Reserves under Certain Economic and Technological Conditions
Petroleum	11.2	21–37‡
Natural gas	10.9	20–36‡
Coal	169	~440‡
Oil shale	16.9	82
Nuclear fission		
Conventional reactors	25.3	
Breeder technology		~1,800
Nuclear fusion		
Deuterium-deuterium		~10^9§
Deuterium-tritium		~275‖
Geothermal heat		
Steam, hot water, and		
geopressured fluids	0.2§	~11#
Hot rock		>100#

	Renewable Resources§
Resource	Amount of Energy Continuously Supplied Per Year
Solar radiation	650
Wind power	4
Ocean thermal gradients	>5
Hydropower	0.12
Photosynthesis	0.20
Organic wastes	0.1
Tidal energy	0.1

*Numbers in both tables are in units of total U.S. energy consumption in 1975, or 1.79×10^{19} calories. They are equivalent to the number of years the resource would last if all energy came from that source alone.

†Except as noted, data are from "A National Plan for Energy Research, Development and Demonstration: Creating Energy Choices for the Future," Vol. I, ERDA (Washington, D.C.: U.S. Government Printing Office, 1975), chap. II.

‡"Energy Facts, II" Subcommittee on Energy Research, Development, and Demonstration, U.S. House of Representatives, 94th Congress, Library of Congress, Serial H, August 1975, p. 44.

§Adapted from A. Hammond, *Science* 177 (1972): 875, using 1975 energy consumption value.

‖Assumes tritium is obtained from lithium-6, the U.S. supply of which is ~74×10^9 g; from A. Hammond, *Science* 191 (1976): 1037.

#D. E. White and D. L. Williams, eds., "Assessment of Geothermal Resources of the U.S.—1975," Geological Survey, Circular 726 (Washington, D.C., 1975).

however, and the efficiency with which the energy can be extracted is very low. Also, the energy would have to be transported over large distances.

The amount of energy potentially available in hydropower is limited, and most of the suitable dam sites have already been developed. Photosynthesis taking place on the surface of the United States represents a relatively small fraction of the total energy consumption, but there are possibilities for increasing the photosynthetic yield and putting it to better use. Organic wastes represent that part of the current yield that is discarded. Converting these wastes to fuel would solve an environmental problem as well as contribute to the energy supply. Tidal energy is difficult to harness and represents a relatively unimportant resource.

7 | Coal

Having looked at the overall picture with respect to the magnitude of energy resources that are potential alternatives to oil and gas, let us now examine these forms of energy in greater detail. The first one to look at is coal, which is, of course, a resource that is already in use.

The size of the U.S. coal reserve is substantially larger than that of oil and gas. There are potential coal deposits to meet the total 1975 U.S. domestic energy consumption at current prices for 169 years and considerably more than that which would be more expensive to extract. Coal is also substantially more abundant than oil or gas on a worldwide basis.

As shown in Figure 1.7, worldwide recoverable reserves of coal are estimated to be about 7.4×10^{12} metric tons, with the Soviet Union and the United States owning about 75% of the supply. Countries in Latin America and other parts of the world would have to depend heavily on foreign imports if coal were to become the chief energy currency. The total coal reserve is equivalent to about 4.7×10^{22} calories. This is almost 800 times the value of world energy consumption from all fuel sources in 1975.

One major problem with coal is that it is a dirty fuel to burn. Of particular concern is the sulfur dioxide emitted, which is a serious health hazard in urban areas. Also, being a solid, coal is much less convenient to use than petroleum or natural gas. One can imagine the inconvenience of running automobiles with steam engines into which the coal has to be shoveled. Even for railroad locomotives, the advantages of liquid fuel long ago led to the replacement of the steam engine by the diesel engine.

It is possible to convert coal to liquid or gaseous fuels by appropriate chemistry. The reduced carbon in coal, in which most of its energy content resides, can be transformed into hydrocarbon molecules which are either liquid or gaseous, depending on their molecular weights and structures. The simplest hydrocarbon molecule, and the one for which the most practical current coal conversion technology has been developed, is methane, CH_4. Figure 1.8 shows the chemical reactions, in simplified form, that are associated with coal gasification technology. Equation (1) shows the hydrogasification reaction, the conversion of carbon to methane by the addition of molecular hydrogen. To run this reaction, a supply of hydrogen is needed. The most abundant source of hydrogen and the only one that is practical to use on a wide scale is water. In order to produce hydrogen, water must be reduced. Equations (2) and (3) show that the same carbon found in coal can serve as a reducing agent, producing successively carbon monoxide and then carbon dioxide, with the release of two molecules of hydrogen. The overall reaction, reaction (4), involves a combination of two atoms of carbon with two molecules of water to produce one molecule of methane and one of carbon dioxide. It appears that we are throwing half the carbon away to produce methane, but the energy value of the methane is about twice that of carbon, and if the reaction could be carried out with 100% efficiency, no energy would be lost. In practice, of course, this efficiency cannot be achieved and some fraction of the energy content in coal must be used in its conversion to gas.

An additional advantage of coal gasification is that it makes the removal of sulfur quite straightforward, as shown in reactionns (5) and (6) in Figure 1.8. In

Figure 1.7 Remaining Identified Worldwide Coal Reserves*

*Total reserve includes sources that could be made available under certain economic and technological conditions.

Gasification:
  Individual steps
    Methane production

$$C + 2H_2 \quad \rightarrow \quad CH_4 \qquad \text{hydrogasification (1)}$$

  Hydrogen production

$$C + H_2O \quad \rightarrow \quad CO + H_2 \qquad \text{water-gas reaction (2)}$$

$$CO + H_2O \quad \rightarrow \quad CO_2 + H_2 \qquad \text{water-gas shift (3)}$$

Overall reaction: (1) + (2) + (3)

$$2C + 2H_2O \quad \xrightarrow{900° C} \quad CH_4 + CO_2 \qquad (4)$$

Desulfurization:

$$S + H_2 \quad \rightarrow \quad H_2S \qquad (5)$$

$$CaCO_3 + H_2S \quad \rightleftharpoons \quad CaS + CO_2 + H_2O \qquad (6)$$

Liquefaction:
  Hydrocarbon liquids by Fischer-Tropsch synthesis

$$nCO + (2n + 1)H_2 \quad \xrightarrow[\sim 15\ \text{atm}]{\substack{\text{catalyst} \\ 200°\ C}} \quad C_nH_{2n+2} + nH_2O \qquad (7)$$

Methanol synthesis

$$CO + 2H_2 \quad \xrightarrow[>200\ \text{atm}]{\substack{\text{catalyst} \\ >300°\ C}} \quad CH_3OH \qquad (8)$$

Direct catalytic hydrogenation

$$nC + (n + 1)H_2 \quad \xrightarrow[>100\ \text{atm}]{\substack{\text{catalyst} \\ 450°\ C}} \quad C_nH_{2n+2} \qquad (9)$$

Figure 1.8 Conversion of Coal to Natural Gas and Liquid Fuels

the presence of the hydrogen that is needed to convert carbon to methane, sulfur is converted to hydrogen sulfide, which is easily trapped in a calcium carbonate bed, with the release of carbon dioxide and water, as in reaction (6). This reaction is reversible on heating, and the hydrogen sulfide can be regenerated in another location and used in a variety of industrial processes such as the production of sulfuric acid. Since the sulfur in coal would otherwise be converted to sulfur dioxide on combustion, coal gasification has the attractive feature of converting a source of pollution into a resource.

Natural gas, which contains mostly methane, is the most convenient energy source for heating and for generating electricity. It is also transported quite easily. Coal gasification would augment the dwindling supplies of this desirable fuel. Once carbon monoxide is generated via reaction (2), it is possible to convert it to higher molecular weight hydrocarbons, in the gasoline range, using what is

Table 1.4   Composition and Heat Content of Common Coals Found in the United States

Rank	Location by State	Moisture	Volatile Matter	Fixed Carbon	Ash	Heating Value (calories/g)
			Chemical Analysis			
Anthracite	Pa.	4.4%	4.8%	81.8%	9.0%	7,288
Bituminous						
Low volatile	Md.	2.3	19.6	65.8	12.3	7,338
High volatile	Ky.	3.2	36.8	56.4	3.6	7,821
Subbituminous	Wyo.	22.2	32.2	40.3	4.3	5,334
Lignite	N. Dak.	36.8	27.8	30.2	5.2	3,863

Source: U.S. Bureau of Mines, Information Circular, No. 769, 1954.

known as Fischer-Tropsch chemistry, shown in reaction (7). This technology is not so advanced as coal gasification, and it is somewhat less efficient in its energy requirements. Another alternative is to convert carbon monoxide to methanol, CH_3OH, via reaction (8). Methanol is nearly as useful as gasoline in internal combustion engines. Finally, recent technology has been developed for the direct catalytic hydrogenation of coal to produce liquid hydrocarbons, under the conditions shown in reaction (9).

It is possible in principle to switch from an oil economy to a coal economy with the assurance of a much larger resource base. Coal can be burned directly in stationary furnaces and can be gasified or liquefied for use as a fuel in transportation. This scenario, however, has formidable problems. In the first place, coal is quite variable in its composition and also in its geographic distribution. Table 1.4 lists various kinds of coal in order of their carbon content. The heating value of the coal depends on the amount of reduced carbon and hydrogen in relation to the amount of nonfuel constituents, such as water, listed in the moisture column, and inorganic materials, listed under the heading of ash. Volatile matter refers to the hydrocarbons, mostly methane, that are released upon heating, while fixed carbon is the combustible fuel that is left behind after the volatile matter is removed. There are basically four types of coal distributed throughout the United States as shown in Figure 1.9. The hard coal, anthracite, is found in only a few deposits in the East and constitutes a small fraction of the total resource. The extensive coal deposits in Appalachia and the Midwest are bituminous or soft coal, which has a relatively high fraction of volatile matter. Western coal reserves amount to more than half the total and consist of subbituminous coal and lignite. These have a high water content, and therefore their heating value per gram is much less than that of eastern and midwestern coal. This factor magnifies the expense involved in transporting western coal to major urban centers.

The sulfur content is highest in the bituminous coals of the East and lowest in the subbituminous and lignite coals of the West. The table in Figure 1.9 shows

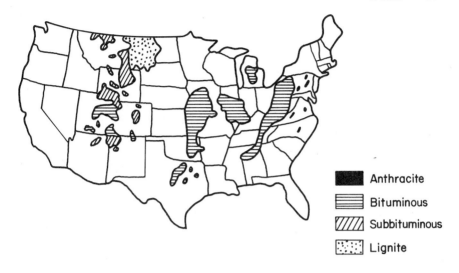

Anthracite
Bituminous
Subbituminous
Lignite

Average Sulfur Content of Coal by Rank

Rank	% of total coal reserves	% with sulfur content >1%
Anthracite	0.9	2.9
Bituminous	46.0	70.2
Subbituminous	24.7	0.4
Lignite	28.4	9.3
Total, all ranks	100	35.0

Figure 1.9 Coal Distribution in the United States and Average Sulfur Content of Coal
Source: P. Averitt, U.S. Geological Survey, Bulletin 1136, January 1960.

that 70% of the bituminous but only 0.4% of the subbituminous and 9% of the lignite have more than 1% sulfur by weight. U.S. air quality standards set an upper limit for the amount of sulfur dioxide that can be emitted per calorie of coal energy consumed in power plants. Currently it stands at 1.2 mg of sulfur dioxide emitted per kilocalorie of coal burned. At first glance it may appear that western coals are safer for the environment because of their lower sulfur content per unit weight. Actually, there is no marked advantage to western coals, since their low percentage of sulfur is offset by their low heating value. Consequently, more western coal has to be burned to obtain a given amount of energy. Moreover, much of the sulfur in bituminous coal is present as iron sulfide, the mineral pyrites, which can be removed fairly readily by grinding and screening the coal, whereas the sulfur of western coal is almost all organically bound and cannot be removed in this fashion.

A major cost of coal consumption, in both economic and human terms, is the mining operation. Deep mines are expensive to dig and maintain and notoriously dangerous for miners. Accident rates have historically been high, and black lung disease is a serious occupational hazard. Compensatory payments to U.S. miners who suffer from black lung disease is expected to reach $8 billion by 1980. The recent operating experience of some mines shows, however, that the institution of proper safety procedures can cut the accident rate to those of other industries, and that exposure to coal dust can be significantly reduced. In recent years strip mining, in which the surface soils are removed to expose the seams of coal, has increased steadily in importance and now accounts for almost half the total coal produced. Strip mining is safer and costs much less than deep mining, but takes its toll on the ecology of the land. In Appalachia, strip mining on steep hillsides has led to serious erosion and fouling of local waterways. Equally serious problems are encountered in the western states, where the topsoil is thin and the climate is semiarid. With considerable effort and expense, it is possible to restore strip-mined land to productive use, although restoration to the original condition is problematic.

Probably the most difficult environmental questions concern the exploitation of the extensive western U.S. coal deposits. As we have seen, these deposits are relatively low grade and are expensive to transport over long distances. The energy companies are thinking of building coal conversion plants on site and shipping the upgraded fuel, gas or liquid, instead. The difficulty here is the lack of water in the region. As shown in Figure 1.8, coal gasification requires the generation of hydrogen, which only water can supply in sufficient quantities. Two molecules of water are required for each molecule of methane that is produced. Large quantities of water are required for the reactions and for cooling. Additional water would be required for the mining activities themselves and for reclamation of the strip-mined land. Water resources, however, have historically been in short supply in the western part of the United States. A study by the National Academy of Sciences concluded that there might be adequate water for mining but not for the coal conversion industries that are envisioned.* This is disputed, however, by the energy companies. The mining activities also present difficult problems. Many of the seams of coal in the West are also natural aquifers, and their stripping might disrupt water tables and water circulation

---

*"Study Committee on the Potential for Rehabilitating Lands Surface Mined for Coal in the Western United States" (Washington, D.C.: National Academy of Sciences, 1973).

patterns. Also, the social and economic disruption of small communities in the West as large energy enterprises get under way has recently caused much concern.

8 | Nuclear Fission

Nuclear power is presently the most highly developed alternative to energy supplied by coal. The one significant form of energy on earth that is not related to the sun either directly or indirectly is energy that resides in the nuclei of atoms. Nuclei are made up of collections of protons and neutrons called *nucleons,* which are held together by strong nuclear forces. As indicated in Table 1.5, protons are positively charged, while neutrons are neutral. The number of protons determines the number of negatively charged electrons that surround the nucleus, which determines the chemical properties of the element. The mass of the atoms is determined by the total number of nucleons. Isotopes of the elements, such as He-3 and He-4, have the same number of protons but different numbers of neutrons. The nuclear forces increase as the number of nucleons increases, but so does the electrostatic repulsion among the positively charged protons. Figure 1.10 is a graph of the total binding energy per nucleon with increasing mass of the nuclei. The highest nuclear stability is associated with atoms of intermediate atomic weight, in the vicinity of the element iron. For heavier elements, the repulsive forces gradually become more important, and elements heavier than bismuth, with 83 protons, are unstable. As illustrated in Figure 1.11, these heavier elements split off alpha particles, which are nuclei of the element helium

Table 1.5 Simple Nuclear Particles

Type	Schematic Representation	Charge	Mass*	Chemical Symbol†
Neutron	●	0	1.0087	$_0^1 n$
Proton	⊕	+1	1.0078	$_1^1 p$
Helium-4 (alpha particle)		+2	4.0026	$_2^4 He$
Helium-3		+2	3.0160	$_2^3 He$

*In atomic mass units (amu), where 1 amu = 1.6606×10^{-24} g.
†The superscript is the *mass number,* equivalent to the number of protons and neutrons in the nucleus; the subscript is the *atomic number,* equivalent to the number of protons. $_2^4 He$ and $_2^3 He$ are isotopes.

that contain two protons and two neutrons. Some of these heavy elements can also undergo spontaneous fission, in which they split into two daughter atoms of intermediate atomic weights, with the release of a great deal of energy.

Isotopes of the elements can also be unstable with respect to the number of neutrons they contain. The ratio of neutrons to protons needed for stability increases slowly with increasing atomic number, as shown in Figure 1.12. Isotopes with too many neutrons can convert a neutron to a proton with the emission of a high-energy electron, called a beta ray. This corresponds to moving diagonally across the graph of Figure 1.12 toward the stability curve. Both alpha particle emission and nuclear fission produce isotopes with too many neutrons, and the products therefore are beta emitters. Unstable isotopes can also release some of their energy in the form of high-energy electromagnetic radiation, called gamma rays. The rate of nuclear decay, whether by alpha, beta, or gamma emission, varies from one isotope to another. It is generally expressed as the half-life, which is the time required for half of the nuclei to decay, as illustrated in Figure 1.13 for plutonium. Plutonium no longer exists naturally in the earth's crust but is produced in nuclear reactors. Half the plutonium that was initially formed on earth decayed after 24,360 years. After 100,000 years, i.e., approxi-

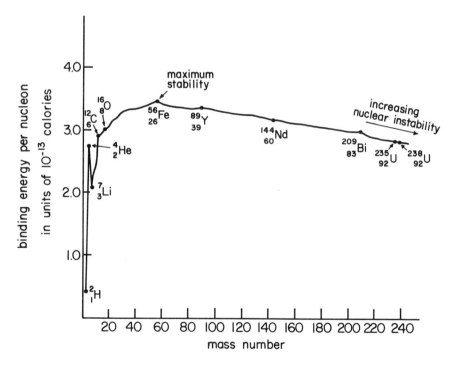

Figure 1.10 Nuclear Binding Energy Curve

Alpha Decay

example:

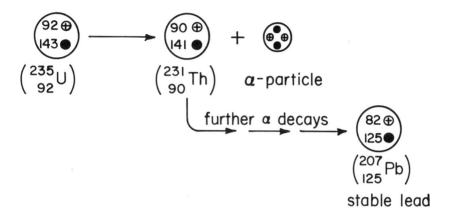

$$\left(^{235}_{92}U\right) \longrightarrow \left(^{231}_{90}Th\right) + \alpha\text{-particle}$$

further α decays

$$\left(^{207}_{125}Pb\right)$$

stable lead

Spontaneous Fission

example*:

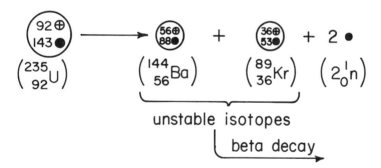

$$\left(^{235}_{92}U\right) \longrightarrow \left(^{144}_{56}Ba\right) + \left(^{89}_{36}Kr\right) + 2 \left(^{1}_{0}n\right)$$

unstable isotopes

beta decay

Figure 1.11 Reactions of Heavy Nuclei

*Example shows just one of more than 30 possible pairs of primary fission products that can occur when $^{235}_{92}U$ splits up.

mately four half-lives, the original quantity of plutonium was reduced to one-sixteenth of its initial value. Thus, plutonium and other unstable elements have long since disappeared over the course of the earth's history. However, a few of them decay so slowly that they are still present in significant abundance. Among these, uranium is the only element that can undergo fission.

Spontaneous fission is an extremely rare event, but one of the isotopes of

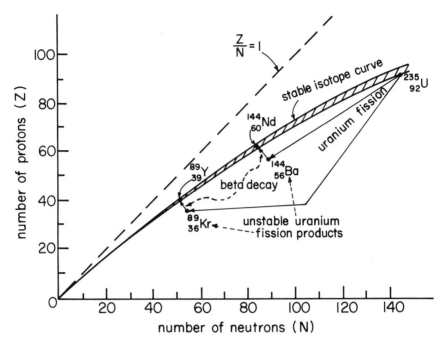

Figure 1.12 Proton-Neutron Ratio for Stable Isotopes: Beta Emission*

*Beta emission: neutron $(_0^1 n) \rightarrow$ proton $(_1^1 p) + \beta^-$ (high-energy electron)

Figure 1.13 Half-Life ($t_{1/2}$) of Radioactive Isotopes

Pressurized Light Water Reactor

Figure 1.14 Chain Reaction by Induced with Slow (Thermal) Neutrons; Pressurized Light Water Reactor

*FP and FP' represent various fission products.

uranium, the one containing 235 nucleons and called U-235, can be induced to undergo fission with high probability if it encounters a neutron. In addition to the two fission fragments, two or three neutrons are produced in this process, as shown in the top part of Figure 1.14. If these neutrons, in turn, strike other atoms of uranium-235, they can produce further fission. Since the ratio of neutrons released to neutrons absorbed in each fission event is greater than one, a chain reaction can be built up in which all the atoms in a piece of uranium-235 undergo fission in a short period of time with a large release of energy. This is the basis of the first atom bomb, which was tested in New Mexico and exploded over Hiroshima in 1945.

9 | Nuclear Power

Pressurized light water reactor

Since the grim dawn of the nuclear age, scientists have dreamed of harnessing the power of the nucleus for peaceful purposes, and from this impetus the nuclear power reactor program arose. The lower part of Figure 1.14 shows the operating principles of one common nuclear reactor design—the pressurized light water reactor. The fuel rods of this reactor contain pellets of uranium or uranium oxide. Naturally occurring uranium is made up mostly of the isotope that contains 238 nucleons, U-238, which does not fission. U-235 constitutes only 1 out of 140 uranium atoms. In order to build up a chain reaction in the light water reactor, the uranium is concentrated in the U-235 isotope to a level of 2–3%. Control rods containing cadmium or boron, which absorb neutrons effectively, are lowered automatically among the fuel rods to a level that adjusts the neutron flux so that the chain reaction is maintained but does not run out of control. Surrounding the fuel and control rods is a bath of water, which acts both as a coolant to carry away the energy generated in the fission reaction and as a moderator, that is, a substance that slows down the neutrons to increase the fission probability. Neutrons released by the fission travel at such high velocities that, in the absence of a moderator, they would escape before inducing further fission. The water circulates through a heat exchanger that generates steam from a secondary water coolant, and this steam is then used to drive a turbine to generate electricity. Basically the reactor is a conventional steam generator in which the heat source is fissioning uranium instead of burning coal. The amount of energy concentrated in uranium, however, is vastly greater than that in coal. Whereas the highest heating value found for coal is about 7,000 calories/g, a gram of U-235 can release 20 billion calories. One gram of uranium-235 is equivalent to about 3 metric tons of high-grade coal. The U-235 cannot be completely used up in the reactor, however, because of the buildup of fission products, which themselves absorb the neutrons and eventually slow the chain reaction down. After about a year, the fuel rods must be replaced with new ones. The spent fuel can be reprocessed by chemical extraction of the fission products and reconcentration of the U-235.

Breeder reactor

Although U-235 represents an extremely concentrated form of energy, there is not a great deal of it present in the world. As we saw in Table 1.3, at present uranium prices, the total U-235 resource in the United States amounts to 25.3 units of the annual energy consumption in 1975. Nuclear fission would therefore represent a short-lived energy resource if it were not for the potential of breeder reactions, one of which is diagrammed in the upper part of Figure 1.15. While

Liquid Sodium Breeder Reactor

Figure 1.15   Breeder Reaction with Fast Neutrons; Liquid Sodium Breeder Reactor

U-235 is the only naturally occurring fissionable isotope, isotopes of other heavy elements, which are no longer present on earth naturally, can also undergo induced fission. Of particular interest is plutonium-239, which can be made by neutron bombardment of uranium-238, the abundant form of uranium. The scheme, shown in the figure, offers the promise of converting inactive uranium-238 to fissionable plutonium-239, thereby converting all the uranium to nuclear fuel. As diagrammed, uranium-238 absorbs a fast-moving neutron to produce a very unstable isotope, uranium-239. This isotope forms a new element, neptunium-239, by beta emission. Neptunium undergoes a similar transformation to plutonium-239.

The reactions for the formation of plutonium can be carried out in a breeder reactor, which is shown in the lower part of Figure 1.15. This reactor is designed to extract power from the fission of either U-235 or Pu-239, but at the same time to produce plutonium from U-238 at a fast rate so that more fuel is produced than is consumed. Again, the reactor core contains uranium fuel rods and cadmium or boron control rods but in this case there is also a blanket of U-238 from which the plutonium is to be bred. A moderator is not wanted because the conversion of uranium-238 to plutonium-239 is most efficient with fast neutrons. With the faster neutrons, however, the induced fission reaction is less efficient, so the fuel must be enriched to the extent of 15–20% with a fissionable isotope, either uranium-235 or plutonium-239. The chosen coolant is liquid sodium, which does not slow down the neutrons, has good heat transfer properties, and is a liquid over a wide temperature range, 98–808° C. The primary sodium coolant transfers its heat to a secondary liquid sodium coolant, which in turn transfers heat to a steam generator that runs the turbine for producing electricity. The purpose of the secondary sodium coolant is to prevent any accidental contact of the primary sodium coolant with water, since some of the sodium atoms do absorb neutrons and become radioactive.

There are inevitable losses in the system, but use of the breeder reactor would still stretch the supply of uranium fuel by at least a factor of 50 and would transform nuclear fission into an energy resource much larger than coal. The technology of the breeder reactor is far more complex than that of the ordinary fission reactor, however, and it is still being developed. The most formidable problem seems to be associated with the plumbing of the heat exchanger, since leaks between the liquid sodium and the water would be disastrous. A practical breeder reactor is not yet in operation, although the British and French programs are quite far advanced.

10 | Weapons Proliferation

Despite its promise for providing cheap and abundant energy, nuclear power presents unique problems that have placed it at the center of the growing controversy about the whole direction of energy policy. One concern has to do with the relative ease with which fission fuel could be diverted to the production of nuclear weapons. Table 1.6 lists the sources, processes, and levels of technology required to construct nuclear weapons from nuclear fuels. The uranium fuel of ordinary fission reactors is only slightly enriched in the fissionable U-235 and is not itself of weapons grade. In order to produce a nuclear explosion, U-235 must be concentrated to at least 90%. Isotope separation is a difficult process and currently is done only at large industrial facilities. In the United States isotope separation plants are of the gaseous diffusion variety, in which the volatile compound, uranium hexafluoride, is passed through many diffusion barriers. The lighter molecules containing U-235 move slightly ahead of their counterparts containing U-238 and are gradually enriched. Other feasible methods involve gas centrifugation or gas nozzle technologies. All these require large and expensive plants.

Table 1.6   Weapons from Nuclear Fuels

Source	Process of Attainment of Weapons-Grade Material	Level of Technology Required
Uranium-235	Enrichment of natural uranium (0.7% U-235) to 90% U-235 by gaseous diffusion, gas centrifuge, or laser techniques	Extremely sophisticated
Plutonium-239	Chemical separation of plutonium from other elements (there are no other plutonium isotopes)	Simple

One of the more acute controversies surrounding nuclear power is the question of whether such plants would be built in countries that import nuclear fission reactors. From the point of view of the importing countries, such plants are highly desirable in that they eliminate dependence on foreign supplies of enriched uranium fuel. The same plants can, however, be used to enrich U-235 to weapons-grade material and could directly contribute to the spread of nuclear armaments. Moreover, it is likely that a new and less costly isotope separation process, based on the use of lasers, will become available before long.

Plutonium presents an even more immediate concern. Since it is a different element than uranium, plutonium is easily extractable from nuclear fuel by conventional chemical methods. Indeed, India has recently demonstrated that it is possible to extract sufficient plutonium from spent reactor fuel to build and explode an atom bomb.

Fuel reprocessing plants routinely separate plutonium during the regeneration of the spent uranium. If this plutonium is then itself used to fashion new fuel rods, substantial quantities of plutonium could be transported from reprocessing plants to fuel fabrication plants and then to the reactors themselves. There is much concern that the plutonium fuel could be stolen, perhaps by criminal or terrorist groups, to manufacture clandestine nuclear weapons. It has been claimed that 5 kg of plutonium could be assembled into a crude but usable weapon by a small group, or even a single individual, working from unclassified published government documents.

These problems of nuclear proliferation and diversion will be greatly magnified when large quantities of plutonium are in circulation, which will happen when plutonium breeder reactors come into widespread use. The issues are sufficiently serious and difficult that, as of the summer of 1979, the entire U.S. breeder program was under reevaluation and its future was in doubt. In the meantime nuclear alternatives to the plutonium breeding cycle have been dis-

Figure 1.16 Thorium-232–Uranium-233 Cycle

cussed increasingly. One of these is based on the conversion of the element thorium to a fissionable isotope. As shown in Figure 1.16, the reaction of thorium-232 with a neutron leads to the production of fissionable uranium-233, which can be used as nuclear fuel. A breeder reactor to convert thorium to uranium-233 would be similar to a plutonium breeder reactor, except that the thorium reaction works best with slow neutrons, so a moderator is needed. Thorium-232 is almost as plentiful as uranium-238, the abundant isotope of uranium; consequently, a thorium breeding cycle would extend the nuclear fuel supply by about the same amount as would the plutonium breeder. The security advantage is that the fissionable uranium-233 could be denatured by the addition of uranium-238, making it unsuitable for the manufacture of bombs. Similar denaturing is not possible with plutonium-239, for which no naturally occurring isotope is available. The technical feasibility of the thorium cycle, as well as other alternatives to the plutonium breeder, have only begun to be seriously evaluated.

11 | Radioactivity

Another major nuclear safety concern is with radioactivity and radioactive isotopes. Table 1.7 indicates some of the hazards. We have seen that elements that are too heavy to be stable decay by the loss of alpha particles. These particles are ejected with high energy. Since they are helium nuclei, with a doubly positive charge, they efficiently ionize atoms in their path, losing energy with each ionization. They do not travel far but produce intense ionization within a short path. In water or biological tissue, their range is only 0.005 cm, so alpha emitters are not harmful to us if they remain external to our bodies. The danger lies in their being inhaled as small particles. Once lodged in the lungs, an alpha particle can produce intense damage in a localized region. One of the known consequences is the eventual induction of cancer.

The absorption of neutrons by uranium produces very unstable heavy isotopes

Table 1.7   Radioactivity

Paths of Energetic Particles in Biological Tissue

Type of Radiation	Range in Biological Tissue	Relative Biological Effectiveness*
alpha	0.005 cm	10–20
beta	3 cm	1
gamma	~20 cm	1

Some Hazardous Radioactive Isotopes

Element	Type of Radiation	Half-Life	Site of Concentration
$^{239}_{94}$Pu	alpha	24,360 years	Bone, lung
$^{90}_{38}$Sr	beta	28.8 years	Bone, teeth
$^{131}_{53}$I	beta, gamma	8 days	Thyroid
$^{137}_{55}$Cs	beta, gamma	30 years	Whole body

*Accounts for the fact that cell damage increases as the density of the damage sites increases.

including plutonium-239, which not only is fissionable but also emits alpha particles. As we noted earlier, the half-life of plutonium-239 is about 24,000 years. Once created, plutonium-239 will be around for much longer than all of recorded history. Because of its cancer-inducing potential, plutonium is one of the most dangerous substances to humans. Its oxide is a finely divided powder and susceptible to inhalation. The maximum permissible dose is a matter of considerable controversy, however. At the moment, it is set at 6 μg for the total body burden. By the end of the century there may be as much as 80,000 kg of plutonium produced per year if plutonium breeder technology is fully developed. Keeping these quantities of plutonium from contaminating the environment will be a formidable problem.

The products of uranium or plutonium fission are also radioactive, decaying by beta and gamma emission, as we have seen. Both forms of radiation travel greater distances than do alpha rays, although they produce a lower intensity of damage. Most fission products decay very rapidly, but some are relatively long-lived, with half-lives on the order of 30 years. Some of these radioisotopes are particularly hazardous because they are specifically concentrated in biological tissue. For example, strontium-90, which has a half-life of 29 years, can replace calcium in bones. During the period of atmospheric testing of nuclear weapons, there was much concern that strontium-90 from the radioactive fallout was being concentrated in the milk of cows that grazed on contaminated grass. Children were particularly at risk since their bone development, and consequently the deposition of strontium-90 from the affected milk, is rapid. Another isotope of particular concern is iodine-131. Although it has a half-life of only eight days, it selectively concentrates in the thyroid where it can produce thyroid cancer. Cesium-137 has a half-life of 30 years. It can replace potassium, an essential biological element, and is distributed throughout the body.

The problem of radioactivity should be viewed against the background of natural and anthropogenic sources of radiation to which we are all exposed even in the absence of the nuclear industry. The major sources of radiation are tabulated in Table 1.8 in which the units are millirads, a convenient measure of radiation dose. We receive a total of about 115 millirads per year in radiation from cosmic rays and from radioisotopes in the earth around us as well as internal to our own bodies. In addition, we receive about 100 millirads per year of radiation due to human activity, chiefly from diagnostic x-rays. Current guidelines for the operation of nuclear reactors call for the release of radiation that produces no more than 20 millirads per year for any individual. This is less than one-fifth of the background dose, and most nuclear plants currently operate well within this limit. (See the Appendix for definitions of the common units of radiation.)

While the radiation released from nuclear reactors in normal operation is quite low, the reactors themselves contain a huge quantity of intense radioactivity, roughly equivalent to that in a Hiroshima-sized atomic bomb. This radioactivity

Table 1.8   Sources of Radiation Dose to Persons
in the United States

Source	Average dose per year (millirads*)	
Human activity (1978)		
Diagnostic x-ray		75
Therapeutic x-ray		15
Radioactive fallout		5
Nuclear industry, including mining and fuel processing		5
	Subtotal	100
Natural background		
Terrestrial radiation, external to body		60
Cosmic rays		30
Radioisotopes, internal to body		25
	Subtotal	115
	Total	215

*1 millirad = absorption of 0.1 erg of energy per gram of tissue.
Sources: J. Harte and R. H. Socolow, *Patient Earth* (New York: Holt, Rinehart and Winston, Inc., 1971), p. 309.; J. L. Marx, *Science* 204 (1979): 162.

could be released in the event of a disastrous accident, which might be caused by a violent earthquake or a crash from a large aircraft. There is also concern about the possibility of massive rupture of the primary plumbing system with rapid loss of the coolant. Although control rods would come down immediately to stop the chain reaction, intense heat generated by radioactivity would accumulate in the reactor. This heat could be sufficient to melt the core and the concrete floor beneath the reactor. Under these circumstances it is feared that the containment vessel itself would be breached and the radioactive fuel spread around the countryside. To avoid such a loss of coolant, each reactor is provided with a backup emergency cooling system designed to flood the reactor core with water. However, there is some concern that this system might fail in an actual crisis situation.

This concern was raised considerably after an accident at the Three Mile Island nuclear plant hear Harrisburg, Pennsylvania, in March, 1979. The sequence of events in the accident scenario demonstrated the inherent probability, however small it might be, of mechanical and human failure leading to a core meltdown.

The problem began when a pump in the primary cooling system shut down. Auxiliary feedwater pumps were not operational, although they should have been, as prescribed by governmental regulations. The temperature of the water in the reactor soared and pressure within the reactor vessel caused a relief valve in the primary coolant loop to open, as it should have, to let out the overheated water. Then the valve failed to close. This caused the pressure to drop low enough for thousands of gallons of water to vaporize and escape out of the reactor core. Thus the fuel rods were left partially exposed above the cooling water level, and they became so hot that some melting of the fuel rod cladding occurred.

At least one water level indicator appears to have given a faulty reading, causing a technician to think the system was full of water when it was not. This made him think wrongly that the situation was under control. The high temperatures caused water molecules to break up into hydrogen and oxygen gas with the formation of a 1000 cubic foot gas bubble in the upper part of the core. Within minutes the emergency cooling system had gone into operation, but the gas bubble kept the coolant from reaching the top of the fuel rods, causing them to remain overheated and dangerously close to complete melting. To exasperate the problem, a technician confusedly turned off the emergency cooling system for a short time at the peak of the crisis.

The bubble formation was a new and unexpected event and for some time left the experts, who arrived on the scene after the accident, perplexed as to how to cope with it. A catastrophe was averted when the bubble was gradually reduced and the core was cooled off.

The consequences of a major accident, in terms of the potential for dispersal of long-lived radioactive materials, are so disastrous that it is difficult to establish a rational notion of the risk involved. This is reflected in the inability of the nuclear industry to obtain accident insurance through normal commercial channels. Under the long-standing Price-Anderson Act, the U.S. Congress has limited the liability for an accident to $560 million and has underwritten the bulk of the insurance for this sum. Critics of the nuclear industry have long called for repeal of this act on the grounds that actual damage might well be considerably greater than the $560 million limit, and that whatever risks are involved with nuclear reactors should be assessed against their operation through appropriate insurance premiums. Such premium payments are a standard market device for encouraging the development of more effective safety procedures, from which the nuclear industry is currently exempt. Proponents of the industry argue that calling for a repeal of the Price-Anderson Act is tantamount to destroying the industry, which needs government backing in this form if it is to provide energy for U.S. needs.

Aside from the question of nuclear reactor operations, there are several points in the entire nuclear fuel cycle, diagrammed in Figure 1.17, where the dispersal of radioactive materials is an actual or potential problem. In the first place, uranium mining itself is a hazardous occupation. Miners have a high risk of developing lung cancer because they inhale dust that contains radioactive radium, which is present in uranium deposits, as well as daughter products of radium decay including the radioactive gas, radon. Moreover, uranium mining produces large hills of waste tailings, fine particles that are left over after the uranium ore is extracted from the rocks. The tailings also contain radium and are dispersed by winds over the surrounding area, posing a threat to people in nearby

Figure 1.17 Light Water Reactor Nuclear Fuel Cycle

Source: "Energy Facts II," Subcommittee on Energy Research, Development and Demonstration, U.S. House of Representatives, 94th Congress, Library of Congress, Serial H, August 1975, p. **262**.

communities. Another place where the release of radiation is potentially serious is the fuel reprocessing plant, where the spent fuel rods are dissolved in acid and the fission products and the heavy element contaminants are separated before the uranium or plutonium is sent back to the fuel fabrication plants. The operation of a reprocessing plant is much more difficult than that of a reactor because of the need to handle intensely radioactive materials, and the release of radiation from such plants is more difficult to prevent. Because of safety and other technical difficulties, no reprocessing plant is currently operating in the United States and spent fuel rods are simply piling up in storage tanks filled with water. A new plant has been built in South Carolina, but current uncertainties about the reprocessing of plutonium leave its opening in doubt.

Another area of uncertainty concerns the eventual disposal of the radioisotopes that are extracted at the reprocessing plant. They must be isolated from the human environment for exceedingly long periods of time. A rule of thumb is that radiation sinks to negligible levels after ten half-lives. For the fission products this is a few hundred years, but for plutonium and the other heavy elements ten half-lives is on the order of a quarter of a million years. Various waste disposal schemes have been suggested, including melting the hot wastes into the Antarctic snow cap or firing them with rockets into space or into the sun. The scheme currently favored, however, involves burying the wastes in underground salt domes, which are extremely dry and geologically stable. There is concern, however, that in due course water could intrude into the salt formation and dissolve the radioisotopes along with the salt. A site chosen near Lyons, Kansas, had to be abandoned when it was subsequently discovered that the area had been infiltrated with water from a salt-mining operation. At present, new sites are being sought in New Mexico.

Finally, the elaborate transportation network required in the nuclear fuel cycle presents many opportunities for accidents or sabotage.

In summary, the energy stored in uranium or in thorium atoms can provide us with a significant energy resource if breeder technology can be mastered. On the other hand, the price of fission energy includes unprecedented possibilities of long-term harm resulting from the unique hazards of nuclear weapons and radioactive isotopes.

12 | Fusion Power

Much greater energy is available from nuclear sources via the fusion reaction. As we saw in Figure 1.10, the most stable nuclei are those of elements with intermediate masses. Consequently the lighter elements are potentially unstable with respect to fusion to heavier ones, and very large amounts of energy could be released in the process. Extreme reaction conditions are necessary, however, because in order for two nuclei to fuse, they must overcome a huge energy barrier caused by the repulsion between their positive charges before the strong nuclear forces take over when the nucleons actually intermingle. Such conditions are achieved in the centers of stars, including our sun, whose energy outputs are due to fusion reactions. They can also be observed in hydrogen bombs, which use the explosive force of a fission bomb as a trigger. The easiest fusion reactions to carry out are those of the heavy isotopes of hydrogen. These are deuterium, with one neutron and one proton, and tritium, with two neutrons and one proton. Fusion reactions of these particles are shown schematically in the first part of Figure 1.18. Reaction 1 shows that two deuterium nuclei can fuse to produce a helium-3 nucleus, with one neutron and two protons, plus a free neutron; or, as in reaction 2, they can produce a tritium nucleus with the release of a proton. Reaction 3 shows that a deuterium nucleus can fuse with a tritium nucleus to produce helium plus a neutron. Tritium, with a half-life of 12.3 days, does not exist in nature and must be synthesized from lithium as shown in reactions 4 and 5. Since reaction 3 has the lowest activation barrier, it is the one that scientists are concentrating on for the production of useful energy. Even so, the temperature required for this reaction, the so-called ignition temperature is 40,000,000° C. Needless to say, at this high temperature, which is characteristic of the interior of the sun, all earthly materials would be vaporized. The overriding obstacle to harnessing the fusion reaction is that there is no conceivable container capable of withstanding such high temperatures.

One answer to this dilemma is to suspend the fusion fuels in free space with the use of powerful magnetic fields. At the high temperatures under consideration, the atoms are completely ionized and can therefore be controlled with magnetic fields. The upper part of Figure 1.19 shows a diagram of a proposed magnetic containment fusion reactor. The plasma would be in a doughnut-shaped electromagnetic field and would be heated to the desired temperature by the induction of an electric current. The tritium would be supplied by a blanket of liquid lithium surrounding the plasma. This blanket absorbs the neutrons given off in the fusion reaction and produces tritium as a by-product, via reactions 4 and 5 in Figure 1.18.

Lithium itself is a relatively scarce element, and high-grade deposits are not plentiful. They probably correspond to an energy resource comparable to the fossil fuels themselves. On the other hand, with appropriate technology for extracting lithium from lower grade sources, the energy available may be much larger. If the deuterium-deuterium reactions can be made to work, then the supply of energy available from fusion is essentially limitless. Deuterium is a naturally occurring isotope of hydrogen and is readily separated in the form of heavy water. There is enough of it in the ocean to provide a resource 50 million times larger than the fossil fuel deposits. However, the deuterium-deuterium

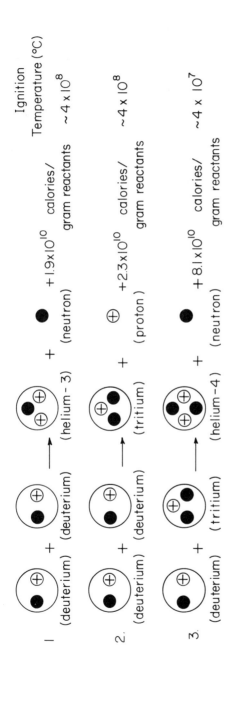

				Ignition Temperature (°C)
1. (deuterium)	+ (deuterium)	→ (helium-3)	+ (neutron) $+1.9 \times 10^{10}$ calories/gram reactants	$\sim 4 \times 10^{8}$
2. (deuterium)	+ (deuterium)	→ (tritium)	+ (proton) $+2.3 \times 10^{10}$ calories/gram reactants	$\sim 4 \times 10^{8}$
3. (deuterium)	+ (tritium)	→ (helium-4)	+ (neutron) $+8.1 \times 10^{10}$ calories/gram reactants	$\sim 4 \times 10^{7}$

Breeding of Tritium from Lithium

4. $^{6}_{3}\text{Li}$ + slow neutron $\longrightarrow$ tritium + $^{4}_{2}\text{He}$ + 1.5×10^{10} calories/gram reactants

5. $^{7}_{3}\text{Li}$ + fast neutron $\longrightarrow$ tritium + $^{4}_{2}\text{He}$ + neutron − 0.8×10^{10} calories/gram reactants

Figure 1.18 Some Energy-Producing Fusion Reactions

35

(i)
Magnetic Containment

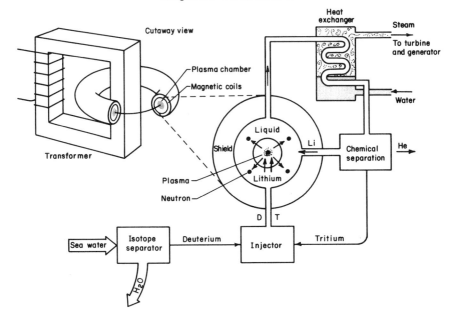

(ii)
Laser Induced

Figure 1.19 Deuterium-Tritium Fusion Reactors

Source: G. Gordon and W. Zoller, *Chemistry in Modern Perspective* (Reading, Mass.: Addison-Wesley Publishing Company Inc., 1975), figs. 6–3 and 6–4. Copyright © 1975. Reprinted with permission.

fusion process has a higher activation energy and the temperature would have to be ten times higher than that for the deuterium-tritium reaction.

At the present time, fusion technology is far from practical. The high-temperature plasmas are subject to various instabilities, and they escape from their confining magnetic fields in short order. These instabilities are gradually being eliminated in experimental plasma machines, but there is still a long way to go before hot plasma can be contained long enough to produce more energy than the machine consumes. Even after this point is reached, the problems of constructing a practical power source are formidable. Among these is the neutron flux produced by the reactor, which is so intense that most ordinary construction materials would have a very short lifetime.

A different design for a fusion reactor has recently been proposed and is shown schematically in the lower part of Figure 1.19. In this method, a small pellet of frozen deuterium and tritium is dropped into a laser beam that has sufficient intensity to compress the pellet suddenly and produce a tiny fusion explosion. Again, a blanket of lithium would absorb the neutrons and the energy produced. Repeated firings of the laser at successive pellets would then produce a steady energy source. This design has the advantage of eliminating the need for very large magnets, but it is presently uncertain whether lasers of sufficient power and stability can be produced.

In terms of environmental hazards, fusion reactors would avoid the problems associated with fission products. Nevertheless, the radioactivity involved is not negligible because large quantities of radioactive tritium would be used. Tritium is a fairly dangerous material because it is readily incorporated into water and biological tissues. Tritium gas, like hydrogen gas, can diffuse through metals and is difficult to contain. Moreover, the material in the reactor structure itself becomes radioactive from the constant neutron bombardment. The reactors will have a finite lifetime, perhaps 20 years, due to the gradual breakdown of materials, and dismantling the structures will present a problem in radioactive waste disposal.

Current research on fusion is being pursued vigorously in several countries. The scientists involved in the work are optimistic that all outstanding problems will be overcome, but no one can be sure whether the concept will work. If it can, it will still take many years to produce useful power.

13 | Solar Energy

The alternative to fossil and nuclear fuels is to harness renewable energy sources that are derived directly or indirectly from sunlight. We have already seen in Table 1.3 that the annual energy deposited by sunlight on the continental United States is 650 times the total annual external energy consumption. Enough sunlight falls yearly on each square meter to equal the energy content of 420 pounds of high-grade bituminous coal. The sun already provides us, in fact, with our most basic energy needs including heat, freshwater, and plant life. There is plenty left over for our other cultural energy needs if we develop the technology to harness it. The difficulty is that sunlight is diffuse and intermittent. The technology required to harness and store solar energy is currently expensive; until now it has been much cheaper to pump oil from the ground and burn it. With fuel prices rising and the end of petroleum deposits in sight, however, the economic balance is shifting. There is now considerable interest in developing solar technology, with a reasonable prospect of substantial cost reductions from engineering improvements and mass production.

The most convenient and straightforward application of solar energy is in heating buildings and providing hot water, which currently consumes 20–25% of our fuel supply. This is an ideal application for a uniformly dispersed energy source. Figure 1.20 shows a detailed design for a solar-heated house. The sunlight is collected on plates in the roof and the heat is transferred to a circulating water system. It has been estimated that the average house in the central United States could obtain its energy needs for heating and hot water in December with a collection area of 1,300 ft^2, well within the average roof area. Various solar-heating designs are currently being tested, and there is little doubt that they will come into widespread use in the coming years. The main problem is that it is relatively expensive to refit older houses with solar units.

A more difficult application is the generation of electricity from sunlight. It would take an area of 1,600 mi^2 to supply the total electrical energy needs of the United States if sunlight were converted to electricity with 30% efficiency. While this area is only slightly larger than Rhode Island, it still represents a very large collection surface. One approach to this is to use collected heat to run a boiler in a steam generator. To achieve high enough temperatures for efficient operation, the sunlight must be focused from many collecting units. One possible design is diagrammed in Figure 1.21. To achieve efficient operation throughout the day, the mirrors must track the path of the sun. The cost of reliable collectors and tracking machinery is one uncertainty surrounding the design of solar thermal plants. Keeping the mirrors clean and scratch-free, especially in deserts, is another major problem.

Another approach is direct transformation of sunlight into electricity via the photovoltaic effect. Light is absorbed in a material with the generation of positive and negative charges that are collected at electrodes at either side. The most successful current design is the silicon solar cell diagrammed in Figure 1.22, which was developed for the space program. This consists of a sandwich of n-type and p-type silicon semiconductors; the charge separation is developed across the junction between them. The silicon cell produces electricity reliably, but it is quite expensive, since very high-grade crystalline silicon is required. The

Details of Heating System

Figure 1.20 Conventional Solar-Heated House

Source: W. E. Morrow, *Technol. Rev.*, December 1973, p. 34.

CHARACTERISTICS	
TOWER HEIGHT	260 m
COLLECTOR AREA	0.5 km^2
AREA UTILIZATION	38.6%
TOTAL LAND AREA	1.3 km^2
No. OF COLLECTORS	15,400
SIZE OF COLLECTORS	32.4 m^2
POWER	33.3 MW

Figure 1.21   Electricity from Sunlight: Central Receiver Design

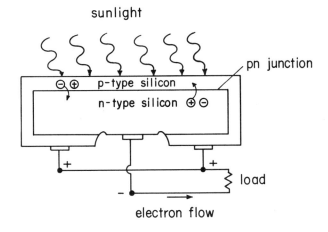

p - type silicon conducts positive charges
n - type silicon conducts negative charges

Figure 1.22   Diagram of Solar Cell for Generation of Electricity efficiency of conversion of light is 10–15%, and an array of such cells sufficiently large to produce a substantial amount of electricity would be prohibitively expensive at current prices. It is hoped, however, that the price can be reduced substantially through new manufacturing processes and more advanced technology. The recent development of cells that contain amorphous rather than crystalline semiconductor materials is one of the most promising avenues for reducing the cost of photovoltaic devices in the future.

Meanwhile, indirect forms of solar energy can be harnessed for the production of electricity. Hydroelectric generation has been with us for a long time, and its potential has been largely tapped. Another source is wind power which, as indicated in Table 1.3, has an energy potential each year of four times the current U.S. consumption. Windmills have a long history of use throughout the world, and in the midwestern United States there were 50,000 backyard windmills generating electricity until 1950, after which they were phased out by the Rural

(i)

lOO kW NASA Windmill

l25 ft.

(ii)

Tornado-like Wind Generator

Figure 1.23   Wind Power

Source: Upper diagram: N. Wade, *Science* 184 (1974):1056. Lower diagram: A. Hammond, *Science* 190 (1975):257. Copyright 1975 by the American Association for the Advancement of Science.

Figure 1.24 Electricity from Ocean Thermal Gradients

Electricity Administration. The strongest and steadiest winds are those on the Great Plains and on the Atlantic seaboard. As shown in Figure 1.23, there have been many technical advances in the design of windmills and wind turbines, and it seems quite likely that wind power will be an economical source of electricity in the near future.

Much solar energy is also stored in the ocean as thermal gradients between the warm surface layer and the colder waters beneath. Extracting this energy requires new and difficult technology. Figure 1.24 illustrates a design for a large-scale low-temperature heat engine for producing electric power from the thermal gradients.

14 | Energy Storage

The main drawback to the production of direct solar or wind electricity is the intermittent nature of the energy source. Electricity is produced only when the sun shines or the wind blows. What is needed is a means of storing energy to provide an even and continuous supply. This would be desirable even with current power plants, since there are large fluctuations in the daily demand for electricity. Extra generating capacity is required to meet the peak demands during daylight hours, particularly during the summer when air-conditioners draw a heavy load, and the extra capacity is left idle much of the time. A few electric companies have developed water pump storage, in which excess electricity is used to pump water uphill to reservoirs and the water running back downhill can then be used to run turbines to meet peak demands. Other energy storage schemes under consideration include storage of compressed air in caverns, mechanical energy storage in flywheels, and direct electrical storage in large superconducting magnets. We are all familiar with the lead storage battery, which represents chemical storage of electrical energy in portable form. While it is very efficient in converting electrical to chemical energy and back, the chemical battery is a heavy and expensive storage medium. Much research is now being directed to finding lighter and cheaper versions.

Probably the most attractive general storage scheme is chemical storage in the form of molecular hydrogen. This can be generated directly by electrolysis of water as shown in the upper diagram of Figure 1.25. Electric current is passed between electrodes immersed in a conducting water solution. Hydrogen is generated at the negative electrode and oxygen at the positive one. The energy stored in the hydrogen can then be reconverted into electricity using the reverse of the electrolytic cell, called the *fuel cell,* diagrammed in the lower diagram of Figure 1.25. Here hydrogen is oxidized at the negative electrode, where electrons are produced and passed through the circuit to the positive electrode, where oxygen is reduced. The overall efficiency of this conversion and reconversion is fairly low because of various energy barriers connected with the electrode processes. Lowering these barriers is an important target of current electrochemical research.

The ability to store energy in the form of hydrogen would help also to solve the problem of energy transport. The cost of electrical transmission over large distances is high, and there are serious losses. The areas with the greatest amount of sunlight, where solar plants would be most efficient, are far from northern centers of population. Transmission problems for ocean-generating plants are even more severe. Hydrogen transport by pipeline is much more efficient and less expensive. Instead of electricity, remote plants could generate hydrogen, which could be piped to urban centers. These considerations have led to the concept of the hydrogen economy shown graphically in Figure 1.26 in which hydrogen gas would become the main energy currency. It would be consumed directly for electrical generation and heating and could be used to synthesize liquid fuels by chemistry similar to that described in connection with coal gasification.

Another possibility is to generate hydrogen directly from sunlight by photochemistry. The energy of visible light is sufficient to split water molecules into hydrogen and oxygen atoms. Water is transparent to sunlight, however, and therefore some other agent must be used such as a catalyst that absorbs light and transfers the energy to the water-splitting reaction. Figure 1.27 shows one scheme for doing this. It consists of an electrochemical cell with platinum and strontium titanate electrodes dipped into a sodium hydroxide solution. When light strikes the strontium titanate electrode, oxygen is produced and electrons flow through the circuit to the platinum electrode, where they generate hydrogen. The main problem is that light in the ultraviolet region is required to activate the strontium titanate. A satisfactory electrode that works with visible light has not

electrode
reactions: $2 OH^- \rightarrow H_2O + \frac{1}{2}O_2 + 2e^-$ $2H_2O + 2e^- \rightarrow H_2 + 2OH^-$

overall
reaction: $H_2O \rightarrow H_2 + \frac{1}{2}O_2$

Electricity Production from Hydrogen−Oxygen Fuel Cell

electrode
reactions: $\frac{1}{2}O_2 + H_2O + 2e^- \rightarrow 2OH^-$ $H_2 + 2OH^- \rightarrow 2H_2O + 2e^-$

overall
reaction: $H_2 + \frac{1}{2}O_2 \rightarrow H_2O$

Figure 1.25 Storage and Production of Electricity with Hydrogen

Figure 1.26 The Hydrogen Economy

yet been found; however, there is considerable interest in the possibility of developing chemicals that can absorb light and transfer the energy directly to the splitting of water molecules.

Of course, green plants have been carrying out photochemical synthesis for millions of years and we use their products for our food supply as well as for fiber and wood. The entire biomass of plants represents an energy resource, some of which could practically be tapped for our energy needs. Figure 1.28 shows one simple scheme for doing this. Bacteria that live in the absence of oxygen can effectively convert plant tissue into methane gas, which we have already seen is a high-grade fuel. Simple methane digesters of well-established design can produce methane from crop residues and manure—materials that are often wasted and in fact may cause pollution problems, as in the case of wastes from massive cattle feedlots. The methane digesters work on any nonwoody plant materials and it would be possible to harvest energy plantations, for example, swamp land that is photosynthetically productive but unsuited for agriculture. In wet areas of the world, this could be a simple and effective way of increasing the energy supply, particularly for poor countries with tropical climates. In addition to methane, the digester leaves a solid residue that is rich in nutrients and could be used as a soil conditioner or converted into animal feed.

Woody tissue is not appropriate for the methane digesters and neither is urban solid refuse, which is contaminated with metals and other substantially toxic

Figure 1.27   Direct Production of Hydrogen from Sunlight by Photoassisted Electrolysis

*0.5 ma of current flows at 0 applied volt; 2 ma (50% of maximum) flows at 0.25 applied volt.
†This prototype photoelectrode system is not an efficient device for converting solar energy into stored chemical energy, since only ~3% of solar energy comes from light in the ultraviolet range.
Source: M. S. Wrighton, et al., *J. Am. Chem. Soc.* 98 (1976):2774.

Figure 1.28   Flower Power: Energy from Decay Products of Photosynthesis

materials. The energy content of urban waste as well as logging and pulp waste is significant, however, amounting to about 3% of our annual energy consumption. Some of this could be recovered through a pyrolysis technique shown in Figure 1.29 from which the product is methanol—a useful fuel. The same process could be used on trees harvested from forest plantations that are designed for energy production.

Overall, then, we can see many ways in which the energy of the sun can be tapped for human purposes. Because of the abundance of sunlight, the long-term prospects for renewable energy supplies are quite good. Some of the technologies, such as solar heating, conversion of plant matter to methane and methanol, and wind power generation of electricity, are already well developed and require only appropriate economic conditions for their implementation. Other techniques such as thermal or photovoltaic solar electricity production are well understood but require engineering development to reduce their costs before they will be attractive. Still other technologies such as direct photochemical production of hydrogen and ocean power generation are somewhat further off, but they have a long-term potential for the provision of abundant energy supplies.

oxygen refuse converter

Figure 1.29   Fuel from Refuse

Source: T. B. Reed and R. M. Lerner, *Science* 182 (1973):1303. Copyright by the American Association for the Advancement of Science.

15 | Thermal Pollution

Even if we could be supplied with unlimited amounts of energy, there are still difficulties associated with the ever-increasing use of energy. One general problem, which comes under the heading of thermal pollution, is how to get rid of all the heat that accompanies energy utilization. A station that generates electricity uses heat, whether it is supplied by the burning of fossil or nuclear fuels, to produce steam, which in turn runs a turbine. Only a fraction of the heat can be converted to useful work, however, even if everything works with perfect efficiency. The situation is illustrated in Figure 1.30. Heat is delivered to a boiler at a temperature of T_2, and after driving the turbine, the steam is condensed at a temperature of T_1. The maximum ratio of work output to heat input is given by the temperature difference, $T_2 - T_1$, divided by the input temperature, T_2. This ratio is a consequence of the second law of thermodynamics and is a fundamental property of nature. No matter what the design of the power plant, the ratio can never be exceeded.

The temperatures in the formula are absolute temperatures. On the centigrade scale, absolute zero is $-273°$. To obtain the absolute temperature, we add 273 to the centigrade temperature. This is called the *Kelvin scale*. Since the temperature at the surface of the earth is, on the average, not far from 27° C, we know that T_1 in the formula will always be roughly 300° K. This means that if the boiler is run at 327° C, or 600° K, the maximum theoretical efficiency would be 50%. Actual efficiencies of generating plants are always lower than the theoretical maximum because of inevitable losses in transferring heat in real systems. The efficiency of coal-fired plants has been improved from initial values of about 10% to about 40% in the most modern one. A plant operating at 40% efficiency produces 4 calories of electrical energy and 6 calories of waste heat for every 10 calories of

$$\frac{W\,max}{Q} = \frac{T_2 - T_1}{T_2} \qquad Q - W_{max} = (\text{waste heat}) = Q \times \frac{T_1}{T_2}$$

Figure 1.30 Maximum Work and Waste Heat from Steam Electric Power Plant fuel burned. This means that for every calorie of electricity produced, 1½ calories of waste heat have to be carried away. The operating efficiency of current pressurized water nuclear reactors is about 30%, because of the relatively low temperature, 300° C, of the primary water coolant. This means that 3 calories of electricity and 7 calories of waste heat are produced for each 10 calories of nuclear energy input. For every calorie of electricity produced, 2.3 calories of waste heat must be removed, which is about 50% more than with modern coal-fired plants. Moreover, in nuclear plants all the waste heat must be removed at the steam condenser, whereas in a coal plant, some of the waste heat exits from the boiler chimney with the exhaust gases.

The condenser coils are cooled with water, which in most designs flows straight through from some nearby source and is discharged back to the environment, with its temperature increased by about 10° C. Already more than 10% of the total water streamflow in the United States is used for this purpose. Immense amounts of flowing water are needed for the very large power plants of current design, and it is becoming increasingly difficult to find sites where this much water is available. Moreover, there are ecological consequences of the cooling water streamflow. For one thing, fish and other marine life can be sucked into the intake and killed in large numbers. There is also concern that the increase in the temperature of the discharge water may be deleterious to aquatic life, although few effects have actually been observed so far. In the case of nuclear reactors on lakes with slow outflows, there is a possibility that traces of radioactivity released in the discharge water might eventually build up to a dangerous level.

It is possible to transfer the waste heat to the atmosphere rather than to the surrounding waters through cooling towers. As shown in Figure 1.31, these can be of the wet or dry variety. In the case of wet cooling towers, the waste heat is removed through the evaporation of water. We recall that it takes 540 calories to evaporate a gram of water but only 10 calories to heat it by 10° C, so that the amount of water needed for wet cooling towers is a factor of 50 less than that used for direct flow cooling. However, this water is now transferred to the atmosphere and may disturb the local climate. Wet cooling towers often produce fog in the local area. Dry cooling towers operate by direct heat exchange from the closed loop condenser coolant to the atmosphere. Large fans are needed to force sufficient air past the heat exchange surfaces, and this produces a high noise level in the vicinity and drains power from the plant. Because heat transfer to the air is appreciably less efficient than transfer to water, dry cooling towers lower the overall efficiency of electricity generation.

In addition to the acute problem of cooling power plants, there is concern about the more general effects of increasing thermal pollution. As we use more and more energy, we disturb the natural energy balances. Cities such as Manhattan already produce more heat than they absorb from the sun, and the effects on the local climate are noticeable. In the long run, it is conceivable that we could upset the overall energy balance of the earth if energy production continues to

(i)
Wet Cooling Tower

(ii)
Dry Cooling Tower

Figure 1.31 Transfer of Waste Heat from Electric Power Generation to the Atmosphere from Cooling Towers

Source: W. L. Masterton and E. J. Slowinski, *Chemical Principles,* 3rd ed. (Philadelphia: W. B. Saunders Company, 1973). Copyright © 1973. Figure 11.11 reprinted with permission.

grow exponentially. We saw in Table 1.1 that the total energy consumed is currently only about 0.007% of the total energy absorbed from the sun. However, the annual energy consumption growth rate is 3.1%, as shown in Figure 1.2, which corresponds to a doubling time of 23 years. At that rate, heat from fuel energy consumption would equal the energy absorbed from the sun in another 320 years. This would certainly produce a marked increase in the earth's surface temperature, as we will see in the next part. Long before this, serious effects on the climate would be observed, including melting of the polar ice caps and flooding of coastal cities as a result of the rising levels of seawater. This sort of problem would be caused by any energy source that adds to the total heat budget, whether it is fossil or nuclear fuel. The only significant exception is solar energy, since the sun's rays are being converted to heat in any event. If we divert some of this solar energy flow to useful purposes, there is no net increase in the earth's energy budget. It is conceivable, of course, that if we begin to absorb a significantly larger fraction of the solar radiation than the earth does already, by blanketing the deserts with solar collectors, for example, then the total heat flow could increase. The increase would be much smaller, however, than that from the direct burning of fossil or nuclear fuels.

16 | Energy Consumption and Conservation

We have learned that there are limits to energy growth. Although there are large energy resources that can be tapped to replace our dwindling supplies of petroleum and natural gas, we cannot continue to increase the energy supply exponentially without upsetting the earth's energy flows. There are also other environmental costs of energy production such as air and water pollution and the exhaustion of mineral resources, which become increasingly important as energy consumption increases.

It is useful at this point to look at the other side of the ledger and ask how much energy we actually need. It is generally assumed that the standard of living increases with increasing energy consumption. This assumption is supported by Figure 1.32, which is a plot of per capita energy consumption against per capita gross national product for many countries. There seems to be a roughly linear correlation between the two, with poor countries clustered near the bottom and

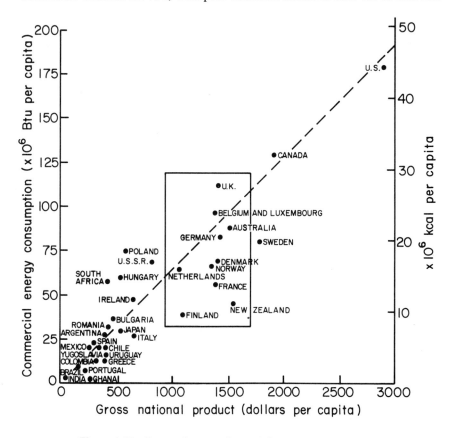

Figure 1.32 Energy Consumption and Gross National Product

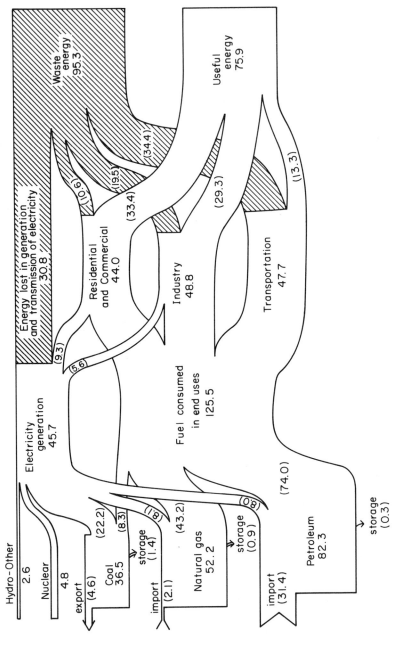

Figure 1.33 Production and Consumption of Energy in the United States, 1975 (in 10^{17} calories)

Waste energy 95.3

Useful energy 75.9

Energy lost in generation and transmission of electricity 30.8

Residential and Commercial 44.0

Industry 48.8

Transportation 47.7

(10.6)

(19.5)

(34.4)

(33.4)

(29.3)

(13.3)

(9.3)

(5.6)

Electricity generation 45.7

Fuel consumed in end uses 125.5

Hydro–Other 2.6

Nuclear 4.8

export (4.6)

Coal 36.5

(22.2)

(8.3)

storage (1.4)

import (2.1)

Natural gas 52.2

(1.8)

(43.2)

storage (0.9)

(0.8)

(74.0)

Petroleum 82.3

import (31.4)

storage (0.3)

the United States at the top. It is arguable, however, whether gross national product, which is the aggregate value of all economic activities, is an accurate measure of the standard of living. Most people who have lived in both countries would agree that the average standard of living is as high in Sweden as it is in the United States, despite a substantially lower per capita gross national product in Sweden. Yet the per capita energy consumption in Sweden is less than half that of the United States. Even within the terms of the overall correlation in Figure 1.32, one can draw a box around the countries of Western Europe and see that in this limited range there is no correlation, with wide variations in per capita energy consumption for comparable per capita gross national product.

These differences may reflect peculiarities of the economies of the individual countries, but they may also reflect the effectiveness with which energy is actually used. It is reasonable that the amount of energy we need depends on how efficiently we use it. Figure 1.33 is a diagram of how energy actually flows through the U.S. economy. On the left side are the inputs from coal, petroleum, natural gas, water, and nuclear power in units of 10^{17} calories. The total consumption is 171.2 units. Of this, 45.7 goes to electricity production and the rest for other uses—household and commercial heating, transportation, and industry all taking comparable shares. Finally, on the right we have a division into useful energy versus waste heat. Fully 95.3 units, or 56% of the total, is wasted. Electricity production results in 30.8 units of waste, representing the inevitable waste heat mentioned earlier, as well as transmission losses.

Transportation produces 34.4 units of waste out of 47.7 total units, an efficiency of only 28%. Some of this waste has to do with inevitable losses in converting heat into motion, but much of it is due to inefficient modes of transportation. Table 1.9 compares the energy efficiency as well as the current economic cost of various modes of transportation for both freight and passengers. We see that pipelines and railroads are far more energy-efficient than trucks in freight transport and that airplanes are extremely inefficient. For passenger transport the differences are less extreme, but airplanes are still more than twice as wasteful as railroads and automobiles, whereas mass transit is twice as efficient as the automobile for urban transportation. These efficiency factors have to be balanced against convenience in making transportation choices, but it is clear that there is much room for energy savings when planning a transportation system. For example, rapid intercity trains would be both more efficient and more convenient up to a distance of about 500 miles, considering the time spent in traveling to and from airports.

In assessing the potential for energy conservation, a flow diagram such as that in Figure 1.33 is only a starting point. Some of the numbers in the waste column actually underestimate the potential. For example, household and commercial heating seems to be fairly efficient, wasting only 10.6 units or 24% of the input energy. However, the figure for waste includes only calories that are expelled directly to the environment rather than used for heating. If electrical resistance heating is used, for example, the conversion from electricity to heat is nearly 100% efficient, but this ignores the approximately 65% heat loss of the electrical generating plant. A more effective way to use the electricity would be to run a heat pump, which is diagrammed in Figure 1.34. This is just an air-conditioner run in reverse, with heat transferred from the colder outdoors to the warmer indoors. The theoretical amount of heat that can be produced from a unit of work is the inverse of the amount of work that can be extracted from heat in a heat engine; that is, the theoretical heat output of the heat pump is given by the ratio of the interior temperature to the difference in temperature between the outside and the inside. If the interior temperature is about 300° on the absolute scale, and the outside temperature is 20° colder, the heat pump could theoretically deliver 15 calories of heat for every calorie of electricity needed to run it. Because of resistances to heat transfer, actual pumps are much less efficient than this, but they nevertheless can be expected to deliver at least 2 calories of heat for every calorie of electricity. This is twice as good as electrical resistance heating and recovers some of the energy wasted at the electrical generating plant.

There are ways to use the waste heat from electrical generation purposefully. As diagrammed in Figure 1.35, one way is simply to use the hot water outflow to

Table 1.9   Efficiencies of Freight and Passenger Transport

Energy and Price Data for Intercity Freight Transport		
Mode	Energy (kcal/ton-mile)	Price (cents/ton-mile)
Pipeline	110	0.27
Railroad	170	1.4
Waterway	170	0.30
Truck	710	7.5
Airplane	11,000	21.9

Energy and Price Data for Passenger Transport		
Mode	Energy (kcal/ton-mile)	Price (cents/passenger-mile)
Intercity		
Bus	400	3.6
Railroad	730	4.0
Automobile	860	4.0
Airplane	2,100	6.0
Urban		
Mass transit	960	8.3
Automobile	2,000	9.6

Source: E. Hirst and J. C. Moyers, *Science* 179 (1973): 1299.

$$\text{Theoretical Efficiency:} \quad \frac{Q_h \text{(heat delivered)}}{W \text{(work)}} = \frac{T_h}{T_h - T_c} = \frac{300}{20} = 15$$

Figure 1.34   The Heat Pump: An Efficient Means of Residential Space Heating

Figure 1.35   Integrated Electric Power Plant—Residential Heating Source

$$CaBr_2 + 2H_2O \rightarrow Ca(OH)_2 + 2HBr \qquad \text{at } 730° \text{ C (1)}$$
$$Hg + 2HBr \rightarrow HgBr_2 + H_2 \qquad \text{at } 250° \text{ C (2)}$$
$$HgBr_2 + Ca(OH)_2 \rightarrow CaBr_2 + HgO + H_2O \qquad \text{at } 100° \text{ C (3)}$$
$$HgO \rightarrow Hg + \tfrac{1}{2}O_2 \qquad \text{at } 500° \text{ C (4)}$$

$$\text{Net: } H_2O \rightarrow H_2 + \tfrac{1}{2}O_2$$

Figure 1.36 Thermochemical Cycle

Source: G. DeBeni and C. Marchetti, *Eur. Spectra* (1970): 46.

heat residential or commercial buildings. This is already being done in urban areas such as New York, but it requires close proximity of the power plant and the units to be heated.

Another possibility is to combine electrical generation with the production of industrial process heat. At the moment much of the fuel consumed by industry goes to generate heat for various chemical and manufacturing processes. These industrial heating plants could be combined with electricity generators to extract greater energy value from the fuel. The main obstacle to this is that all electricity production is currently centralized in a single electrical utility in a given area. Another possibility that depends on further technical development is the use of some of the wasted heat to generate hydrogen through a thermochemical cycle of reactions. For example, Figure 1.36 shows a set of simple chemical reactions that sum up to give the water-splitting reaction. Although the direct thermal dissociation of water requires temperatures of about 2,500° C, all the individual reactions in the cycle shown occur at temperatures below 730° C. In essence, calcium bromide and mercury serve as catalysts for the dissociation of water by the four reaction steps shown. The overall reaction still requires energy and represents an energy-storing mechanism, but lower grade heat can be used for that purpose. The hydrogen produced in this fashion would be an input into the overall hydrogen economy discussed previously.

There are many opportunities to save substantial amounts of energy in manufacturing processes as well. The production of steel, aluminum, and paper consumes more than 20% of the total industrial energy expenditure in the United States. A substantial savings would arise from more systematic recycling of these and other industrial commodities. The bar graph in Figure 1.37 shows the amount of energy required to produce a metric ton of steel, paper, and aluminum from primary materials compared with the energy required for production from recycled materials. We see that aluminum production from ore is particularly energy-intensive. Recycled aluminum requires only 5% as much energy to process as primary aluminum ore. The savings from using steel scrap and paper waste are not so high—52% and 70%, respectively. Nevertheless, the potential for energy conservation is substantial when we consider the volume of these materials produced annually. Effective solid waste management could transform the environmental liability of millions of tons of waste products into new raw

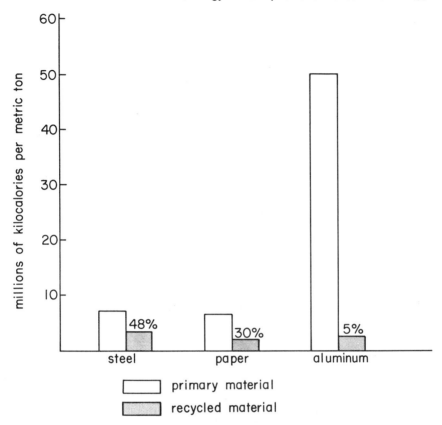

Figure 1.37 Comparison of Energy Requirements for Production of Steel, Paper, and Aluminum from Primary and Recycled Materials

Source: Ford Foundation, *A Time to Choose America's Energy Future* (Cambridge, Mass.: Ballinger Publishing Company, 1975), pp. 458, 464. E. T. Hays, "Energy Implications of Materials Processing," in *Materials: Renewable and Nonrenewable Resources,* ed. P. H. Abelson and A. L. Hammond (Washington, D.C.: American Association for the Advancement of Science, 1976), p. 33.

material assets. It would also help to eliminate the problem of finding more land for landfill disposal operations.

Historically, U.S. government policy has been skewed in favor of using primary materials rather than recycled materials. Most companies that mine primary ores are given about a 15% depletion allowance—a favorable tax incentive. Furthermore, federally regulated freight rates for transporting scrap iron and steel, nonferrous metals, paper, rubber, and textile wastes have been considerably higher than the freight rates paid by producers of competitive primary materials. These policies have made it more profitable to continue to rely on production from primary materials despite the major energy savings that recycling would provide.

The trend is changing, however, and recycled wastes will come to play a more important role in materials production. As part of the 1978 United States National Energy Act, equipment purchased for recycling wastes was given a 10% investment tax credit in addition to the 10% credit that already exists. Furthermore, the energy legislation contains a recycling targets provision, which authorizes the Department of Energy to set industrial goals maximizing the use of recycled materials. Specific targets are to be set for each industry for the next ten years. Also, the Interstate Commerce Commission has been mandated to review the freight rate structure for primary and scrap material.

The trend toward recycling is one example of how energy can be saved by examining the energy flow patterns in our society in depth, from both technological and social perspectives. Energy analysis is a new and rapidly developing area of study that is very important for energy policy. It is becoming clear that answers to the questions of what energy supplies are available to us and over what period of years they must be developed depend critically on having an accurate assessment of how much energy we really need. We cannot rely on extrapolations from past consumption patterns since they are based on the assumption of plentiful, cheap energy.

17 | Summary

Our survey of sources has shown that energy is supplied to us in abundance by the sun, and this steady energy flow is sufficient to maintain the human population at a steady state, which we must, in any event, achieve over a period of time. Capturing the sun's energy and putting it to useful work are challenges to science and technology. At the moment it is much more expensive to do this than to tap the solar energy that has been stored over the millennia in fossil fuels, which we have used to develop our industrial civilization. We are currently completely dependent on fossil fuels and particularly on petroleum and natural gas. These fuel stocks are being drawn down and will inevitably run out, in a matter of decades for oil and gas and perhaps in a few centuries for coal. In the meantime, the development of atomic science has begun to release the very large amounts of energy stored in the nuclei of uranium atoms, and potentially in hydrogen atoms as well, both for destructive and for constructive purposes. The development of nuclear power on a large scale, however, poses unprecedented problems for humanity in terms of the dangers of nuclear weapons proliferation and the long-term hazards associated with massive amounts of radioisotopes.

On the supply side of the energy equation, the key questions are to what extent coal and nuclear fuels can be used safely with acceptable environmental costs, and how long it will take to introduce alternative technologies involving solar power and possibly the fusion reaction. Equally important questions exist on the demand side of the energy equation; these are just beginning to be recognized. It is obvious that energy consumption cannot continue to grow exponentially forever. A close examination of how energy is actually used shows that significant savings are possible in situations where the use of energy has been historically predicated on the availability of a cheap and plentiful supply. Energy savings have a greater impact on the equation than energy supplies because of the low efficiency with which fuels are used. Each calorie of electricity that is not used represents a saving of 3 calories of oil, coal, or nuclear fuels. Savings on the demand side of the energy equation are desirable because they increase the range of human choices with respect to the energy supply. The lower the projected energy requirements, the greater is the flexibility for providing energy from a variety of sources, and the more time there is to develop the safest, most efficient, and least environmentally harmful technologies.

Problem Set

The following table refers to problems 1 and 2. It lists the heating requirements for a typical well insulated one family house in the central United States, along with the sunlight per day (24 hour average) falling on a fixed 45° flat plate collector facing south.

	Monthly heating requirements	Daily sunlight (calories/cm^2) 45° tilt
January	4.2×10^9 cal	283
February	4.0×10^9 cal	411
March	3.2×10^9 cal	383
April	1.7×10^9 cal	396
May	0.7×10^9 cal	391
June	0.2×10^9 cal	399
July	0	478
August	0	438
September	0.3×10^9 cal	428
October	1.3×10^9 cal	405
November	3.0×10^9 cal	243
December	4.1×10^9 cal	211

1. Plot energy need versus time over the course of a year. On the same graph draw a plot of available daily sunlight versus time. Comment on why most solar energy systems are not designed to provide 100% of the heating needs (typically, they may provide 50%).
2. Consider a house fitted with 50 m^2 of solar collectors capable of converting 40% of the available sunlight to warm the house. Calculate the amount of heat that can be extracted from the system to meet the heating needs of the house for one year. If the solar collectors are installed at a cost of $375 per m^2 what is the total cost of the

system? Assume that the cost of home heating oil will be an average of $3 per gallon over the next 20 years and that the heat value of the oil is 2.50×10^7 calories/gal. Assume further that the oil is burned at 90% efficiency. What would be the return on the investment over the 20 year period?

3. Describe three major environmental and security problems associated with nuclear power.

4. Explain how nuclear power based on the thorium breeding cycle has a security advantage in terms of nuclear proliferation over the plutonium breeding cycle.

5. How great an increase in the present genetically significant radiation background, 0.2 rad/year, would be expected to increase the estimated mutation rate, 10 per 10^6 genes per generation, by 10%? Assume that radiation induces 0.06 mutations per 10^6 genes per rad. One generation equals 30 years.

6. Plutonium is very damaging when inhaled as small particles because of the ionization of tissue by its emitted alpha particles. One microgram of plutonium is known to produce cancer in experimental animals. From its atomic weight (239) and half-life (24,000 years), calculate how many alpha particles are emitted by a microgram of plutonium over the course of a year. About how many ionizations do the particles produce?

7. A neutron generated by fission typically possesses a kinetic energy of 2 Mev. When such a neutron collides with a hydrogen atom 18 times, its energy is reduced to its thermal energy of 0.025 ev, i.e., the kinetic energy it would possess by virtue of the temperature of its surroundings. The same neutron would have to collide with a sodium atom more than 200 times to reduce its energy by the same amount. Explain how these characteristics make water a suitable coolant in the pressurized light water reactor that utilizes U-235 as the fuel, whereas sodium is the suitable coolant in the breeder reactor.

8. If world energy consumption continues to increase at the present annual rate of 3.6%, how long will it take to double? At this rate of increase, how long would it be before human energy consumption equals 1% of the solar energy absorbed by the earth, 2.1 $\times 10^{23}$ calories/year? The present world energy consumption is 4.8×10^{19} calories/ year.

9. a) Compare the costs per unit of the energy of electricity and gasoline. Current prices are $0.05 per kwh for the former and $1.50 per gallon for the latter. Gasoline weighs 5.51 lb/gal, and its energy release on combustion is 19,000 Btu (British thermal units) per pound. Energy units: 1 calorie = 4.18 joules = 1.16×10^{-6} kwh = 3.97×10^{-3} Btu.

b) Is this comparison fair?

10. An electric hot-water heater has a standard efficiency rating of 90% (i.e., for every 10 calories of electricity consumed, 9 go into heating the water). If the heater normally heats water from the ambient temperature, 68° F, to 176° F, what is its "second law" efficiency (i.e., what is the ratio of the amount of energy that an ideal heat pump would use to do the same job, to the amount of energy actually consumed)?

11. Calculate the theoretical efficiency of a heat pump when the room temperature is 65° F (18.3° C) and the outside temperature is -10° F (-23.3° C). If the heat pump were drawing heat from a water tank at 40° F (4.4° C) what would be the theoretical efficiency? Describe how solar energy in conjunction with a heat pump can provide an efficient means of heating a house.

12. 23% of total national energy consumption is used for space heating of residential and commercial buildings. Total national energy consumption is currently about 2.0×10^{19} calories/year. It is estimated that on the average space heating can be reduced by 50% by adding more efficient insulation, caulking, and weatherstripping. Using the heat value of oil given in problem 13 calculate the barrels of oil saved if all houses in the U.S. were efficiently insulated. In the peak year of 1977, 8.8×10^6 barrels per day were imported. By what percentage could our foreign oil imports be reduced if 50% better insulation were adopted?

13. a) The energy equivalent of how many barrels of crude oil are saved by recycling one ton of scrap aluminum rather than producing the ton from the ore. Use the following information:

    1 barrel of oil $= 1.46 \times 10^9$ calories
    1 ton of finished aluminum requires 4.79×10^{10} calories from ore and 2.39×10^9 calories from recycled aluminum.

    b) In 1979 about 8.0 million tons of aluminum were produced in the U.S. Of this about 2.0 million tons were produced from scrap metal. The equivalent of how many barrels of oil could have been saved if half of the total aluminum were produced from scrap metal? At \$25 a barrel, how much money can be saved?

14. A large power plant is being constructed that will produce 1.6×10^{10} kcal/day of electrical energy. For every kcalorie of energy produced, 2 kcal of waste heat is discharged. If the plant draws 2×10^9 l/day of river water at 20° C into its cooling condensers, calculate the rise in temperature of the cooling water. If the river has a flow rate of 10^{10} l/day, estimate the rise in temperature of the water downstream from the plant.

15. Assume you are asked by an electric utility in Chicago to assess the feasibility of using low sulfur subbituminous coal from Wyoming rather than locally available bituminous coal in order to meet EPA SO_2 emission standards (1.2 mg SO_2/kcalorie coal burned). Environmental impact and energy conservation should be considered in your assessment. You are given the following information:

	% S (by weight)	heat value (calorie/gram)
Bituminous (Chicago)	1.00	8,000
Subbituminous (Wyoming)	0.34	5,500

50% of the sulfur in the bituminous coal is in the mineral form of pyrite which is easily removed by mechanical means. The remainder of the sulfur is organically bound within the coal structure. All the sulfur in the subbituminuous coal is organically bound. The energy cost of transporting the coal by train is 170 kcalories/ton-mile. The distance from Wyoming to Chicago is 1,000 miles.

Suggestions for Further Reading

Energy

"Energy and Power" issue of *Scientific American* 225 (September 1971).
a) Energy issue of *Science* 184 (April 19, 1974).

b) This issue was also published along with other relevant *Science* articles in: Abelson, P. H., ed. *Energy—Use, Conservation and Supply.* Washington, D.C.: American Association for the Advancement of Science, 1974.

Science 199 (February 10, 1978), devoted largely to articles on energy.

Abelson, P. H., and Hammond, A. L., eds. *Energy II: Use, Conservation and Supply.* Washington, D.C.: American Association for the Advancement of Science, 1978.

"Energy Review." *Nature* 249 (June 21, 1974):697–737.

Ford Foundation. *A Time to Choose America's Energy Future,* final report by the Energy Policy Project of the Ford Foundation. Cambridge, Mass.: Ballinger Publishing Company, 1974.

Makhijani, A., and Poole, A. *Energy and Agriculture in the Third World.* Cambridge, Mass.: Ballinger Publishing Company, 1975.

Commoner, B. *The Poverty of Power. Energy and the Economic Crisis.* New York: Alfred A. Knopf, Inc., 1976.

Fossil fuels

Levorsen, A. *Geology of Petroleum.* San Francisco: W. H. Freeman and Co. Publishers, 1967, pp. 499–537.

Murchison, D. *Coal and Coal-Bearing Strata,* edited by T. S. Westoll. London: Oliver and Boyd, Ltd., 1968, pp. 197–268.

Griffith, E. D., and Clarke, A. W. "World Coal Production." *Sci. Am.* 240 (January 1979):38.

Flower, A. R. "World Oil Production." *Sci. Am.* 238 (March 1978):42.

Myerhoff, A. A. "Economic Impact and Geopolitical Implications of Giant Petroleum Fields." *Am. Sci.* 64 (September–October 1976):536.

Klass, D. L. "Synthetic Crude Oil from Shale and Coal." *Chem. Technol.* August 1975, p. 499.

Hammond, O. H., and Baron, R. E. "Synthetic Fuels: Prices, Prospects and Prior Art." *Am. Sci.* 64 (July–August 1976):407.

Worthy, W. "Synfuels: Uncertain and Costly Fuel Option." *Chem. Eng. News,* August 27, 1979, p. 20.

Maugh, T. "Tar Sands: A New Fuels Industry Takes Shape." *Science* 199 (1978):756.

Gillette, R. "Western Coal: Does the Debate Follow Irreversible Commitment?" *Science* 182 (1973):456.

Koppenaal, D., and Manahan, S. "Hazardous Chemicals from Coal Conversion Processes." *Environ. Sci. Technol.* 12 (1976):1104.

Fission

Harvey, B. G. *Introduction to Nuclear Physics and Chemistry,* 2nd ed. Englewood Cliffs, N.J.: Prentice-Hall, Inc., 1969.

Vendryes, G. A. "Superphénix: A Full-Scale Breeder Reactor." *Sci. Am.* 236 (March 1977):26.

Metz, W. D. "European Breeders (II): The Nuclear Parts Are Not the Problem." *Science* 191 (1976):368.

Zare, R. N. "Laser Separation of Isotopes." *Sci. Am.* 236 (February 1977):86.

Kubo, A. S., and Rose, D. J. "Disposal of Nuclear Wastes." *Science* 182 (1973): 1205.

Rochlin, G. I. "Nuclear Waste Disposal: Two Social Criteria." *Science* 195 (1977):23.

deMarsily, G., Ledoux, E., Barbreau, A., and Margat, J. "Nuclear Waste Disposal: Can the Geologist Guarantee Isolation?" *Science* 197 (1977):519.

Cohen, B. L. "The Disposal of Radioactive Wastes from Fission Reactors." *Sci. Am.* 236 (June 1977):21.

Sagan, L. A. "Human Costs of Nuclear Power." *Science* 177 (1972):487.

Lovins, A. B., and Patterson, W. C. "Plutonium Particles: Some Like Them Hot." *Nature* 254 (1975):278.

Lichtenstein, G. "Ill Wind Blows No Good in Uranium County." *New York Times,* May 22, 1976, p. 27.

Cohen, B. L. "Impacts of the Nuclear Energy Industry on Human Health and Safety." *Am. Sci.* 64 (September–October 1976):550.

Morgan, K. "Cancer and Low-Level Ionizing Radiation." *Bull. Atom. Sci.* 34 (September 1978):30.

Roblat, J. "The Risks for Radiation Workers." *Bull. Atom. Sci.* 34 (September 1978):41.

Edsall, J. T. "Toxicity of Plutonium and Some Other Actinides." *Bull. Atom. Sci.* 32 (September 1976):27.

Kerr, R. "Geologic Disposal of Nuclear Wastes: Salt's Lead Is Challenged." *Science* 204 (1979):603.

Marx, J. "Low-Level Radiation: Just How Bad Is It?" *Science* 204 (1979):160.

Carter, L. "Uranium Mill Tailings: Congress Addresses a Long-Neglected Problem." *Science* 202 (1978):191.

Angino, E. "High Level and Long-Lived Radioactive Waste Disposal." *Science* 198 (1977):885.

Hammond, R. P. "Nuclear Wastes and Public Acceptance." *Am. Sci.* 67 (March–April 1979):146.

Marshall, E., Carter, L., and Holden, C. "The Crisis at Three Mile Island: Nuclear Risks Are Reconsidered." *Science* 204 (1979):152.

Burwell, C. C., Ohanian, M. J., and Weinberg, A. M. "A Siting Policy for an Acceptable Nuclear Future." *Science* 204 (1979):1043.

Hammond, A. L. "Nuclear Proliferation (I): Warnings from the Arms Control Community." *Science* 193 (1976):126.

Feiveson, H. A., Taylor, T. B., von Hippel, F., and Williams, R. H. "The Plutonium Economy, Why We Should Wait and Why We Can Wait." *Bull. Atom. Sci.* 32 (December 1976):10.

Feiveson, H. A., and Taylor, T. B. "Security Implications of Alternative Fission Futures." *Bull. Atom. Sci.* 32 (December 1976):14.

von Hippel, F., and Williams, R. H. "Energy Waste and Nuclear Power Growth." *Bull. Atom. Sci.* 32 (December 1976):18.

Lovins, A. B. "Thorium Cycles and Proliferation." *Bull. Atom. Sci.* 35 (February 1979):16.

Kross, A. S. "Laser Enrichment of Uranium: The Proliferation Connection." *Science* 196 (1977):721.

Wilson, R. "How to Have Nuclear Power Without Weapons Proliferation." *Bull. Atom. Sci.* 33 (November 1977):39.

Roblat, J. "Controlling Weapons-Grade Fissile Material." *Bull. Atom. Sci.* 33 (June 1977):37.

Bebbington, W. P. "The Processing of Nuclear Fuels." *Sci. Am.* 235 (December 1976):30.

Walsh, J. "Fuel Reprocessing Still the Focus of U.S. Nonproliferation Policy." *Science* 201 (1978):692.

Lewis, K. N. "The Prompt and Delayed Effects of Nuclear War." *Sci. Am.* 241 (July 1979):35.

Rose, D., and Lester, R. "Nuclear Power, Nuclear Weapons and International Stability." *Sci. Am.* 238 (April 1978):45.

Rose, D. J., Walsh, P. W., and Leskovjan, L. L. "Nuclear Power Compared to What?" *Am. Sci.* 64 (May–June 1976):291.

Hohenemser, C., Kasperson, R., and Kates, R. "The Distrust of Nuclear Power." *Science* 196 (1977):25.

Flowers, B. "Nuclear Power." *Bull. Atom. Sci.* 34 (March 1978):21.

Weinberg, A. M. "Is Nuclear Energy Acceptable?" *Bull. Atom. Sci.* 33 (April 1977):54.

Rossin, A., and Rieck, T. "Economics of Nuclear Power." *Science* 201 (1978):582.

Kulcinski, G. L., et al. "Energy for the Long Run—Fission or Fusion?" *Am. Sci.* 67 (January–February 1979):78.

Fusion

Post, R. F., and Ribe, F. L. "Fusion Reactors As Future Energy Sources." *Science* 186 (1974):397.

Emmett, J. L., Nuckolls, J., and Wood, L. "Fusion Power by Laser Implosion." *Sci. Am.* 230 (June 1974):24.

Ashby, D. "Laser Fusion." *J. Br. Nucl. Energy Soc.* 14 (1975):311.

Holmes-Siedle, A. "Radiation Effects in the Fusion Power Programme." *Nature* 251 (September 20, 1974):191.

Metz, W. D. "Fusion Research (I): What Is the Program Buying the Country?" 192 (1976):1320.

Metz, W. D. "Fusion Research (II): Detailed Reactor Studies Identify More Problems." *Science* 193 (1976):38.

"Fusion Focus Shifts to Practical Aspects." *Chem. Eng. News,* October 11, 1976, p. 24.

Holdren, J. "Fusion Energy in Context: Its Fitness for the Long Term." *Science* 200 (1978):168.

Steiner, D., and Clarke, J. "The Tokamak: Model T Fusion Reactor." *Science* 194 (1978):1395.

Parkins, W. E. "Engineering Limitations of Fusion Power Plants." *Science* 199 (1978):1403.

Furth, H. P. "Progress Toward a Tokamak Fusion Reactor." *Sci. Am.* 241 (August 1979):50.

Yonas, G. "Fusion Power with Particle Beams." *Sci. Am.* 239 (November 1979):50.

Dingee, D. "Fusion Power." *Chem. Eng. News,* April 12, 1979, p. 32.

Solar Energy

Daniels, F. *Direct Use of the Sun's Energy,* (New York: Ballantine Books, Inc., 1974.

Wrighton, M. S. "Photochemistry: Power and Fuel from the Sun." *Chem. Eng. News,* September 3, 1979, p. 29.

Calvin, M. "Photosynthesis As a Resource for Energy and Materials." *Am. Sci.* 64 (May–June 1976):260.

Poole, A. D., and Williams, R. H. "Flower Power: Prospects for Photosynthetic Energy." *Bull. Atom. Sci.* 32 (May 1976):48.

Hammond, A. L. "Alcohol: A Brazilian Answer to the Energy Crisis." *Science* 195 (1977):564.

Burwell, C. "Solar Biomass Energy: An Overview of U.S. Potential." *Science* 199 (1978):1041.

Anderson, E. V. "Gasohol: Energy Mountain or Molehill?" *Chem. Eng. News,* July 31, 1978, p. 8.

Wade, N. "Windmills: The Resurrection of an Ancient Energy Technology." *Science* 184 (1974):1055.

Gustavson, M. R. "Limits to Wind Power." *Science* 204 (1979):13.

Pollard, W. G. "The Long-Range Prospects for Solar-Derived Fuels." *Am. Sci.* 64 (September–October 1976):509.

Bezdek, R., Hirshberg, A., and Babcock, W. "Economic Feasibility of Solar Water and Space Heating." *Science* 203 (1979):1214.

Hammond, A., and Metz, W. "Capturing Sunlight: A Revolution in Collector Design." *Science* 201 (1978):36.

Metz, W. "Energy Storage and Solar Power: An Exaggerated Problem." *Science* 200 (1978):1471.

Worthy, W. "Passive Solar Heating Systems Show Promise." *Chem. Eng. News,* September 11, 1978, p. 23.

Chalmers, B. "The Photovoltaic Generation of Electricity." *Sci. Am.* 235 (October 1976):34.

Hildebrandt, A. F., and Vant-Hull, L. L. "Power with Heliostats." *Science* 197 (1977):1139.

Duguay, M. A. "Solar Electricity: The Hybrid System Approach." *Am. Sci.* 65 (July–August 1977):422.

Hammond, A. L., and Metz, W. D. "Solar Energy Research: Making Solar After the Nuclear Model?" *Science* 197 (1977):241.

Caputo, R. S. "Solar Power Plants: Dark Horse in the Energy Stable." *Bull. Atom. Sci.* 33 (May 1977):46.

Johnston, W. D. "The Prospects for Photovoltaic Conversion." *Am. Sci.* 65 (November–December 1977):729.

Pollard, W. G. "The Long-Range Prospects for Solar Energy." *Am. Sci.* 64 (July–August 1976):424.

Rawls, R. "Prospects Improving for Wider Solar Energy Use." *Chem. Eng. News,* August 20, 1979, p. 22.

von Hippel, F., and Williams, R. H. "Toward a Solar Civilization." *Bull. Atom. Sci.* 33 (October 1977):12.

Lovins, A. "Energy Strategy: The Road Not Taken?" *Foreign Affairs,* October 1976.

Energy Conservation

Ford, K. W., et al., eds. "Efficient Use of Energy: A Physics Perspective, American Physics Society Studies on the Technical Aspects of the More Efficient Use of Energy." New York: American Institute of Physics, 1975.

Socolow, R. H. "Efficient Use of Energy."*Phys. Today* 28 (August 1975):23.

Schipper, L., and Lichtenberg, A. J. "Efficient Energy Use and Well-Being: The Swedish Example." *Science* 194 (1976):100.

Robinson, A. L. "Energy Storage (I): Using Electricity More Efficiently." *Science* 184 (1974):785.

Robinson, A. L. "Energy Storage (II): Developing Advanced Technologies." *Science* 184 (1974):884.

Fickett, A. P. "Fuel-Cell Power Plants." *Sci. Am.* 239 (December 1978):70.

Hirst, E. "Residential Energy Use Alternatives: 1976 to 2000." *Science* 194 (1976):1247.

Karkheck, J., Powell, J., and Beardsworth, E. "Prospects for District Heating in the United States." *Science* 195 (1977):948.

Hayes, E. T. "Energy Implications of Materials Processing." *Science* 191 (1976):661.

Hayes, E. "Energy Resources Available to the United States, 1985 to 2000." *Science* 203 (1979):233.

Reddy, A. K. "Energy Options for the Third World." *Bull. Atom. Sci.* 34 (May 1978):28.

PART II | ATMOSPHERE

1 | Earth's Radiation Balance

As we have seen, the sun provides us with a very large input of energy every day. Consequently, the earth must get rid of this energy at the same rate if it is to maintain a steady state. It does so by radiating light. Of course, the earth does not glow the way the sun does. The wavelengths of the earth's rays are too long to be detected by our eyes. A hot body gives off radiation with a range of wavelengths that decreases with increasing temperature. This is why a piece of iron when heated in a furnace glows red and then white as its temperature increases. Wavelengths are expressed in terms of billionths of meters, or nanometers (nm). The eye is sensitive to wavelengths between 400 and 700 nm, corresponding to the blue and red ends of the spectrum.

Figure 2.1 shows the spectral distribution of radiation from the sun as well as from the earth. The sun is a very hot body, and most of its rays fall in the region of visible wavelength. This is reasonable since our visual organs have evolved in response to sunlight. As shown by equation 1 in Figure 2.1, known at *Wein's law,* one can calculate the peak wavelength of the rays given off by a hot body by dividing its absolute temperature into a constant number, 2,900,000. The solar spectrum peaks at 483 nm, giving an estimate of the temperature at the surface of the sun of about 6,000° K. The earth, of course, is much cooler than this. If we take the average temperature to be about 290° K, we would expect from equation 1 a peak wavelength of about 10,000 nm, which is in good agreement with the earth's spectrum shown in Figure 2.1. In summary, while the earth absorbs radiation mainly in the visible region, characteristic of the high temperature at the surface of the sun, it gives off radiation at the same rate but at the much longer wavelengths characteristic of the earth's surface temperature.

The rate at which a hot body radiates energy is proportional to the fourth power of its absolute temperature, as shown by equation 2 in Figure 2.1, known as the *Stefan-Boltzmann law.* From the rate at which the earth absorbs energy from the sun, one can calculate the steady state temperature.

The solar flux incident on the earth is known to be 1.95 calories/cm^2-minute. The fraction absorbed by the earth is one minus the average albedo, or 0.66.

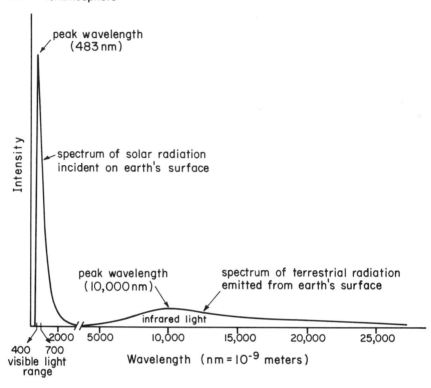

I.   peak wavelength = $\dfrac{2.90 \times 10^6}{T}$ nm

2.   total energy flux from
     surface of radiator = $82 \times 10^{-12} \, T^4$ calories/cm^2-minute

(T = temperature in degrees Kelvin)

Figure 2.1   Spectral Distribution of Solar and Terrestrial Radiation

Averaging over the surface of the earth means dividing by four, because as seen from the sun the earth is a disk of area πr^2, where r is the earth's radius, whereas the total surface area of the earth is $4\pi r^2$. If the rate of radiation follows the Stefan-Boltzmann law, then energy balance requires that

$$82 \times 10^{-12} T^4 = \frac{1.95}{4} \times 0.7 \text{ calories/cm}^2\text{-minute}$$

This gives $T = 254°$ K, or $-30°$ C, which is actually the average temperature that prevails about 5 km above the surface of the earth. The earth-air system acts as if it radiates from somewhere in the middle of the atmosphere.

If the heat input to the earth is increased or decreased, the outflux will adjust accordingly, and the average temperature will move up or down. In the first part of this book, we mentioned that human consumption of energy in the form of fossil or nuclear fuels will equal the solar heat flux within another 14 doubling periods, which at current rates of increase corresponds to about 320 years. Using the fourth-power dependence of the total heat flux on the temperature, it is easy to calculate that the average temperature would then increase by 19%, or 46° C. Long before then severe effects, including the melting of the polar ice caps, would be felt.

Another way that human activities could upset the heat balance is by inadvertently changing the albedo. As mentioned earlier, the average value for the fraction of sunlight reflected and scattered back into space without being absorbed is about 34%. As illustrated in Figure 2.2, this represents an average over very large local variations, which could be affected by human activities. For example, the clearing of forest land for agriculture increases the albedo from about 15% to 20%. If erosion sets in, leading to dust bowl and eventually desert conditions, the albedo is further increased to about 28%. An area of particular

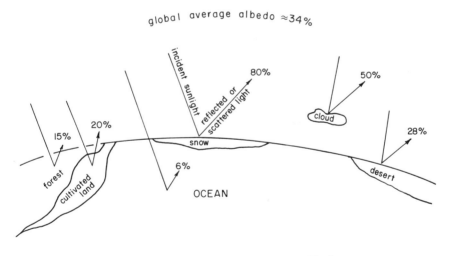

Surface Type	Average Albedo
forest land	15%
agricutural land	20%
deserts	28%
snow covered (above 60° latitude)	80%
oceans (70° latitude)	9- 23%
oceans (below 70° latitude)	3- 8%
clouds (average over all types)	50%
over entire surface	~ 34%

Figure 2.2 Variations in Albedo with Type of Surface on Earth

concern is the Arctic ice sheet—large masses of ice that melt and reform every year. This is a potentially unstable situation since the melting of ice leads to a decrease in the albedo from 80% to less than 25%. Therefore, a greater absorption of solar heat would cause an increased degree of melting with an accompanying decrease in the overall albedo. This would cause even more ice to melt in a positive feedback loop. There is a possibility that the instability might be increased if areas of the ice were covered with foreign matter that decreases the albedo, for example, oil that might spill and spread on the ice as a result of drilling and transporting petroleum in the Arctic region.

A related concern has to do with the dispersal of airborne particles in the atmosphere as a result of human activities. Both agriculture and industry release quantities of dust and fumes into the air, as do heating plants and automobiles. The increased particle loading of the atmosphere might affect the radiation balance. Figure 2.3 is a graphical estimate of the amounts of particles dispersed in the atmosphere over the past 100 years. The contribution from human activity, shown by the solid curve, is much less than the contribution from wind and other natural sources, but it is rising rapidly. Large temporary increases in particle concentrations have resulted from volcanic eruptions in the past. The effect of more particles in the atmosphere has generally been thought to be a cooling of the earth's surface as a result of increased scattering of the sun's rays. However, particles can absorb light as well as scatter it, as shown in Figure 2.4. Dark particles absorb light, whereas light particles reflect light. The absorbed light contributes to the heating of the earth's atmosphere, while the reflected light

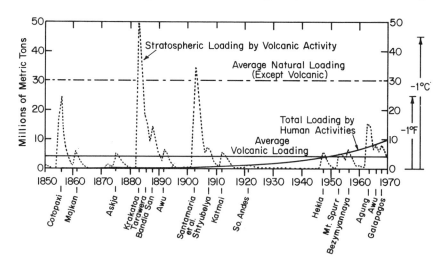

Figure 2.3   Natural and Man-made Particle Loading of Atmosphere

Source: "The Natural Stratosphere of 1974," Monograph 1, U.S. Department of Transportation, Climatic Impact Assessment Program (DOT-TST-75-51), September 1975, p. 8-24.

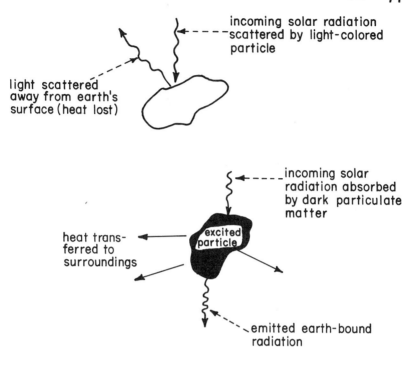

incoming solar radiation
scattered by light-colored
particle

light scattered
away from earth's
surface (heat lost)

incoming solar
radiation absorbed
by dark particulate
matter

excited
particle

heat trans-
ferred to
surroundings

emitted earth-bound
radiation

Earth's   Surface

Figure 2.4   Scattering and Absorption of Radiation from Particulate Matter

takes heat away. Consequently, whether particles have a cooling or heating effect depends on their optical properties, which vary depending on their source. Coal dust absorbs more light than does sand. Understanding the effect of particles on climate therefore requires a detailed analysis of the sources as well as the overall loading.

2 | Greenhouse Effect

What about the air molecules through which radiation passes to and from the earth? How do they affect the heat flow? Table 2.1 shows the gaseous composition of the atmosphere. It is 78% nitrogen, by volume, 21% oxygen, 0.9% inert gas argon, and 0.03% carbon dioxide. There are many other gases present in trace quantities. All of them together make up less than 0.01% of the total. The units usually used for measuring atmospheric gases present at low concentrations are parts per million, which can be obtained from the percentage by multiplying by 10,000.

The table gives no value for water vapor, whose contribution varies greatly from place to place. While all the other constituents are well mixed throughout the atmosphere, this is not true of water. The amount of water in the air depends on the vapor pressure of liquid water, which depends strongly on the temperature. Moreover, water molecules are being constantly evaporated and reprecipitated as rain. The total number of water molecules in the atmosphere at any time is about 0.4% of the air molecules.

All the constituents listed in Table 2.1 are transparent to most of the sun's rays. None of them absorbs light significantly in the visible region of the spectrum. The situation is different in the infrared region, however, where the earth emits its radiation. Neither nitrogen nor oxygen absorbs infrared rays, but carbon dioxide and water vapor do. Figure 2.5 shows the absorption spectra of these molecules, that is, the intensity of light absorption as a function of wavelength. These two spectra add up to effectively block a large fraction of the earth's emitted radiation, as illustrated in the top graph of the figure. Some of the terrestrial radiation does escape without absorption in a relatively small frequency range between 8,000 and 13,000 nm. This is called the *atmospheric window*.

The absorption of the earth's rays by carbon dioxide and water is of great importance to the climate on our planet. The overall effect is to heat up the

Table 2.1   The Gaseous Composition
of Unpolluted Air (dry basis)

	Volume (%)	Volume (ppm)
Nitrogen	78.09	780,900
Oxygen	20.94	209,400
Water	—	—
Argon	0.93	9,300
Carbon dioxide	0.03	325
Neon	Trace	18
Helium	Trace	5.2
Methane	Trace	1.0–1.2
Krypton	Trace	1.0
Nitrous oxide	Trace	0.5
Hydrogen	Trace	0.5
Xenon	Trace	0.08
Organic vapors	Trace	~0.02

Source: A. C. Stern, H. C. Wohlers, R. W. Boubel, and W. P. Lowry, *Fundamentals of Air Pollution* (New York: Academic Press, 1973), p. 21.

earth's surface by a phenomenon commonly called the *greenhouse effect,* which is shown schematically in Figure 2.6. The light absorbed by carbon dioxide and water can be emitted again. The radiation can be reemitted in all directions, with equal probability upward and downward. The net result of this is that part of the earth's radiation returns to the surface and raises the surface temperature to warmer than what it would be in the absence of an atmosphere. This effect causes a change of about 35° C, the difference between the 254° K temperature calculated earlier for the earth as a radiating body and the actual average temperature at the surface. The overall radiation balance is not affected by this, of course, since the earth must still lose as much energy as it absorbs; what changes is the temperature distribution in the atmosphere. The surface of the earth is heated up at the expense of the upper layers of the air.

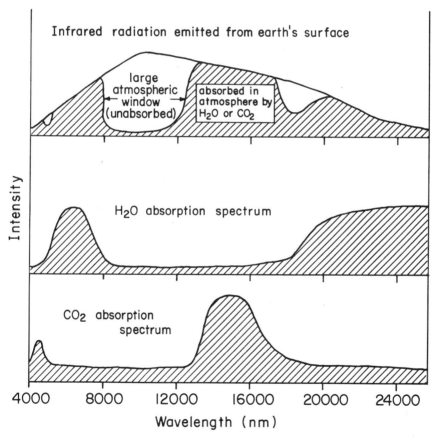

Figure 2.5 Absorption of Terrestrial Radiation by Water and Carbon Dioxide

Figure 2.6   The Greenhouse Effect

As far as we surface dwellers are concerned, however, it is the surface temperature that counts, and there has been concern that the greenhouse effect will be magnified by the increasing amounts of carbon dioxide produced by the rapid burning of the fossil fuel stores. We saw earlier that the burning of fossil fuels has a negligible effect on the oxygen content of the atmosphere, which is very large, but an appreciable effect on the carbon dioxide content which is currently only 325 ppm. The upper part of Figure 2.7 shows the increase in industrial carbon dioxide production during the last century. The curve is exponential, paralleling the curve of energy consumption. The second graph in the figure shows the mean monthly carbon dioxide concentrations in the atmosphere over a measuring station in Hawaii for the past two decades. There are large seasonal fluctuations associated with the yearly cycle of plant life. The plants grow in the spring and summer and decay in the fall and winter, giving their carbon dioxide back to the atmosphere. Underlying this seasonal variation is a steady upward trend in the average value. Since 1958, the value has increased from about 312 ppm to the present average value of 325 ppm.

However, the rate of increase is only about 50% of that expected if all the carbon dioxide emitted by human activity during those years were added to the total. Evidently 50% of the carbon dioxide produced does not stay in the atmosphere. Figure 2.8 diagrams the sources of atmospheric carbon dioxide and also the removal mechanisms, commonly known as the *sinks*. One sink is the ocean, which contains very large amounts of carbon dioxide in the form of the bicarbonate ion and accounts for most of the carbon dioxide removal, according to recent studies. Another possible sink is the biomass, that is, the living green plants

(i)
Industrial CO_2 Production Since 1860

(ii)
Mean Monthly Values of CO_2 Concentration at Mauna Loa, Hawaii
(1958 – 1971)

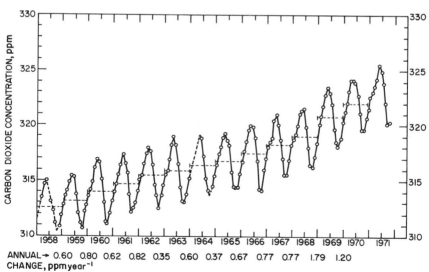

ANNUAL→ 0.60 0.80 0.62 0.82 0.35 0.60 0.37 0.67 0.77 0.77 1.79 1.20
CHANGE, ppm year^{-1}

Figure 2.7   Buildup of Carbon Dioxide in the Atmosphere

Source: G. M. Woodwell and E. V. Pecan, eds., *Carbon and the Biosphere* (Springfield, Va.: Technical Information Center, U.S. Atomic Energy Commission, August 1973), pp. 22, 90.

themselves. It is known from laboratory experiments that green plants increase their rate of photosynthesis in response to an increase in the carbon dioxide concentration. This could be happening on a global scale. But the growth and shrinkage of the biomass depend on much more than the carbon dioxide concentration. They depend on other factors that affect plant growth and on human activities, particularly the widespread clearing of forested areas for agricultural purposes. It is very difficult to estimate the size of the total biomass, and we do not know whether it is presently growing or shrinking.

The temperature effects of carbon dioxide and water vapor are coupled. As the surface temperature rises, because of increased amounts of carbon dioxide, more water evaporates, and the water vapor increases the temperature further. The combined effect can be calculated to be a 3° C rise in the surface temperature for a doubling of the carbon dioxide concentration. Also general precipitation increases by 7% because of the increased rate of water evaporation. Extrapolation of the present trend suggests that the carbon dioxide concentration will double by the year 2050.

New considerations in studying the greenhouse effect are the chlorofluoromethane gases, called CFMs, which are used in refrigerators and as spray can propellants. There are two kinds of CFMs: $CFCl_3$ and CF_2Cl_2. Both are very inert, which is one of their desirable properties from the point of view of the consumer, and they accumulate in the atmosphere. The major controversy about CFMs has to do with their impact on the ozone layer, which we will discuss shortly. It has been pointed out that these molecules also absorb infrared light strongly and that their absorption bands fall in the window region of carbon dioxide and water absorption, which, as we saw in Figure 2.5, is the region of maximum radiation from the earth. The CFM spectra and the window region are shown in Figure 2.9. The effect is strong enough so that an increase in the surface temperature of nearly a degree might result from CFM concentrations on the order of 2 parts per billion (ppb), which would be expected by the year 2000 if

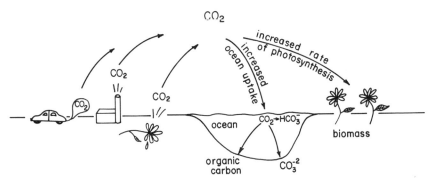

Figure 2.8 Sources and Sinks of Carbon Dioxide

levels of injection of CFMs into the atmosphere were maintained at the 1975 level.

The mean global temperature has been increasing gradually throughout the first half of this century, as shown in the top graph of Figure 2.10, in which a smooth curve is drawn through the yearly temperature fluctuation. This rise correlates with the increase in carbon dioxide production associated with the Industrial Revolution. It has been suggested that the greenhouse effect is responsible. On the other hand, the temperature seems to have peaked in about 1940 and has been declining perceptibly since then. This downward trend might be associated with the increasing production of particles, according to our previous discussion. The second graph in Figure 2.10 shows the solar radiation flux at the

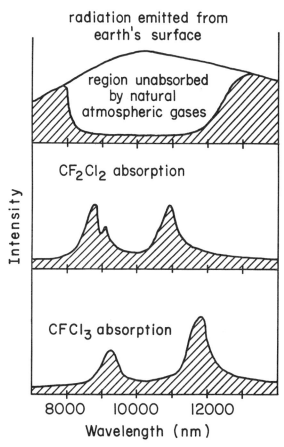

Figure 2.9 Absorption Spectra of Chlorofluoromethanes, CFCl and CFCl₇ Coincidence with Atmospheric Window Region*

*Region from 8,000 to 13,000 nm (See Figure 2.5)

surface of the earth. There is a suggestive similarity with the overall shape of the temperature record including the dip in the early 1900s. This dip and the earlier one before 1890 can be associated with atmospheric dust from large volcanic eruptions, as shown in Figure 2.3, and it is likely that the radiation curve reflects the amount of particles in the air.

The average temperature can be traced back over a longer period of time using a variety of geophysical techniques as well as fossil records. When this is done, much larger temperature fluctuations are observed, as illustrated in Figure 2.11. The graph on the left shows that over the past few hundred years, temperature fluctuations of more than 1° C were experienced. Temperatures were appreciably lower from about 1400 to 1850. This period is known as the Little Ice Age in Europe. As seen in the graph on the right, there were larger fluctuations over a

(i)
Mean Temperatures (1880-1970)*

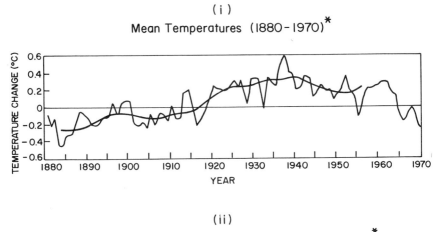

(ii)
Solar Flux Striking Earth's Surface (1880-1970)*

Figure 2.10   Recent Trends in Temperature and Solar Radiation Flux (Northern Hemisphere)

*Baselines have been arbitrarily set.
Source: Adapted from "The Natural Stratosphere of 1974," Monograph 1, U.S. Department of Transportation, Climatic Impact Assessment Program (DOT-TST-75-51), September 1975, p. 8–47.

span of hundreds of thousands of years. These reflect the Ice Ages, the last one of which reached its lowest temperature about 20,000 years ago.

We see that the assessment of human impacts on the climate must be superimposed on this large natural variation. Figure 2.12 shows an attempt to do this for the carbon dioxide greenhouse effect. The expected 0.3° C rise per 10% increase in carbon dioxide concentration is added to a projection of the natural temperature fluctuations obtained from an examination of the temperature record over the past several hundred years. If this approach is correct, then the current cooling trend should soon level off and be followed by a rather steep rise in temperature. This calculation does not consider contributions to the greenhouse effect by the chlorofluoromethanes, and conceivably by other organic molecules currently being emitted into the atmosphere, which would magnify the predicted temperature increase.

Relatively small average temperature changes could seriously disrupt world food production. A 1° C decline would decrease the growing period in the

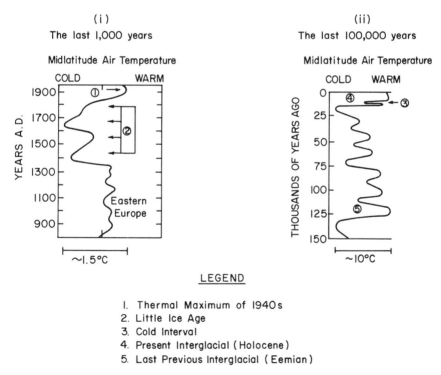

LEGEND

1. Thermal Maximum of 1940s
2. Little Ice Age
3. Cold Interval
4. Present Interglacial (Holocene)
5. Last Previous Interglacial (Eemian)

Figure 2.11 Natural Fluctuations in Earth's Temperature

Source: *Understanding Climatic Change, A Program for Action* (Washington, D.C.: National Academy of Sciences, 1975), p. 130.

Figure 2.12   A Model for Projected Trend in Global Temperature Due to the Greenhouse Effect

Source: W. S. Broecker, *Science* **189** (1975):461.

northern latitudes sufficiently to eliminate much of the wheat crop in Canada and large areas in the Soviet Union. On the other hand, an increase in average temperature would shift the wheat-growing zones toward the poles, away from fertile soils and onto poorer quality ground. Also, a warming of the surface layers of the ocean would reduce the vertical circulation that carries nutrients to the surface from the deeper layers. Biological productivity would therefore decrease.

At the moment we simply do not know enough about the determinants of long-term effects on climate to make any predictions with confidence. This is an active and important area of research.

3 | Atmospheric Structure

Our gaseous envelope extends many miles up from the surface of the earth. With respect to its major chemical constituents, which we examined in Table 2.1, the atmosphere is quite uniform throughout its extent, except for water vapor, which is concentrated in the lower region. In other respects, the air is far from uniform. It grows thinner with increasing altitude. The density falls off roughly logarithmically with increasing distance from the surface. About 70% of the mass of the atmosphere is contained in a blanket 10 km thick. Even less uniform than the density is the temperature, which depends on altitude as shown in Figure 2.13. The slope of the curve of temperature versus altitude is called the *lapse rate*. Figure 2.13 shows several reversals of the lapse rate. Up to about 10 km, temperature decreases uniformly with increasing altitude. This reflects the fact that the atmosphere in this lower region is heated from below by the earth's radiation. Above 10 km, however, the temperature increases again with increasing altitude, reaching a maximum near 50 km and decreasing once again beyond this. The maximum in the temperature profile reflects a heating process high in the atmosphere due to the absorption of solar radiation in the near ultraviolet region by a band of ozone, O_3. We will examine the ozone layer and its properties shortly. Beyond about 90 km, the temperature rises once more due to the absorption of solar rays in the far ultraviolet region by atmospheric gases, principally oxygen. These far ultraviolet rays are sufficiently energetic to ionize molecules and break them into their constituent atoms. Because of the thinness of the atmosphere at such high altitudes, fragments recombine only rarely, and an appreciable fraction of the gases in this region, called the *thermosphere,* exist as atoms or ions.

The structure of the temperature profile reflects a physical layering of the atmosphere as well. A negative lapse rate leads to convection of the air; warm air rises from below and cool air sinks. But a positive lapse rate reflects a region of stability with respect to convection, since warm air overlies cool air. The change from negative to positive lapse rate is called a *temperature inversion,* and the point at which this change occurs marks a stable boundary between two physically distinct layers of air. Local temperature inversions are quite common over many cities, particularly those nestled in surrounding mountains or, as in the case of Los Angeles, where prevailing winds from the ocean blow cool air into a region ringed on three sides by mountains. Warm air flowing over the mountain tops traps the cool air below, allowing pollutants to build up for considerable periods. Anyone flying into Los Angeles on a sunny day is likely to see the local temperature inversion and the quite distinct boundary between the clear air above and the brown smoggy air below.

The temperature inversion shown in Figure 2.13 at an altitude of about 10 km is called the *tropopause.* It marks a global layering of the atmosphere into the troposphere below and the stratosphere above. The troposphere contains 70% of the mass of the atmosphere. Because of its negative lapse rate, the air it contains is mixed rapidly by convection. It is also a region of much turbulence due to the global energy flow that results from the imbalances of heating and cooling rates between the equator and the poles. The stratosphere, on the other hand, is a quiescent layer; because of its positive lapse rate, it mixes slowly. The tropopause itself is a stable boundary and the flux of air across it is low. Residence times of molecules or particles in the stratosphere are measured on a scale of years. The air in it is quite thin so that pollutants that reach, or are injected into, the stratosphere have a relatively greater global impact than they would in the much denser troposphere.

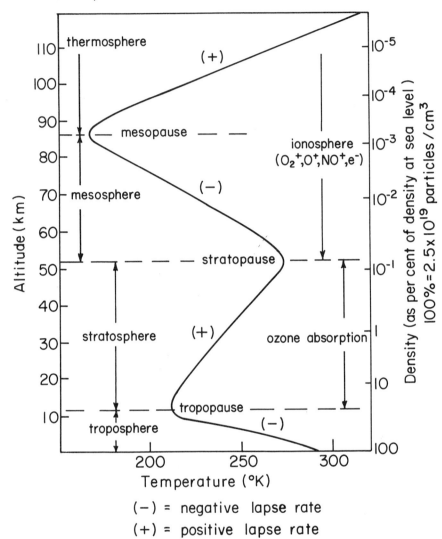

Figure 2.13 Layer Structure of the Atmosphere

Concern about pollution of the stratosphere centers on possible threats to the layer of ozone it contains. This triatomic form of the element oxygen serves two essential functions in the stratosphere. It protects living matter on earth from the harmful effects of the sun's ultraviolet rays, and it provides the heat source for layering the atmosphere into a quiescent stratosphere and a turbulent troposphere.

Figure 2.14 shows the spectrum of the sun's rays in the visible and ultraviolet regions. Also shown is part of the absorption spectrum of ozone. It has a peak at about 260 nm. Although the ozone layer extends over tens of kilometers in altitude, if compressed to 1 atm pressure its thickness would be only 3 mm on the average. Nevertheless, its ultraviolet absorption is strong enough to eliminate much of the ultraviolet tail of the solar radiation spectrum at the surface of the earth. These ultraviolet rays are harmful to life. They carry enough energy to break the bonds of organic molecules and produce reactive fragments. Ultraviolet radiation produces sunburn and also skin cancer, particularly in people who have

visible light: 400 - 700 nm   ultraviolet light: < 400 nm

Figure 2.14 Absorption of Sun's Ultraviolet Light by Ozone light pigmentation. The damage done to living tissue as a function of solar wavelength is shown in Figure 2.15 and is commonly known as the *action spectrum*. The solid curve in the figure shows the spectrum of the skin's sunburn sensitivity at constant light intensity. Also shown is the spectrum of the solar rays at ground level. The product of these two curves gives the actual action spectrum for sunburn, that is, the response of the skin to solar radiation. The overlap of ground-level radiation with the sunburn sensitivity curve would be much greater if it were not for the filtering effects of the ozone layer.

Figure 2.16 shows data that support the connection between exposure to solar ultraviolet radiation and the incidence of skin cancer. Both the incidence of skin cancer and the solar ultraviolet flux decrease with increasing distance from the equator. The sun's rays fall more directly at lower latitudes, and also the ozone layer is thinner over the equator than over the poles. As shown in the figure, between 30 and 46 degrees latitude north, the ultraviolet flux is reduced by a factor of three, the incidence of malignant skin cancer appears to decrease by a factor of nearly three, and nonmalignant cancer decreases by a factor of nearly four. Green plants are also susceptible to damage by ultraviolet rays. Their light-harvesting photosynthetic apparatus is tuned to visible radiation and can be destroyed by sufficiently intense ultraviolet radiation. Also, the genetic material of both plants and animals, the DNA molecules, is known to be susceptible to ultraviolet radiation damage. It is likely that higher forms of life could not have evolved on earth until the protective ozone layer had developed.

Figure 2.15   Action Spectrum of Ultraviolet Radiation Damage to Living Tissue

UV exposure by latitude

Malignant melanoma skin cancer by latitude

Figure 2.16 Correlation Between Skin Cancer Incidence* and Ultraviolet Exposure

Source: Top graph: Adapted from data of F.S. Johnson, et al., *Photochem. Photobiol.* 23 (1976): 179. Middle and bottom graphs: A.J. Grobecker, et al., "The Effects of Stratospheric Pollution by Aircraft" (DOT-TST-75-50) (Springfield, Va.: National Technical Information Service, U.S. Atomic Energy Commission, December 1974), p. 35.

*Caucasian total age-adjusted incidence in the United States, 1970.

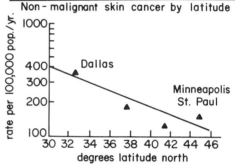

Non-malignant skin cancer by latitude

4 | Ozone Chemistry

Figure 2.17 shows the reactions that are responsible for the buildup of ozone in the stratosphere. As we mentioned earlier, the ultraviolet photons of the sun have enough energy to split oxygen molecules into oxygen atoms high in the atmosphere. This is shown in reaction 1. Reaction 2 shows an oxygen atom combining with another oxygen molecule to form the triatomic molecule, ozone. Because the oxygen atom is very energetic, a third molecule labeled M must be present at the encounter in order to carry away some of the excess energy, otherwise the ozone molecule would fly apart as fast as it was formed. M can be any molecule that happens to be present. In the atmosphere it is most likely to be nitrogen or

O_3 Formation

photon = $h\nu$ < 242 nm

I.

O——O   →   O
oxygen   highly energetic
molecule   →   O   oxygen atoms

2.

O   +   O   energy transfer →   M   ⟶   (stable ozone)   +   M
high energy oxygen atom   (low kinetic energy)   (high kinetic energy)

highly energetic collision

(M is a third body, e.g. N_2, O_2)

O_3 Destruction

photon = $h\nu$ (200-320nm)

3.

ozone   ⟶   O   +   O
             oxygen   oxygen
             atom   molecule

4.

O   +   (ozone)   ⟶   O—O   +   O
two body collision   oxygen molecules

Figure 2.17 Reactions of Ozone

another molecule of oxygen. Reactions 3 and 4 are ozone destruction reactions. As we have seen, ozone can absorb solar rays in the ultraviolet region. When this happens, there is a high probability that the excited ozone molecule will dissociate into an oxygen molecule and an oxygen atom, as shown in reaction 3. Also, an oxygen atom can combine with an ozone molecule to form two oxygen molecules, as in reaction 4.

Ozone is highly unstable compared with the normal form of oxygen, O_2. At equilibrium, less than 1 part in 10^{25} of the oxygen in the atmosphere is present as ozone. The actual ratio of ozone to oxygen reaches values as high as about 1 part in 30,000 at an altitude of 30 km. Evidently the ozone layer is very far from being at equilibrium because the ozone-destroying reactions are not instantaneous. The actual ozone concentration depends on the rate of the destruction reactions compared with the rate of the formation reactions. The rate of formation depends on the flux of ultraviolet solar radiation in the stratosphere. If this flux were constant, we would have a steady-state condition in which the rate of formation is equal to the rate of destruction. We could then write down the rate equations and solve them for the steady-state concentration of ozone.

At any given place in the atmosphere the solar flux is, of course, not constant. It varies throughout the day and also with the seasons. The ozone concentration is therefore subject to large variations. These variations are fairly regular, however, and on the average the ultraviolet solar flux depends only on the altitude, becoming smaller at lower altitudes as most of the rays are absorbed. When these average values are used in the steady-state equation, the ozone profile shown as the dashed line in Figure 2.18 can be calculated. Also shown, as the solid line, is the actual ozone profile as obtained from averaged measurements. The two curves are quite similar in shape, but the calculated curve gives ozone concentrations that are about a factor of two too high, at least at the maximum in the curve.

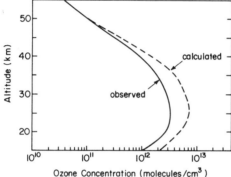

Figure 2.18 Plot of Observed and Calculated Atmospheric Ozone Concentrations.

Ref.: *Report of the Study of Man's Impact on Climate (SMIC)*, op. cit. (Fig. 2(B)), p. 268.

5 | Nitrogen Oxides

The likeliest reason for the discrepancy between the actual and the calculated ozone concentrations is that we have not considered reactions that can significantly speed up the destruction of ozone. Many such reactions have been considered. The most important ones appear to be reactions 5 and 6 in Figure 2.19. In reaction 5, a molecule of nitric oxide, NO, reacts with ozone to give molecular oxygen and a molecule of nitrogen dioxide, NO_2. In reaction 6, the nitrogen dioxide reacts with an oxygen atom to regenerate nitric oxide and produce another molecule of oxygen. The sum of reactions 5 and 6 is reaction 4 of Figure 2.17. In other words, reactions 5 and 6 act to speed up the combination of ozone and atomic oxygen to give molecular oxygen. The nitrogen oxides are not used up in this process; they are simply interconverted between nitric oxide and nitrogen dioxide. Therefore they act as a catalyst in the destruction of ozone. Although present in relatively small amounts, nitrogen oxides are natural constituents of the atmosphere. The largest source of nitrogen oxides on a worldwide basis is microbial action, which produces nitrous oxide, N_2O. As shown in the lower part of Figure 2.19, nitrous oxide is quite inert in the lower atmosphere, but it can react with oxygen atoms that are available in the stratosphere to produce nitric oxide, and thereby enter the ozone destruction cycle. Eventually this cycle is broken when the nitrogen dioxide reacts with the hydroxyl radical, OH, to produce nitric acid, HNO_3, and nitric oxide reacts similarly to produce nitrous acid, HNO_2. These acids diffuse back out of the stratosphere and, being very soluble in water, are quickly rained out. As shown in Figure 2.19, hydroxyl radicals arise from the interaction of water molecules with oxygen atoms that are produced by photochemical reactions in the atmosphere.

We therefore have a picture in which the ozone concentration in the stratosphere is maintained at a value of about half of what it would be in pure oxygen because of catalytic destruction by a reaction cycle involving nitrogen oxides. The nitrogen oxide pool is depleted by gradual conversion to nitric and nitrous acids, which are rained out, and it is replenished by the activation of nitrous oxide resulting from microbial action on the earth below. Estimates of the nitrous oxide flux are uncertain, but they appear to be in the right range to account for the observed depression in the calculated ozone concentration.

This picture of the ozone chemistry is highly simplified. There are many more reactions involving ozone than those shown in Figures 2.17 and 2.19. Moreover, the rates at which the reactions occur in many parts of the stratosphere are sufficiently slow so that transport processes—the movement of air masses from one location to the other—are as important as the chemistry. In order to deal with these complexities, elaborate computer programs have been devised to model the distribution of gases in the stratosphere. These calculations have highlighted the need for better measurements of stratospheric constituents than are currently available. As the new measurements are obtained, they permit better refinement of the computer models. The results obtained so far do indicate that the reactions that we have considered are probably the most important ones, even though many more reactions may have to be taken into account to obtain an accurate picture.

If human activities lead to a significant increase in the load of stratospheric nitrogen oxides, then there could be a further reduction in the ozone shield and a corresponding increase in ultraviolet radiation at the surface of the earth. As indicated in the lower diagram of Figure 2.19, one concern is with supersonic aircraft, which must fly in the stratosphere where air resistance is minimized. Jet engines are designed to operate at high temperature with the result that exhaust gases contain considerable quantities of nitric oxide, which is injected directly into the stratosphere. The supersonic speeds require high rates of fuel consump-

Ozone Destruction by NO$_x$ in Stratosphere

Figure 2.19 NO$_x$ Reactions in the Stratosphere

Source: Lower diagram: From reactions given in "The Natural Stratosphere of 1974," Monograph 1, U.S. Department of Transportation, Climatic Impact Assessment Program (DOT-TST-75-51), September 1975, chaps. 1 and 5.

tion and produce large quantities of exhaust. Before its development was forestalled by congressional refusal to provide further funding, the American design for the supersonic transport, the SST, was estimated to produce nitric oxide at a rate of one million grams per hour. An eventual fleet of 500 SSTs, as initially projected, flying 7 hours per day might have produced about as much nitric oxide per year as is presently found in the stratosphere. Since residence times of gases in the stratosphere are generally on the order of a year or so, this could have led to a doubling of the stratospheric concentration of nitrogen oxides with a resultant further decrease of the ozone concentration by a factor of about 40%, predicted by the steady-state approximation. The more complicated and realistic computer calculations project a more modest reduction. Moreover, newly measured rates of important reactions involving the hydroxyl radical have increased the estimated efficiency of nitrogen oxide removal from the stratosphere. At present the problem of SST emissions appears less serious than was thought, although considerable uncertainty persists and studies of the problem are being actively pursued.

A more serious increase in nitrogen oxide levels would be brought about by the explosion of many nuclear weapons, as would occur in a nuclear war. Nuclear explosions heat the surrounding air to very high temperatures, producing large quantities of nitrogen oxides. The force of the explosion causes these oxides to be injected directly into the stratosphere. While the matter is still controversial, it appears likely that the extensive nuclear tests conducted by the United States and the Soviet Union during 1961 and 1962 temporarily reduced the ozone concentration by as much as 4%. There is little doubt that an all-out nuclear war would significantly deplete the ozone layer. The Pentagon estimates the reduction as 50–75% if the nuclear arsenals of the Soviet Union and the United States were unleashed. A similar conclusion was reached by a National Academy of Sciences committee in a 1975 report.* Such a large reduction in the ozone shield might conceivably be disastrous to food production through ultraviolet radiation damage to plants. Thus, the production of nitric oxides by nuclear weapons might put humanity at even greater risk from nuclear war than it would be from the direct effects of the explosions and from radioactive fallout.

6 | Chlorofluoromethanes

Another reaction cycle that could be effective in destroying ozone is shown in Figure 2.20. In reaction 7 a chlorine atom reacts with ozone to produce an oxygen molecule and chlorine oxide, which then combines with an oxygen atom in reaction 8 to produce another oxygen molecule and regenerate the chlorine atom. The sum of reactions 7 and 8 gives reaction 4 in Figure 2.17 and the high rate of these reactions makes this an effective catalytic cycle. In fact, they are six times more efficient than the nitrogen oxide cycle reactions 5 and 6 of Figure 2.19. If present in equal concentration, chlorine atoms would be six times more effective than nitric oxide in destroying ozone.

*"Long-Term Worldwide Effects of Multiple Nuclear-Weapons Detonations" (Washington, D.C.: National Academy of Sciences, 1975).

Ozone Destruction by Cl in Stratosphere

7.   ·Cl + ozone ⟶ Cl—O + oxygen molecule

chlorine radical   ozone   chlorine oxide   oxygen molecule

collision

8.   Cl—O + O ⟶ ·Cl + O—O

chlorine oxide   oxygen atom

collision

Reactions 7 + 8 = Reaction 4 of Fig. 2.21

Coupled Cl – NO$_2$ Removal

9.   Cl—O + NO$_2$ ⟶ Cl—O—N chlorine nitrate

collision

Sources and Sinks for Cl

hν = 200nm

CF$_x$Cl$_{y-1}$

CF$_x$Cl$_y$ ⟶ ·Cl   O$_3$ O$_2$ O O$_2$ CH$_4$ ·CH$_3$

·Cl ⟶ ·ClO ⟶ ·Cl ⟶ HCl

NO$_2$ ⟶ ClONO$_2$

hν(300-400nm)

Cl$_2$ ⟶ ·Cl   ·OH H$_2$O

HCl ⟶ ·Cl

slow downward diffusion

stratosphere

troposphere

direct stratospheric injection

rainout

manufactured chlorofluoromethanes
(CFM'S)   Volcanic activity   earth

Figure 2.20 Chlorine Reactions in the Stratosphere

Source: From reactions given in "The Natural Stratosphere of 1974," Monograph 1, U.S. Department of Transportation, Climatic Impact Assessment Program (DOT-TST-75-51), September 1975, chap. 5; and "Halocarbons: Environmental Effects of Chlorofluoromethane Release" (Washington, D.C.: National Academy of Sciences, 1976).

Concern about this reaction sequence has centered on the production and use of the chlorofluoromethanes (CFMs) as refrigerants and aerosol spray can propellants. In news articles they have often been referred to as fluorocarbons, but it is, in fact, the chlorine they contain that is of central concern to the ozone question. These chemicals undergo no known reactions in the lower atmosphere, and it had been accepted that this inertness precludes any harmful environmental impact. However, in 1974 two scientists, Dr. M. J. Molina and Professor F. S. Rowland, pointed out that a danger does exist in the stratosphere when the CFMs split off chlorine atoms.* As shown in the lower part of Figure 2.20, in this region CFMs are subjected to ultraviolet radiation at wavelengths of around 200 nm. At these short wavelengths the radiation flux is negligible in the troposphere due to the ozone shield, but it becomes significant in the stratosphere. The same ultraviolet radiation that is absorbed by the ozone can convert CFMs into a source of chlorine atoms that can efficiently destroy the ozone. Precisely because the CFMs undergo no known reactions in the troposphere, they eventually diffuse up into the stratosphere and are a continuing source of chlorine atoms. Eventually, by reaction with methane, CH_4, the chlorine atoms are trapped as hydrochloric acid, HCl, which, because of its solubility in water, is rained out of the atmosphere.

It takes a few years for the CFM molecules to diffuse up to the altitude of peak photoefficiency, about 25–35 km. Therefore, there is a considerable time lag between the production of CFM and the eventual effects on the ozone layer that may be observed. These effects may be substantial. However, there are many uncertainties in the calculations that could move the predicted effects upward or downward. For example, it has recently been discovered that chlorine oxide and nitrogen dioxide can react to give a fairly stable product, chlorine nitrate, as shown in reaction 9 of Figure 2.20. This has the effect of lowering the rate of both the chlorine and nitrogen oxide catalytic cycles for ozone destruction, leading to somewhat lower overall ozone depletion rates.

A U.S. government task force concluded that at the 1973 level of chlorofluoromethane production, the eventual ozone reduction would be about 7%, according to the best current estimates. After this study, the federal government decided to ban all CFM use in spray cans as of December 1978. This ban has decreased U.S. production of CFMs by about 50%, since other uses, mainly as refrigerants, accounted for the remaining 50%. Before the ban, the United States made half the CFMs in the world; hence, the ban has reduced the global CFM production by about 25%. With the exception of Sweden, CFM use has not been restricted in other parts of the world, although Canada and Norway are considering similar legislation and the Netherlands has required the labeling of spray cans using CFMs as potentially dangerous. Other countries are aware of the problem

*M. J. Molina and F. S. Rowland, *Nature* 249 (1974):810.

and at an international conference in Munich in December 1978, the general consensus among the world producers was that production would either hold at its present level or decrease in the near future.

Other aerosol spray propellants are readily available, but finding a suitable substitute in refrigeration units is a more difficult problem. It should be possible to design the units so that the CFM does not escape into the atmosphere but is recycled at the end of the refrigerator's lifetime.

7 | Oxide Chemistry

The reactivity of oxygen also dominates the chemistry of the lower atmosphere. In the presence of molecular oxygen, the stable forms of almost all the elements are oxides. This is shown graphically in Figure 2.21. The crust of the earth consists mainly of solid oxides of the various elements, iron, aluminum, magnesium, calcium, carbon, and silicon, while the oceans are filled with the oxide of the element hydrogen. The atmosphere also contains volatile oxides such as carbon dioxide and sulfur dioxide. Nitrogen, however, is stable in the presence of oxygen. The bond connecting the two nitrogen atoms is so strong that energy would be lost in converting N_2 to any of the nitrogen oxides.

Since carbon dioxide is the stable form of carbon in the presence of oxygen, we might wonder how reduced organic compounds, of which plants and animals are made, can exist in contact with the atmosphere. The answer to this is that the reactions of oxygen are quite slow under ordinary conditions. A substantial

Figure 2.21 Most Elements, Except Nitrogen, Are Stable As Oxides

(i)

Uncatalyzed Oxidation (combustion)

(ii)

Biologically Catalyzed Oxidation (respiration)

Figure 2.22 Oxidation Reactions, in the Absence of Catalysts, Are Quite Slow

activation barrier must usually be overcome, as diagrammed in the top part of Figure 2.22. An activation barrier corresponds to the energy that the reactants must acquire before they can form the products, even if the overall reaction releases energy. In the combustion of reduced carbon, such as coal or oil, the activation barrier is manifested by the high ignition temperatures that are required. The energy of the combustion products, carbon dioxide and water, is lower than that of the reduced organic compounds, but the reaction has to travel uphill in terms of energy before the products can be formed, with the liberation of heat.

One factor that determines the activation energy is the requirement that the bond between the oxygen atoms must be broken. Although not as strong as the bond between nitrogen atoms, this is quite a strong bond. The two carbon-oxygen bonds formed in the carbon dioxide product are worth more in energy, but the oxygen-oxygen bond must still be broken first or at least appreciably weakened, and this requires energy. Another factor is that the oxygen molecule has two of its electrons unpaired, whereas most stable molecules have all their electrons paired. It costs energy to pair up electrons, and this is another contribution to the barrier to oxygen reactivity.

For these reasons we exist fairly comfortably with our oxygen atmosphere, except in certain circumstances such as in the intense heat of fire, which can provide the needed activation energy to cause oxygen to react. Indeed, biological organisms have developed a specialized biochemical apparatus inside their cells, called the *mitochondrion,* in order to be able to use oxygen to provide rapid energy through respiration, as illustrated in the lower part of Figure 2.22. The mitochondrion contains atoms of the elements iron and copper, which themselves have unpaired electrons and can lower the activation barrier to oxygen reactivity. The mitochondrion is designed not only to lower the barrier but also to channel the resulting energy into biochemical pathways useful to the organisms. Thus organisms require both the reactivity of oxygen and its control by the biochemical machinery that has evolved for the purpose. Both the energy source and the energy barrier, which can be selectively reduced for productive ends, are essential.

Turning our attention to the top part of Figure 2.23, we see that although molecular nitrogen is stable in the presence of oxygen, nitrogen oxides can be formed at sufficiently high temperature. Since the nitrogen-oxygen bonds that form are not so strong as the nitrogen-nitrogen and oxygen-oxygen bonds that are broken, heat must be supplied to the system to make the reaction go. This is shown for nitric oxide, represented by reaction 1 on the left side of the illustration. The energy diagram is the reverse of the one in Figure 2.22, with the products at a higher energy than the reactants. We know that reactions that absorb heat can be made to go forward if enough heat is supplied. This is the reason high-temperature processes such as combustion or the explosion of bombs

(i)

Pathways of Nitrogen-Oxygen Reactions

(ii)

Oxidation Reactions of Nitrogen, Carbon, and Sulfur[*]

	stable at low temp.	stable at high temp.
1.	heat $+ N_2 + O_2$	$\rightleftharpoons$ 2 NO

	stable at high temp.	stable at low temp.
2.	$NO + \frac{1}{2} O_2$	$\rightleftharpoons$ NO_2 + heat
3.	$CO + \frac{1}{2} O_2$	$\rightleftharpoons$ CO_2 + heat
4.	$SO_2 + \frac{1}{2} O_2$	$\rightleftharpoons$ SO_3 + heat

Figure 2.23 Thermochemical Stability of Oxides

*Reactions are governed by Le Chatelier's principle; i.e., if temperature is lowered, the reaction system compensates by shifting the equilibrium toward the side where heat is given off, and vice versa.

are associated with the formation of nitrogen oxides in the atmosphere. Once the heat is taken away, nitric oxide is unstable with respect to nitrogen and oxygen. However, the reverse of reaction 1 is also slow at low temperature because a high activation barrier must still be overcome, as shown in the diagram. Again, a fairly strong bond between nitrogen and oxygen must be broken or considerably weakened before the stronger nitrogen-nitrogen and oxygen-oxygen bonds can form. Consequently, if the temperature is lowered quickly, as is the case in exhaust gases from a fire or an explosion, the nitric oxide does not have a chance to dissociate and the reaction is so slow that the molecule can last for a long time even though it is potentially unstable. Indeed, another reaction is more probable, namely, the oxidation of nitric oxide to nitrogen dioxide, represented by reaction 2 on the right side of the figure. This reaction is also downhill in energy, and it has a lower activation barrier because, while the oxygen-oxygen bond must still be broken, the nitrogen-oxygen bond remains intact. The reaction is still slow but not so slow as the reformation of nitrogen and oxygen. Since heat is given off in reaction 2, it can be reversed at sufficiently high temperature. Consequently as indicated in reaction 1 in the lower part of Figure 2.23, nitric oxide is the main product of nitrogen oxidation associated with combustion and it is slowly oxidized to nitrogen dioxide as it cools in the atmosphere, as shown in reaction 2. This pattern also holds for other volatile oxides.

The oxidation of carbon monoxide to carbon dioxide, reaction 3 in Figure 2.23, is likewise accompanied by the liberation of heat and can be reversed at high temperature. The internal combustion engine in particular gives off substantial quantities of carbon monoxide, which slowly oxidizes to carbon dioxide in the atmosphere. Similarly, as shown in reaction 4 of Figure 2.23, the oxidation of sulfur dioxide to sulfur trioxide gives off heat and is reversed at high temperature. Sulfur dioxide is emitted by coal-burning power plants and it is slowly oxidized in the atmosphere.

8 | Air Pollution

As shown in Table 2.2, the major air pollutants are sulfur dioxide, which is produced mostly from coal-burning power plants; carbon monoxide, mostly from automobiles; unburned hydrocarbons, from automobiles and industrial processes; and nitrogen oxide, which is contributed both by stationary power sources and by the internal combustion engine.

In addition to these gaseous pollutants, Table 2.2 lists pollution from the direct emission of particles to the atmosphere. These are primary particles, as distinct from secondary particles that are formed from chemical reactions in the atmosphere. Particle size is given in units of microns—a micron being one-millionth of a meter and denoted by μ. As we will see later, health effects are strongly

Table 2.2 Annual Emissions of Pollutants in the United States by Source*
(millions of metric tons per year)

	SO$_2$	CO	Hydrocarbons	NO/NO$_2$	Particles† ≤20 μ	≤3 μ
Transportation	0.8	69.7	10.8	10.1	1.2	1.0
Stationary fuel combustion	21.9	1.2	1.4	11.8	4.6	1.3
Industrial processes	4.1	7.8	9.4	0.7	6.3	2.7
Miscellaneous	0.1	8.5	6.3	0.4	1.3	—
Total	26.9	87.2	27.9	23.0	13.4	5.0

*Except as noted, data are from *National Air Quality and Emissions Trends Report, 1976*, U.S. EPA, Research Triangle Park, EPA-450/1-77-002, December 1977.
†Data for particles smaller than 3 μ are from L. J. Shannon, P. G. Gorman, and W. Park, *Feasibility of Emissions Standards Based on Particle Size*, prepared for the Office of Research and Development, U.S. EPA, EPA-600/5-74-007, March 1974.

related to particle size. The total quantity of each of the pollutants in the table does not reflect its relative impact on our environment since the effect of each pollutant depends on many different factors.

Carbon monoxide

The association of carbon monoxide with automobile traffic is graphically illustrated in Figure 2.24, in which both traffic density and carbon monoxide concentration at street level are shown to rise and fall in a regular daily pattern in Manhattan. A similar graph could be drawn for all other urban areas. Shown in the lower part of Figure 2.24 are carbon monoxide concentrations, averaged over an eight-hour period, for locations with increasing distance from traffic. The eight-hour average is chosen to reflect the fact that carbon monoxide is an asphyxiating poison that competes with oxygen for hemoglobin molecules, which are responsible for transporting oxygen from the lung to the tissues. It takes some time to establish this competition while the gases are breathed in and out and the blood circulates to the tissues. Thus, the eight-hour average represents the best measure of actual exposure. The reactions involved are shown in the upper part of Figure 2.25. Both oxygen and carbon monoxide are bound to the iron atoms in the hemoglobin molecules, but the binding of carbon monoxide is 320 times more effective than that of oxygen. This means that oxygen and carbon monoxide would be on an equal footing in competing for hemoglobin if the carbon monoxide concentration were as high as 1/320 of the oxygen concentration, or about 625 ppm. At this concentration, half the hemoglobin would bind to oxygen and half to carbon monoxide. At 100 ppm, about 16% of the hemoglobin would be tied up in the carbon monoxide complex. As the lower part of Figure 2.24 shows, 100 ppm is a concentration to which people can be exposed in heavy traffic. Bridge and tunnel workers and traffic police officers are espe-

(i)

CO Build-up in Manhattan Air from Heavy Traffic

(ii)

8-Hour Average CO Concentration (ppm)

	exceeded at 5% of sites	exceeded at 50% of sites
Inside vehicles in downtown traffic	115	70
Inside vehicles on expressways	75	50
Commercial areas	40	17
Residential areas	23	16
Background	0.025 – 1.0	

Figure 2.24 Carbon Monoxide Concentrations in Urban Atmospheres

Source: Upper graph: K. L. Johnson, L. H. Dworetzky, and A. N. Heller, *Science* 160 (1968):67. Copyright 1968 by the American Association for the Advancement of Science. Lower table :"Air Quality Criteria for Carbon Monoxide," U.S. Department of Health, Education and Welfare, Washington, D. C., March 1970, p. 6-22.

(i)
Replacement of Oxygen in Hemoglobin

(ii)
Dose-Response Curves of HbCO Uptake in Blood

Figure 2.25 Physiological Effects of Carbon Monoxide Poisoning

Source: Lower diagram: P. C. Wolfe, *Environ. Sci. Technol.* 5 (1971):213.

cially at risk. As seen in the lower diagram in Figure 2.25, acute effects of carbon monoxide poisoning begin to occur at about 20% saturation of the hemoglobin, while 60% saturation can cause death. Some effects on heart and lung function can be seen down to about 5% binding of carbon monoxide. All of us have a background level of about 0.5% carbonmonoxyhemoglobin in our blood, and in smokers this level rises to 2%.

Acute exposure to carbon monoxide is reversible. Once the carbon monoxide is removed, the physiological functions return to normal. It is uncertain whether there are any long-term effects of chronic exposure to the carbon monoxide levels typical of urban areas. No such effects have yet been determined conclusively, although there is some statistical correlation between carbon monoxide levels and mortality rates in urban areas. Certainly individuals with heart problems are particularly at risk when the concentration of carbon monoxide increases.

Nitrogen oxides and hydrocarbons

Nitrogen oxides and unburned hydrocarbons are key ingredients in the formation of smog, a condition that afflicts an increasing number of cities. Smog can form whenever large quantities of automobile exhausts are trapped by an inversion layer over a locality that is, at the same time, exposed to sunshine. Los Angeles, with its dependence on the automobile, abundant sunshine, and frequent inversion layers, is the classic location for smog, but automobile traffic has introduced the problem to other cities as well. Smog is characterized by an accumulation of brown, hazy fumes, which irritate the eye and lung and lead to the cracking of rubber and to extensive damage of plant life.

Figure 2.26 shows the time course of the key atmospheric ingredients for a classic, smoggy day in Los Angeles. The peak in the concentration of hydrocarbons is during the early morning rush hour. The concentration of nitric oxide reaches a peak at the same time, and then begins to decrease as the nitrogen dioxide concentration increases. Subsequently there is a rise in the concentration of oxidants—materials that are active oxidizing agents and contain the irritating ingredients of smog. This coincides with the gradual reduction in the hydrocarbon concentration. Figure 2.27 shows that a somewhat similar time course can be observed in experiments with a smog chamber, a device into which controlled amounts of gases can be introduced and subjected to solar or artificial radiation. The experiment in the figure involves the irradiation of a mixture of pure air, nitric oxide, and the hydrocarbon, *trans*-butene. All these ingredients are needed for the reaction to work. As in the urban air, the concentrations of hydrocarbon and nitric oxide decrease in parallel while the nitrogen dioxide concentration increases and falls again. Replacing the hydrocarbon is an oxidized product, in this case acetaldehyde. Increasing at the same time is one of the most potent eye irritants found in smog—peroxyacetylnitrate (PAN). The computer simulation in Figure 2.27 was achieved by postulating a set of reactions with known rates,

Figure 2.26   Concentration Profiles of Smog-Forming Chemicals in Los Angeles Air
Source: J. A. Kerr, J. G. Calvert, and K. L. Demerjian, *Chem. Br.* 8 (1972):253.

suggesting that the chemistry, at least in the smog chamber, is reasonably well understood.

A flow chart for the chemistry of smog formation is given in Figure 2.28. Basically it involves catalysis of the oxidation of hydrocarbons in air to form products that are themselves reactive and irritating to biological tissue. The catalysis requires sunlight, and the key chemical ingredient is nitrogen dioxide, which is the only molecule present in significant quantities that is capable of absorbing solar light. Its absorption spectrum is shown in Figure 2.29 along with the spectrum of solar radiation. The absorption band of nitrogen dioxide is quite broad and has a peak at about 400 nm, not far from the peak in the solar spectrum. At the beginning of the smog formation reaction, however, there is only nitric oxide, which is transparent to sunlight, and we have to explain how nitric oxide is converted to nitrogen dioxide. As shown by the reaction in Figure

(i)
Smog Chamber

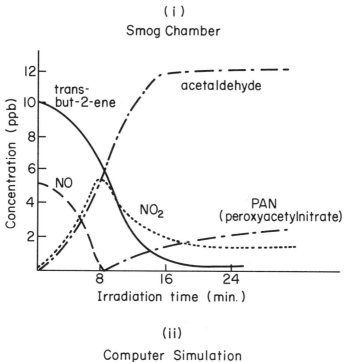

(ii)
Computer Simulation

Figure 2.27 Simulated Smog Formation from *trans*-but-1-ene, Nitric Oxide, Nitrogen Dioxide, and Air

Source: J. A. Kerr, J. G. Calvert, and K. L. Demerjian, *Chem. Br.* 8 (1972):253.

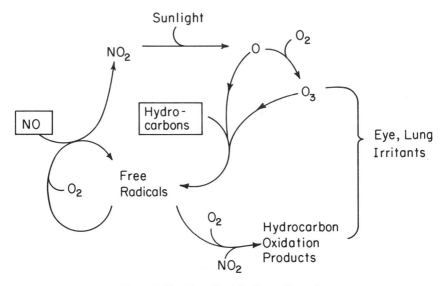

Figure 2.28   Flow Chart for Smog Formation

2.29, when nitrogen dioxide absorbs light, there is a high probability that it will split into nitric oxide and an oxygen atom. Referring back to Figure 2.28, we see that the oxygen atom is picked up by an oxygen molecule to form ozone in the same reaction that is responsible for forming ozone in the stratosphere. The ozone can transfer the oxygen atom back to nitric oxide, thus reforming nitrogen dioxide; but if this happens, we are back where we started. Indeed studies have shown that nitric oxide is not converted to nitrogen dioxide at a significant rate if the hydrocarbon is left out of the cycle. It is the hydrocarbon that accelerates the reaction of oxygen molecules with nitric oxide to form nitrogen dioxide. It does this by first reacting with the ozone to produce hydrocarbon free radicals, highly reactive molecules with an unpaired electron. Because of the unpaired electron, the free radicals combine readily with molecular oxygen, forming reactive oxygen species that can easily transfer an oxygen atom to nitric oxide, forming more nitrogen dioxide. This process regenerates the free radicals, which can continue to react with oxygen and nitric oxide many times in a chain reaction. This is how the absorption of sunlight by nitrogen dioxide, which is initially present in very low concentration, can lead to a rapid buildup of the nitrogen dioxide itself. It amounts to catalysis of the nitric oxide oxidation by the agency of free radicals formed from the hydrocarbons and the ozone, which are photochemically generated from the nitrogen dioxide. The free radicals eventually combine with oxygen and nitrogen dioxide to form the oxidation products, which are eye and lung irritants, and gradually the hydrocarbon supply is depleted.

The upper part of Figure 2.30 shows in more detail some of the free-radical

hν is a photon of light energy

Figure 2.29   Absorption of Solar Light by Nitrogen Dioxide to Form Oxygen Atoms

*The reaction shown under the absorption curve occurs when nitrogen dioxide absorbs light at wavelengths of less than 400 nm. For wavelengths greater than 400 nm, nitrogen dioxide is excited but does not decompose.

reactions that can take place and lead to the buildup of the concentration of nitrogen dioxide and oxidants. There are many other reactions possible, but the cycle shown here serves to illustrate the main features of smog formation. The initial event is the production of a hydrocarbon free radical symbolized by $RCH_2\cdot$, that is, a hydrocarbon with an unpaired electron in place of the bond to a hydrogen atom. This can be produced by the interaction of ozone with hydrocarbons from auto exhaust that have a reactive group, such as a carbon-carbon double bond. Once formed, the hydrocarbon free radical rapidly reacts with oxygen to form a new free radical with the two oxygen atoms incorporated. One of these oxygen atoms is readily donated to nitric oxide, producing nitrogen dioxide and leaving another free radical with only one oxygen atom. This radical can transfer a hydrogen atom to oxygen, thus producing a stable aldehyde molecule, which is an oxidation product of the original hydrocarbon. This reaction produces the hydroperoxyl radical, $HO_2\cdot$, which can donate an oxygen atom

PAN Formation

peroxyacyl nitrate (PAN)

Figure 2.30 Smog-Forming Reactions

to another nitric oxide molecule, leaving the hydroxyl radical, HO . The hydroxyl radical is extremely reactive and can pull a hydrogen atom away from a stable hydrocarbon to produce water and regenerate the hydrocarbon free radical. We thereby close the loop. One circuit around it produces two molecules of nitrogen dioxide and one molecule of oxidized hydrocarbon, and regenerates the free radical to start all over again. It is this sort of chain reaction that leads to the rapid buildup of smog products. The lower part of Figure 2.30 shows another pathway leading to the peroxyacylnitrates, the most potent eye and lung irritants in smog. The hydroxyl radical pulls a hydrogen atom off the aldehyde, leaving an acyl radical, which combines with an oxygen molecule to form a peroxyacyl radical and then with nitrogen dioxide to give the final product, peroxyacylnitrate.

9 | Automotive Emissions

Since smog production depends on nitrogen oxides as well as hydrocarbons, clean air regulations require that both of these pollutants be controlled in automobile emissions. Figure 2.31 shows, however, that this is a difficult task. It shows the concentrations of carbon monoxide, hydrocarbons, and nitrogen oxides in auto exhaust as a function of the ratio of air to fuel, which is controlled by the carburetor. The dashed line shows the stoichiometric ratio, that is, the ratio at which there is just enough oxygen in the fuel to convert all the carbon and hydrogen to carbon dioxide and water, if the combustion were complete. In fact, combustion is not complete under the rapidly varying conditions of an internal combustion engine, and there is a residual amount of carbon monoxide and unburned hydrocarbons well beyond the stoichiometric ratio. At less than this ratio the amounts of both hydrocarbons and carbon monoxide increase rapidly. The formation of nitrogen oxide results, as we have discussed, from the high-temperature combination of nitrogen and oxygen that are present in the air. Combustion is hottest close to the stoichiometric air/fuel ratio and cools off on either side. This explains the bell-shaped curve shown for nitrogen oxide emission. Automobile carburetors are adjusted to the fuel-rich side of the stoichiometric ratio, because if more air is admitted, the engine tends to stall. The exact ratio can be varied somewhat without undue detriment to automobile performance.

When the smog problem in Los Angeles was first recognized to be associated with automobile exhaust, standards were imposed on the hydrocarbon and carbon monoxide levels in automobile emissions. At that time, the involvement of nitrogen oxides in smog production was not clearly appreciated. Automobile manufacturers found that the easiest way to meet the new emission standards was to adjust the carburetor to increase the air/fuel ratio. As we can understand from Figure 2.31, the result was to decrease the concentrations of hydrocarbons and

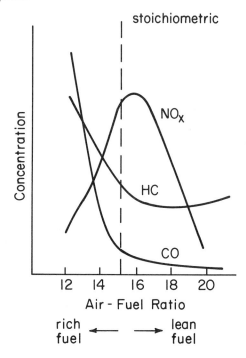

Figure 2.31 Auto Exhaust Composition

carbon monoxide but simultaneously to increase the nitrogen oxide level. It was found that the smog problem grew significantly worse after the initial standards were imposed.

Under the U.S. Federal Clean Air Act, nationwide standards have been set for the concentrations of nitrogen oxides as well as hydrocarbon and carbon monoxide. Imposition of the standards has been postponed repeatedly, however, pending resolution of the technical issues of how the standards can be met. Because of the conflicting requirements for getting rid of the different pollutants, that is, more complete combustion to lower the concentrations of hydrocarbons and carbon monoxide but lower temperatures to decrease the concentration of nitrogen oxides, the emission control problem turned out to be a difficult one.

The solution favored by the Detroit automobile manufacturers is the catalytic converter, which is diagrammed in Figure 2.32. The idea is to eliminate the

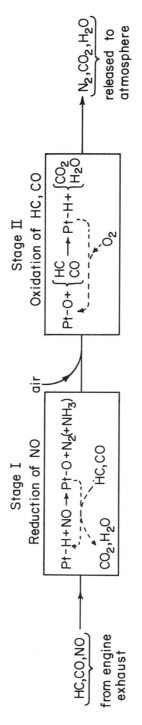

Figure 2.32 Catalytic Converter for Treating Auto Emissions

pollutants from the exhaust gases before they are vented to the atmosphere. Again, the different pollutants require different chemistries. Hydrocarbons and carbon monoxide can be oxidized to carbon dioxide and water, but oxidation of nitric oxide would produce nitrogen dioxide, which is itself a pollutant. Rather, the nitric oxide must be reduced to molecular nitrogen, which, as we have seen, is stable. The solution is to have two catalytic converters, one for reduction and the other for oxidation. Both use the same catalyst, finely divided platinum, but the conditions in each converter are different. In the first stage, reduction is induced by the presence of the hydrocarbons and carbon monoxide, which serve as the reducing agents. The nitric oxide gives up its oxygen to the surface of the catalyst, where it is picked up by the hydrocarbons or carbon monoxide. Following this stage, air is introduced to provide an oxidizing atmosphere for the second stage. Here the oxidation of carbon monoxide and hydrocarbon to carbon dioxide and water is completed. The overall chemistry of catalytic conversion is rather complicated and requires careful control of temperature and gas composition. One problem is that the reduction product of the first stage can be either molecular nitrogen or ammonia, NH_3. Ammonia, however, is rapidly reoxidized to nitrogen oxides in the second-stage unit. Careful control of the reduction stage is essential to minimize the production of ammonia. Another difficulty is that the catalyst itself is subject to poisoning by heavy elements. These combine with the reactive sites of the catalyst surface and inhibit the desired reaction.

Of particular concern is lead, which is normally added to gasoline to improve its combustion performance. Without lead the air/fuel mixture tends to ignite spontaneously as it is heated during the compression stroke in the cylinder. This sets off a small explosion that precedes the desired one, which is induced by the spark when the fuel is maximally compressed. This preignition, or knocking, decreases the efficiency of the engine and also sets up harmful stresses that increase engine wear. Preignition is caused by free radicals like the ones we have encountered in smog chemistry, which form in the engine due to the high temperature produced by the compression. As illustrated in Figure 2.33, tetraethyl lead is a good scavenger of free radicals. It reacts with them before they can build up the chain reaction that leads to combustion. Introduction of the catalytic converter, however, requires that lead be removed from gasoline, which may also be desirable from the point of view of curbing lead pollution. We will consider this subject later in the book.

Removal of lead from gasoline, however, poses difficulties with respect to engine performance. One solution is to change the composition of gasoline so that it is less likely to generate the free radicals that lead to knocking. Aromatic hydrocarbons, those that contain benzene rings, do not easily break down into radicals, and the quality of gasoline can be upgraded by increasing the content of aromatics. This can be done by changing the operating characteristics of refineries, although the process is costly. Another solution that has been introduced

piston of internal combustion engine

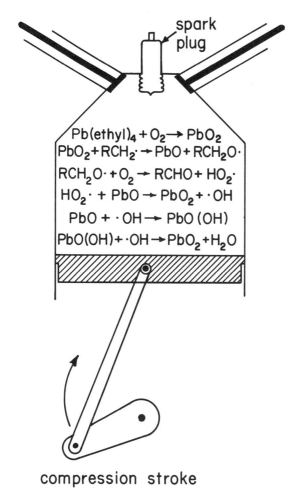

compression stroke

Figure 2.33 Radical Scavenging Reactions of Tetraethyl Lead

Source: Adapted from J. N. Bradley, *Flame and Combustion Phenomena* (London: Chapman and Hall, Ltd., 1972), p. 180.

is to lower the compression ratios of automobile engines, that is, the degree to which the air/fuel mixture is compressed in the cylinder before ignition. The lower the compression, the less tendency there is to produce free radicals. Consequently, ordinary gasoline with little or no lead becomes acceptable. Unfortunately, the engine efficiency also decreases with decreasing compression ratio, and the number of miles per gallon is reduced.

An alternative to the catalytic conversion of pollutants in the exhaust is to try to prevent their formation in the combustion process itself. Figure 2.34 shows one design that has been successfully tested, namely, the stratified charge engine. This is very similar to the normal internal combustion engine, but the head is modified to introduce an extra combustion chamber. In this prechamber, a fuel-rich mixture is introduced and ignited with a spark. Combustion therefore begins at a relatively low temperature which, as we saw in Figure 2.31, is associated with little formation of nitrogen oxides. The burning mixture is then

(piston design of Honda engine)

Figure 2.34 Stratified Charge Engine

Source: *Chem. Eng.* April 30, 1973, p. 39.

introduced into the larger main chamber, where it is mixed with a lean fuel mixture—one that has excess air in it. The combustion has already begun and goes to completion without stalling the engine. The excess air ensures complete combustion of the hydrocarbon and carbon monoxide, but the temperature remains low enough that the buildup of nitrogen oxides is limited. The stratified charge engine introduced by the Honda Corporation has been shown to meet the federal air pollution standards. There seem to be some questions about the extension of this design to large engines. If these can be satisfactorily answered, the stratified charge engine does offer the advantage over catalytic conversion of operating simplicity and more efficient performance.

10 | Sulfur Dioxide

Sulfur dioxide is largely associated with the burning of coal and some crude oils for electric power and heating. The sulfur content of refined petroleum is generally much lower. At the high temperatures of combustion, the sulfur is converted to sulfur dioxide. Sulfur dioxide itself is a lung irritant and is known to be harmful to people who suffer from respiratory disease. However, it is the sulfuric acid aerosol formed from the oxidation of sulfur dioxide that causes the most damaging health effects in urban atmospheres. The conversion process is shown graphically in Figure 2.35. As noted previously, sulfur dioxide is oxidized in the atmosphere to sulfur trioxide, the stable form at ambient temperatures, but the conversion is slow in the absence of a catalyst. Figure 2.35 shows two known pathways by which sulfur dioxide oxidation can be greatly accelerated in the atmosphere. In reaction a, ozone donates an oxygen atom to form sulfur trioxide, which in turn combines rapidly with water to form sulfuric acid. The sulfuric acid can condense to form aerosol droplets. In addition to ozone, other reactive gas-phase oxidants can cause a similar conversion. Alternatively, as shown in reaction b, the normally slow oxidation by oxygen can be catalyzed at the surface of particles such as soot, dust, or heavy metal oxides.

Sulfate aerosols in urban air are generally smaller than $2\ \mu$. Figure 2.36 shows that in the range smaller than $2\ \mu$, particles can quite effectively penetrate the innermost passages of the lung, called the pulmonary region. This is the region where oxygen is exchanged with carbon dioxide in the blood. Sulfuric acid aerosol irritates the fine vessels of the pulmonary region, causing them to swell and block the vessel passages. Severe breathing impairment may occur. The effect appears to be cumulative and older people suffer the most severe respiratory problems.

In order to reduce the level of sulfuric acid aerosols in urban air, power plants are often built with tall smokestacks to disperse the plume over a wide area. This

chemical pathways

a)

$$SO_2 + O_3 \longrightarrow SO_3 + O_2 \xrightarrow{+H_2O} H_2SO_4 \longrightarrow (H_2SO_4)_n$$

sulfuric   aerosol
acid   droplet

b)

$$SO_2 + \tfrac{1}{2}O_2 \xrightarrow[\substack{\text{or} \\ \text{metal oxide}}]{\substack{\text{soot} \\ \text{dust}}} SO_3 \xrightarrow{+H_2O} H_2SO_4 \longrightarrow (H_2SO_4)_n$$

Figure 2.35 Formation of Sulfuric Acid Aerosol from Sulfur Dioxide

reduces the local problem but may increase the problem for areas that are far removed from the source of pollution. The sulfuric acid is washed out in rain or snowfall, resulting in an increase in the acidity of the local waters downwind from power plants and producing a condition that has come to be known as *acid rain*. Prevailing wind patterns bring acid rain to Scandinavia from the industrial areas of Europe and to New England and upstate New York from the industrial cities of the Northeast and Midwest of the United States. We will examine this problem in more detail in the next section.

Another approach to sulfur oxide abatement is to limit the sulfur content of fuels. This is one reason that coal has largely been displaced by petroleum and natural gas as a fuel in urban areas. With the tightening supply and higher prices of gas and petroleum, however, there is a strong incentive to return to coal. Unfortunately the supplies of low-sulfur coal are also quite limited, as mentioned earlier. There is consequently pressure to relax the sulfur emission standards currently in force. An alternative is to remove sulfur dioxide from the stack gases of the power plant by using chemical scrubbers of the type shown in Figure 2.37. In this design the stack gas is passed through a slurry of limestone, calcium carbonate, which removes sulfur dioxide quite efficiently according to the reaction shown to produce mostly calcium sulfite. Limestone is a cheap and abundant

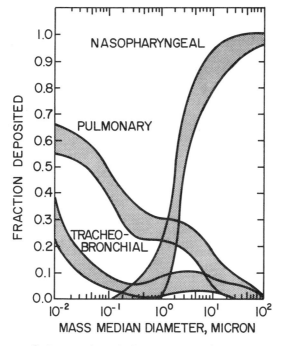

MASS MEDIAN DIAMETER, MICRON

Schematic of Respiratory System

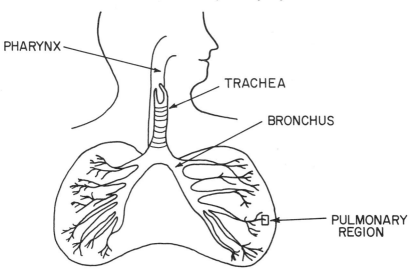

Figure 2.36 Penetration of Particles in the Human Respiratory System As a Function of Particle Size

Source: Upper graph: U.S. Department of Health, Education and Welfare, National Air Pollution Control Boards, "Air Quality Criteria for Particulate Matter," Publication No. AP-49, Washington, D.C., January 1969.

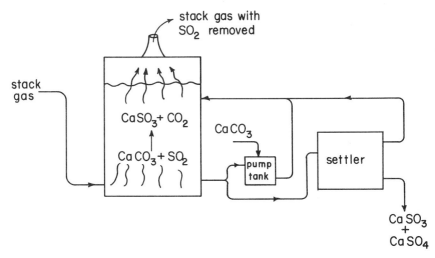

Figure 2.37 Scrubber Addition of Limestone for Removal of Sulfur Dioxide from Waste Gas

absorbent relative to other chemicals that are also under investigation. Power plant officials claim that the technology is expensive and not very reliable, and that the large quantities of calcium sulfite produced are a major waste disposal problem. The U.S. Environmental Protection Agency, on the other hand, asserts that the method is practical and is applying pressure for its widespread introduction. Another possibility is to remove the sulfur from the coal before it is burned. The inorganic sulfur can be removed fairly easily by screening powdered coal. Coal is already pulverized for large furnaces to improve its combustion characteristics. Organically bound sulfur is somewhat more difficult to remove, but several chemical processes are under investigation.

11 | Primary Particles

Sulfuric acid aerosol is a secondary particle since it is formed from a gas-to-particle conversion process in the atmosphere. In contrast, primary particles are emitted directly into the atmosphere with no intermediate conversion steps. They vary widely in their chemical composition, and hence it is difficult to assess their effects quantitatively. Soot, which arises from the residue of fuel combustion from power plants and automobiles, comprises about 50% of the particulate load in urban areas. But other particles from various industrial sources such as the cement and metallurgy industries also contribute.

As we saw in Table 2.2, 13.4 MT of primary particles is emitted annually in the United States, and of this, about 5.0 MT is smaller than 3 μ. These fine particles scatter light effectively and thereby reduce visibility. They are also the worst causes of lung damage because of their ability to penetrate into the deep air passages, as discussed in connection with sulfuric acid and shown in Figure 2.36. The larger particles are trapped in the nose and throat, from which they are easily eliminated. But the finer particles can remain lodged for years in the innermost regions of the lungs, which have no effective mechanism for particle removal.

Lodged particles can cause severe breathing impairment simply by the physical blockage and irritation of the delicate lung capillaries. Coal miners' black-lung disease, asbestos workers' pulmonary fibrosis, and the city dwellers' emphysema are all associated with the accumulation of such small particles.

Some particles are especially dangerous because they may carry toxic chemicals that can interact directly with lung tissue. A key example is soot, which is illustrated in Figure 2.38. Soot is mostly finely divided carbon with a loose structure that possesses a large surface area. It is often associated with toxic trace

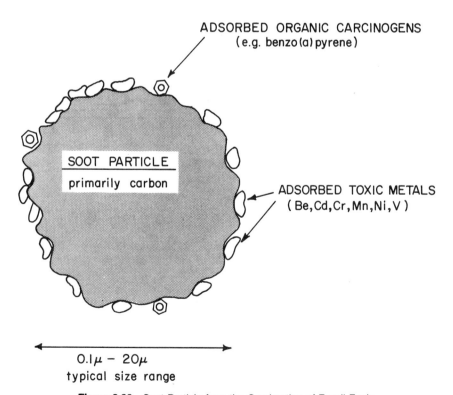

Figure 2.38   Soot Particle from the Combustion of Fossil Fuels

metals such as beryllium, cadmium, chromium, manganese, nickel, and vanadium adsorbed on its surface. Moreover, soot serves as a carrier for toxic organic molecules such as benzo(a)pyrene, which has been implicated as a cancer-causing agent. Asbestos is another insidious particulate that can lodge in the lung and cause cancer.

Control of particle emissions from stationary sources can be achieved by filtering the stack gas, by scrubbing it with a liquid spray, or by electrostatic precipitators, which charge the particles with an electric field and collect them on a grounded surface. These devices are effective for large particles but less so for the more dangerous fine particles. Nevertheless, when well designed, they are capable of achieving more than 90% collection of fine particles.

The amount of fine particles from automobile exhaust has been reduced by the use of nonleaded fuel in combination with the catalytic converter. However, the expanding use of diesel fuels in the 1980s will be an area of increasing concern in terms of particulate pollution. It has been estimated that light-duty diesel engines in passenger vehicles may produce 50 to 80 times as many particles as conventional engines with catalytic converters. Compounding this is the fact that 90% of the particulate matter is smaller than 2.5 μ, and that these particles contain relatively high concentrations of organic carcinogens. Control of diesel emissions will require an intensive research effort.

12 | Summary

Looking back on our survey of atmospheric issues, we see that atmospheric balances can be upset both on a global scale through the greenhouse effect and stratospheric ozone destruction and on a local and regional scale through the buildup of fossil fuel exhaust gases and their oxidation products. These problems are interrelated in complex and sometimes paradoxical ways. For example, nitrogen oxides catalyze ozone destruction in the stratosphere but are partly responsible for ozone formation in polluted urban air. The chlorofluoromethane gases are harmless locally but have potential global contributions to both the greenhouse effect and ozone destruction. Carbon monoxide and hydrocarbons are local pollutants, whose noxious qualities can be eliminated by oxidizing them to carbon dioxide, but an increase in the global carbon dioxide concentration will heat up the earth's surface. We do not know whether this in itself would be good or bad since the long-term trends in the climate are quite unpredictable. While scientists have learned a great deal about the atmosphere, partly in response to recent environmental concerns, there is an urgent need to learn much more in order to assess the human impact on it.

Problem Set

1. The polar ice caps have an albedo of about 0.80, while the polar seas have a maximum albedo of about 0.25. How could this difference in albedo cause the spontaneous melting of much of the ice cap if a small rise in ambient temperature occurred? How could large-scale soot deposition on the ice cap cause a similar melting?

2. The total mass of carbon contained in fossil fuels that was burned in the world from 1860 to 1975 was 14.0×10^{16} g. It is known that the concentration of CO_2 in the atmosphere in 1975 was 330 ppm, corresponding to a total mass of 2.59×10^{15} kg of CO_2. If the concentration of CO_2 in 1860 was 295 ppm, calculate the percentage of burned carbon that has remained in the atmosphere.

3. Which of the molecules in the following table has the potential to cause a greenhouse effect similar to that predicted for CFMs (see Figure 2.9)? For polyatomic molecules, identify the specific vibration involved.

S—C—O (linear)	H—Cl	F_2	H_2S (nonlinear)	Cl_2O (nonlinear)
$\nu_1 = 11{,}641$ nm	$\nu = 3{,}465$ nm	$\nu = 11{,}211$ nm	$\nu_1 = 3{,}830$ nm	$\nu_1 = 14{,}706$ nm
$\nu_2 = 18{,}975$ nm			$\nu_2 = 7{,}752$ nm	$\nu_2 = 30{,}303$ nm
$\nu_3 = 4{,}810$ nm			$\nu_3 = 3{,}726$ nm	$\nu_3 = 10{,}277$ nm

4. Assume that the concentration of suspended particulates in a polluted atmosphere is 170 μg/m^3. The particulates contain adsorbed sulfate and hydrocarbons comprising 14% and 9% of the weight, respectively. An average person respires 8,500 l of air daily and retains 50% of the particles smaller than 1 μm in diameter in the lungs. How much sulfate and hydrocarbon accumulate in the lungs in one year if 75% of the particulate mass is contained in particles smaller than 1 μm? [Concentration data taken from S. I. Rasool, ed., *Chemistry of the Lower Atmosphere* (New York: Plenum Press, 1973), p. 85.]

5. a) The lapse rate of the atmosphere over a certain city is positive up to an altitude of 1,000 m, rising 1° C for each 100 m increase in altitude. At 1,000 m, the lapse rate becomes negative, decreasing by 1° C for each 100 m increase in altitude up to 10,000 m. Plot altitude versus temperature for the 10-km layer of atmosphere over the city. The surface temperature is 20° C.

   b) What climatologic phenomenon is occurring in the city? Describe the public health danger that can result from it.

6. For the conversion reaction of carbon monoxide to carbon dioxide:

$$CO(g) + \tfrac{1}{2}O_2(g) \rightarrow CO_2(g)$$

the equilibrium constant K (at 25° C) = 3×10^{45}. Given this enormous value, why doesn't carbon monoxide convert spontaneously to carbon dioxide in air? How does the use of platinum in the catalytic converter of automobiles facilitate the conversion to carbon dioxide? (Hint: Platinum contains unpaired electrons like iron and copper in biological systems; see Figure 2.22.)

7. Why is NO_2, unlike the higher oxides of carbon and sulfur (CO_2 and SO_3, respectively), unstable at 25° C in the presence of sunlight? Describe briefly how the reaction of NO_2 with sunlight plays a key role in smog formation and in the regeneration of NO_2 itself.

8. Examine the accompanying graph and Figure 2.31, and explain the basic dilemma in automobile pollution control; i.e., more complete combustion leading to the reduc-

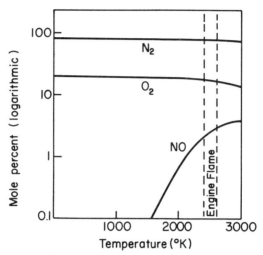

Equilibrium concentrations of nitric oxide in air as a function of temperature

tion of unburned hydrocarbons and CO leads to increased formation of NO. How does the stratified charge engine serve to mitigate this dilemma?

9. The oxidation of SO_2 to SO_3 proceeds very slowly in purified air at ambient temperatures. In the presence of particles that contain iron, the oxidation rate is greatly increased. Why is this true (see Figure 2.22 and problem 6)? Since iron is a common constituent in coal soot, describe the link between burning of high-sulfur coal and sulfuric acid formation in urban atmospheres. Why is the removal of pyrites (iron sulfides) from coal relatively easy and effective in pollution abatement?

10. Give two reasons why the stratosphere is more susceptible to chemical pollution than the troposphere.

11. What is the major natural process that leads to a 50% depletion in the ozone layer? How could a nuclear war lead to a similar process of depletion? Show relevant equations.

12. If the earth's average absolute temperature, T, is given by a balance between the absorbed solar energy, $\Omega\,(1-a)/4$, and black body radiation, sT^4, what would be the direction and magnitude of the temperature change if:

a) Power is generated from fossil or nuclear fuels at a rate equivalent to 1% of the incident solar energy?

b) The albedo increases by 1%?

The solar flux, $\Omega = 2$ calories/minute/cm²; the albedo, $a = 0.4$; and the radiation constant, $S = 1.43 \times 10^{-12}$ calories/sec/cm² per degree.

13. a) The atmosphere weighs 1,000 g/cm² and is 20% oxygen and 80% nitrogen by volume. If all the air was at standard pressure (1 atm) and temperature (0° C), how high would the atmosphere extend? The radius of the earth is 6.4×10^6 m. The gas constant $R = 0.082$ atm-l/mol-degree.

b) It is estimated that the ozone layer would be 0.3 cm thick at standard temperature and pressure. What is the fraction of ozone in the atmosphere by volume? By weight?

Suggestions for Further Reading

Atmosphere

Heicklen, J. *Atmospheric Chemistry.* New York: Academic Press, 1976.

Rasool, S. I., ed. *Chemistry of the Lower Atmosphere.* New York: Plenum Press, 1973.

Barry, R. G., and Chorley, R. J. *Atmosphere, Weather and Climate.* New York: Holt, Rinehart and Winston, Inc., 1970.

Inadvertent Climate Modification. Report of the Study of Man's Impact on Climate (SMIC). Cambridge, Mass.: MIT Press, 1971.

"Understanding Climatic Change. A Program for Action." Washington, D.C.: National Academy of Sciences, 1975.

Schneider, S. H. *The Genesis Strategy. Climate and Global Survival.* New York: Plenum Press, 1976.

Baes, C. F., Goeller, H. E., Olson, J. S., and Rotty, R. M. "The Global Carbon Dioxide Problem," Oak Ridge National Lab (ORNL-5194), August 1976.

Kerr, J. A., Calvert, J. G., and Demerjian, K. L. "Free Radical Reactions in the Production of Photochemical Smog." In *Free Radicals in Biology,* edited by W. A. Pryor, Vol. II. New York: Academic Press, 1976.

"Environmental Impact of Stratospheric Flight." Washington, D.C.: National Academy of Sciences, 1975.

"Halocarbons: Environmental Effects of Chlorofluoromethane Release." Washington, D.C.: National Academy of Sciences, 1976.

Perera, F., and Ahmed, A. *Respirable Particles: Impact of Airborne Fine Particulates on Health and the Environment.* Cambridge, Mass.: Ballinger Publishing Company, 1979.

Pollution and Climate

Bryson, R. A. "A Perspective on Climatic Change." *Science* 184 (1974):753.

Prospero, J. M., and Nees, R. T. "Dust Concentration in the Atmosphere of the Equatorial North Atlantic: Possible Relationship to the Sahelian Drought." *Science* 196 (1977):1196.

Potter, G., Ellsaesser, H. W., MacCracken, M. C., and Luther, F. M. "Possible Climatic Impact of Tropical Deforestation." *Nature* 258 (December 25, 1975):697.

Houghton, H. G. "On the Annual Heat Balance of the Northern Hemisphere." *J. Meteorol.* 11 (February 1954):1.

Manabe, S., and Wetherald, R. T. "Thermal Equilibrium of the Atmosphere with a Given Distribution of Relative Humidity." *J. Atmos. Sci.* 24 (May 1967):241.

Broecker, W. S. "Climatic Change: Are We on the Brink of a Pronounced Global Warming?" *Science* 189 (1975):460.

Wong, C. "Atmospheric Input of Carbon Dioxide from Burning Wood." *Science* 200 (1978):197.

Adams, J. A., Mantorani, M. S., and Lundell, L. L. "Wood Versus Fossil Fuels As a Source of Excess Carbon Dioxide in the Atmosphere: A Preliminary Report." *Science* 196 (1977):54.

Stuiver, M. "Atmospheric Carbon Dioxide and Carbon Reservoir Changes." *Science* 199 (1978):253.

Woodwell, G. M., et al. "The Biota and the World Carbon Budget." *Science* 199 (1978):141.

Kerr, R. "Carbon Dioxide and Climate: Carbon Budget Still Unbalanced." *Science* 197 (1977):1352.

Woodwell, G. "The Carbon Dioxide Question." *Sci. Am.* 238 (January 1978):34.

Baes, C. F., Goeller, H. E., Olson, J. S., and Rotty, R. "Carbon Dioxide and Climate: The Uncontrolled Experiment." *Am. Sci.* 65 (May–June 1977):310.

Siegenthaler, U., and Oeschger, H. "Predicting Future Atmospheric Carbon Dioxide Levels." *Science* 199 (1978):388.

Kellogg, W. W. "Is Mankind Warming the Earth?" *Bull. Atom. Sci.* 34 (February 1978):10.

McLean, D. "A Terminal Mesozoic 'Greenhouse,' Lessons from the Past." *Science* 201 (1979):401.

Ramanathan, V. "Greenhouse Effect Due to Chlorofluorocarbons: Climatic Implications." *Science* 190 (1975):50.

Wang, W. C., Yung, Y. L., Lacis, A. A., Mo, T., and Hansen, J. E. "Greenhouse Effects Due to Man-Made Perturbations of Trace Gases." *Science* 194 (1976):685.

Tropospheric Air Pollution

Newell, R. E. "The Global Circulation of Atmospheric Pollutants." *Sci. Am.* 224 (January 1971):32.

Lee, R. E., and von Lehmden, D. J. "Trace Metal Pollution in the Environment." *J. Air Pollut. Control Assoc.* 23 (October 1973):853.

Shinn, J. H., and Lynn, S. "Do Man-Made Sources Affect the Sulfur Cycle of Northeastern States?" *Environ. Sci. Technol.* 13 (September 1979):1062.

Novakov, T., Chang, S. G., and Harker, A. B. "Sulfates As Pollution Particulates: Catalytic Formation on Carbon (Soot) Particles." *Science* 186 (1974):259.

Natusch, D. F., and Wallace, J. R. "Urban Aerosol Toxicity: The Influence of Particle Size." *Science* 186 (1974):695.

Kerr, J. A., Calvert, J. G., and Demerjian, K. L. "The Mechanism of Photochemical Smog Formation." *Chem. Br.* 8 (1972):252.

Pitts, J. N. "Keys to Photochemical Smog Control." *Environ. Sci. Technol.* 11 (May 1977):456.

Wilson, D. G. "Alternative Automobile Engines." *Sci. Am.* 239 (July 1978):39.

Cleveland, W. S., Kleiner, B., McRae, J. E., Warner, J. L., and Pasceri, R. E. "Geographical Properties of Ozone Concentrations in the Northeastern United States." *J. Air Pollut. Control Assoc.* 27 (April 1977):325.

Gillette, D. G. "Ambient Oxidant Exposure and Health Costs in the United States— 1973." *Science* 199 (1978):329.

Williams, W. T., Brady, M., and Willison, S. C. "Air Pollution Damage to the Forests of the Sierra Nevada Mountains of California." *J. Air Pollut. Control Assoc.* 27 (March 1977):230.

Wolf, P. C. "Carbon Monoxide. Measurement and Monitoring in Urban Air." *Environ. Sci. Technol.* 5 (March 1971):212.

Sze, N. D. "Anthropogenic CO Emissions: Implications for the Atmospheric CO–OH– CH_4 Cycle." *Science* 195 (1977):673.

Carter, L. "Asbestos: Trouble in the Air from Maryland Rock Quarry." *Science* 197 (1977):237.

Stratospheric Pollution

Johnston, H. S. "Ground-Level Effects of Supersonic Transports in the Stratosphere." *Accounts Chem. Res.* 8 (1975):289.

Broderick, A. "Stratospheric Effects from Aviation." *J. Aircraft* 15 (October 1978):643.

Molina, M. J., and Rowland, F. S. "Stratospheric Sink for Chlorofluoromethanes: Chlorine Atom-Catalyzed Destruction of Ozone." *Nature* 249 (June 28, 1974):810.

Cutchis, P. "Stratospheric Ozone Depletion and Solar Ultraviolet Radiation on Earth." *Science* 184 (1974):13.

Johnston, H. "Newly Recognized Vital Nitrogen Cycle." *Proc. Nat. Acad. Sci. USA* 69 (1972):2369.

Council for Agricultural Science and Technology (CAST). "Effect of Increased Nitrogen Fixation on Stratospheric Ozone," Report No. 53. Ames: Iowa State University, 1976.

Other Readings

Brimblecombe, P. "Attitudes and Responses Towards Air Pollution in Medieval England." *J. Air Pollut. Control Assoc.* 26 (October 1976):941.

Garrels, R. M., Lerman, A., and Mackenzie, F. T. "Controls of Atmospheric O_2 and CO_2: Past, Present and Future." *Am. Sci.* 63 (May–June 1976):306.

PART III | HYDROSPHERE

1 | Water Resources

About 97% of the earth's water supply is in the oceans, but its high salt content makes it unfit for human consumption and most other uses. Everyday, however, the sun's rays evaporate a large quantity of the water in the oceans as well as on land and this water falls as rain, which provides us with our supply and reserves of freshwater. We treat water as if it were free and, in a sense, it is free—a by-product of the enormous flux of solar energy on the earth. As noted at the beginning of this book in Figure 1.1, one-third of the solar energy absorbed by the earth's surface goes into the hydrologic cycle. Yet we are using freshwater so fast that we are running into shortages of it from place to place and from year to year.

Table 3.1 shows the amounts of water present on the average in the United States, as atmospheric and soil moisture, and in rivers, reservoirs, and lakes. It also shows the total amount of water in aquifers under the ground. In the right-hand column these figures are translated into units of total annual water consumption in 1975. If water were nonreplenishable and if the hydrologic cycle stopped tomorrow, the United States would, in principle, have enough water available, particularly in groundwater supplies, to last almost 150 years. But, of course, water is recycled continuously through evaporation and precipitation and none of it is literally consumed; it is simply detoured through the various uses that we find for it.

The flow diagram in the top part of Figure 3.1 shows that of the annual precipitation, 70% is evaporated or transpired by plants while the remaining 30% goes into the streamflow. About a quarter of this streamflow is used for various purposes that can be broadly divided into irrigation, municipal water supplies, industrial uses, and electric utilities. Some of the water is evaporated during use, but most of it eventually finds its way to the ocean.

Historically irrigation for agricultural purposes has been the main use of water, but as shown in the lower part of Figure 3.1, the cooling of electric power plants has caught up and is now the chief consumer in the United States. While none of these uses actually destroys the water, the uses contaminate it with pesticides and

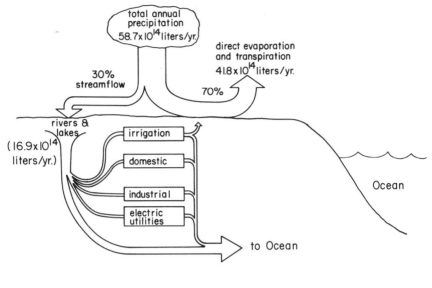

Figure 3.1 Average Distribution of Precipitation in the United States

*Streamflow supplied about 85% of U.S. demand in 1975; the balance was drawn from groundwater.
Source: Data from R. G. Bond, C. P. Straub, and R. Prober, eds., *Handbook of Environmental Control: Water Supply and Treatment,* Vol. III (Cleveland: Chemical Rubber Co., 1973), pp. 6, 131.

fertilizers, animal wastes, suspended soil particles, waste chemicals, and sewage. If the water is to be used again, it must be purified. This can be accomplished by natural means, through bacterial action or evaporation, or by chemical treatment. The use of water is increasing rapidly and, although water reserves are abundant, the amount accessible at a particular location may be quite limited. It will become more and more necessary to find efficient means for recycling wastewater for its immediate reuse. Another reason to insist on better treatment of the wastewater is that the pollutants carried into our rivers and lakes can cause disruptive effects on the ecologies of these water systems and on human health.

Table 3.1   U.S. Freshwater Reserves

Source of Water	Amount (10^{14} l)	Reserve Life*
Atmospheric moisture	2.18	0.4
Soil moisture	7.85	1.5
Rivers	0.56	0.1
Reservoirs	4.51	0.8
Lakes	160.77	30.2
Groundwater	587.43	110.4
Total	763.30	143.4

*Numbers represent units of 5.23×10^{14} l, which equals the total water consumption in the United States in 1975. They represent the number of years the source would last if all water needs were taken from that source alone.
Source: R. G. Bond, C. P. Straub, and R. Prober, eds., *Handbook of Environmental Control: Water Supply and Treatment,* Vol. III (Cleveland: Chemical Rubber Co., 1973), p. 5.

2 | Acidity

We will deal with the topic of water treatment after first considering the chemistry of natural waters and how it is affected by human use. The water molecule has an oxygen atom and two hydrogen atoms; in the liquid state there is a small tendency for the hydrogen-oxygen bonds to dissociate, producing a hydrogen ion and a hydroxide ion, as shown in the upper part of Figure 3.2. In pure water, the concentration of each of these ions is 10^{-7} mol/l. A mole is Avogadro's number, 6.02×10^{23}, of molecules, atoms, or ions. The product of the molar concentrations of the hydrogen and hydroxide ion is 10^{-14}. This is the equilibrium constant, K_w, for the ionization reaction of water shown in the figure. The concentration of hydrogen ions can be increased by the addition of acids to water, such as sulfuric, nitric, or hydrochloric acids, and likewise the concentration of hydroxide ions can be increased by the addition of bases, such as sodium hydroxide or ammonia. As illustrated graphically in the lower part of Figure 3.2, the product of the hydrogen and hydroxide concentrations must remain constant, and thus they are reciprocally related; as one goes up, the other goes down. The acidity or basicity of a solution is expressed quantitatively by the pH scale. The pH is defined as the negative logarithm of the hydrogen ion concentration. Thus, as acidity increases, pH decreases. At neutrality, the pH is 7. Acid solutions have pH values less than 7, and basic solutions have pH values greater than 7.

While pure water should have a pH of 7, the water in the atmosphere is not neutral. As illustrated in Figure 3.3 and shown in equation 1, the water can react with carbon dioxide to form carbonic acid, H_2CO_3. Carbonic acid is a weak acid and dissociates to a slight extent, as indicated by equation 2, to form hydrogen ions and bicarbonate ions, HCO_3^-. The concentration of hydrogen ion and bicar-

Ionization

equilibrium constant $K_w = 10^{-14}$

where $K_w = [H^+] \times [OH^-]$

$[H^+]$ and $[OH^-]$ are concentrations in units of moles per liter of solution

(1 mole = 6.02×10^{23} molecules, atoms or ions)

Acidity and Basicity

$pH = -\log [H^+]$

Figure 3.2 Properties of Water

bonate ion depend on the carbonic acid concentration, which in turn depends on the carbon dioxide concentration in the air. The current level of carbon dioxide is 325 ppm. As shown by the calculations in the lower part of the figure, saturated rainwater has a carbonic acid concentration of 10^{-5} mol/l and a pH of 5.7.

Once the rain has fallen, it percolates through the topsoil as diagrammed in Figure 3.4. The topsoil contains a large amount of carbon dioxide produced by bacterial action. Typically, the carbon dioxide concentration in topsoil is 100 times what it is in the atmosphere and the pH falls to about 4.7. Deeper in the soil there is less bacterial activity and here the carbonic acid can react with basic minerals, such as silicate clays or calcium carbonate, in the neutralization reactions shown in Figure 3.4. The result of these reactions is that carbonic acid is converted into bicarbonate ion and the acidity is lowered. Through these reactions, the pH may rise to neutrality and even a little higher. The pH values of many lakes lie between 7 and 8 and the pH of the oceans is about 8.

The acidity of rain can be significantly increased by industrial pollutants, as we discussed in the preceding part of this book. As shown in Table 3.2, the pH of rain in southern Norway and Sweden, which had a background value in 1956, dropped quite dramatically in the succeeding decades. Similarly, pH values for rain falling in various locales in New England in 1970 were on the order of 4. Such low values imply the presence in the local atmosphere of acids that are

$$1. \quad CO_2 + H_2O \rightleftharpoons H_2CO_3 \qquad K_1 = \frac{[H_2CO_3]\ (mol/l)}{p_{CO_2}\ (atm)} = 10^{-1.5}$$

$$2. \quad H_2CO_3 \rightleftharpoons H^+ + HCO_3^- \qquad K_2 = \frac{[H^+][HCO_3^-]}{[H_2CO_3]}(mol/l) = 10^{-6.4}$$

Atmospheric concentration of $CO_2 = 325$ ppm
Hence, $p_{CO_2} = 0.325 \times 10^{-3}$ atm $= 10^{-3.5}$ atm
Therefore, from equation 1:
$[H_2CO_3] = 10^{-5.0}$ mol/l
From equation 2:
$[H^+] = [HCO_3^-]$
hence, $[H^+]^2 = (10^{-6.4})(10^{-5.0}) = 10^{-11.4}$
$[H^+] = 10^{-5.7}$
$\boxed{pH = 5.7}$

Figure 3.3 Major Reactions with Carbon Dioxide Causing Natural Acidity of Rainwater significantly stronger than carbonic acid. Table 3.2 also shows an analysis of the ions present in rainwater at Hubbard Brook in New England. The fact that 62% of the negative ions are sulfate supports the view that acid rain results mainly from sulfuric acid transported downwind from urban and industrial areas. The particularly severe acid rain conditions encountered in New England and Scandanavia are thought to arise from the concentration of pollutants produced by the industrial cities of the northeastern United States and by the British and German industrial areas, respectively. As shown in the top graph of Figure 3.5, a sufficient drop in the pH in lakes can lead to the elimination of desirable kinds of fish, many of which have rather restricted tolerances for acidity. Lakes in Scandinavia and New York State have already shown marked declines in fish populations. The trend for southern Norway is shown in the bottom graph of Figure 3.5.

Rain (slightly acidic)

$\downarrow \quad \downarrow \quad \downarrow \quad \downarrow \quad \downarrow \quad \downarrow \quad \downarrow$

TOPSOIL

Zone of intense bacterial action $\rightarrow$ CO_2 produced in large amounts
rain (pH = 5.7) +CO_2 $\rightarrow$ rain (pH $\sim$ 4.7)

Some ion exchange with silicate clays that lower acidity

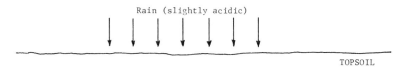

$$[M(SiO_4)]_x + H_2CO_3 \rightarrow \overbrace{M^{n+} + HCO_3^-}^{} + [H(SiO_4)]_x$$
$$\underbrace{\qquad\qquad}_{\text{water soluble}}$$

$M^{n+} = K^+, Na^+, Ca^{2+},$ or Mg^{2+} and small amounts of $Fe^{2+}, Sr^{2+},$ and Mn^{2+}

SUBSOIL

Zone of lesser bacterial action $\rightarrow CO_2$ produced in lesser amounts

Continued chemical action with clays, limestone particles

LIMESTONE BEDROCK
($CaCO_3$)

crevice

Zone of chemical neutralization reactions that lower acidity

$$CaCO_3 + H_2CO_3 \quad \rightarrow \quad Ca^{2+} + 2HCO_3^-$$

$$MgCO_3 + H_2CO_3 \quad \rightarrow \quad Mg^{2+} + 2HCO_3^-$$
$$\underbrace{\qquad\qquad\qquad}_{\text{dissolved ions}}$$

Figure 3.4 Chemistry of Water Hardness

Table 3.2   Examples of Acid Rain Downwind from Industrial Areas

Average Changes in pH of Rain in Southern Norway and Sweden, 1956–1975

Year	pH
1956	6.0–5.5
1961	5.0–4.5
1966	4.5–4.0
1975	4.6–4.3

Average pH of Rain at Selected Sites in New England, 1970

Place	pH
Hubbard Brook, N.H.	4.03
Hubbardston, Mass.	4.29
Thomaston, Conn.	4.27
New Haven, Conn.	3.81

Ions Present in Rain at Hubbard Brook, New Hampshire

Ion	Percent
H^+	69 (of cations)
SO_4^{2-}	62 (of anions)
NO_3^-	23 (of anions)
Cl^-	14 (of anions)

Source: pH values given in G. E. Likens, F. H. Bormann, and N. M. Johnson, *Environment* 14 (March 1972): 33. Percentage of ions given in G. E. Likens and F. H. Bormann, *Science* 184 (1974): 1176. Data for 1975 given in G. E. Likens, *Chem. Eng. News* (November 22, 1976), p. 29.

The increased acidity of runoff and stream water also increases leaching rates, since basic minerals are dissolved in acid. The effects of this on the ecosystem are not known at this time.

A condition somewhat related to acid rain is that of acid mine drainage. Coal mines, especially those that have been abandoned, are known to release substantial quantities of sulfuric acid as well as iron hydroxide into local streams through seepage. As shown in the reactions in Figure 3.6, these chemicals result from the oxidation of iron sulfide, which is present in large quantities in the underground seams that also contain coal. Iron sulfide is stable in the absence of air, but when the coal seams are exposed to air in mining operations, the oxidation reactions shown in Figure 3.6 take place, with the production of substantial quantities of

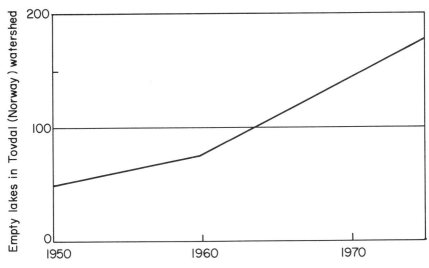

Figure 3.5 Population Declines As the Acidity of Lake Water Increases

Source: G. E. Likens, *Chem. Eng. News*, November 22, 1976, p. 29.

In coal mines, oxidation of sulfide in pyrite (FeS_2) occurs in the presence of water:

$$FeS_2 + \frac{7}{2} O_2 + H_2O \quad \rightarrow \quad Fe^{2+} + 2HSO_4^- \tag{1}$$

In streams, brown precipitate and acid form:

$$Fe^{2+} + \frac{1}{4} O_2 + \frac{1}{2} H_2O \quad \rightarrow \quad Fe^{3+} + OH^- \tag{2a}$$

$$Fe^{3+} + 3H_2O \quad \rightarrow \quad Fe(OH)_3 \downarrow + 3H^+ \tag{2b}$$
brown precipitate

Total reaction: (1) + (2a) + (2b) = (3)

$$\underset{\text{pyrite}}{FeS_2} + \frac{15}{4} O_2 + \frac{7}{2} H_2O \quad \rightarrow \quad Fe(OH)_3 \downarrow + \underbrace{2H^+ + 2HSO_4^-}_{\text{sulfuric acid}} \tag{3}$$

Stream pH is as low as 3; i.e. $[H_2SO_4] \approx 0.5 \times 10^{-3}$ M.

Figure 3.6   Acid Mine Drainage

acid. These reactions continue long after coal-mining operations have ceased. The resulting local pollution problem is quite severe, with many streams in coal-mining areas completely polluted by sulfuric acid. It is difficult to control since sealing up the mines effectively is arduous and expensive. It has been estimated that billions of dollars will be required for adequate cleanup of this problem.

3 | Hardness

In addition to its acidity, an important characteristic of natural water is the concentration of dissolved minerals—a condition known as *hardness*. The same neutralization reactions shown in Figure 3.4 that serve to raise the pH of water as it percolates through the soil also introduce appreciable quantities of calcium and magnesium ions and smaller amounts of strontium, iron, and manganese ions. These doubly charged positive ions become noticeable when we wash because they precipitate soap.

There is a wide variety of cleaning agents used to remove soil and dirt from clothes, dishes, and thousands of other commodities; they are classified under the

(i)

Structure

long hydrocarbon tail
(oil soluble; hydrophobic)

small ionic head
(water soluble; hydrophilic)
examples:

carboxyl ($-COO^-$ Na^+)

sulfonate ($-SO_3^-$ Na^+)

hydroxyl ($-OH$)

(ii)

Cleaning Action of Detergents in Water by Agglomeration
(Micelle Formation)

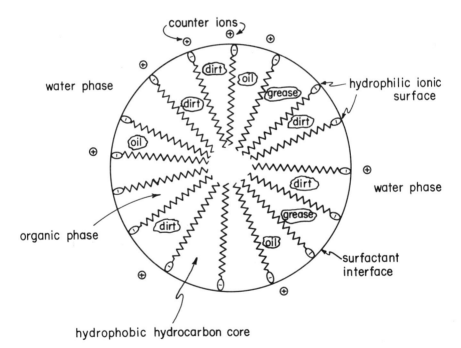

Figure 3.7 General Properties of Detergents

general term "detergent." The upper part of Figure 3.7 shows that a detergent molecule contains two distinct parts: one part, called the *tail* of the molecule, is usually a long organic chain that is soluble in oil but not in water; the tail is called the *hydrophobic* part from the Greek word meaning "fear of water." In contrast, the head of the molecule is polar and readily soluble in water. This part is called *hydrophilic* from the Greek word meaning "love of water." It consists of carboxyl, sulfonate, or hydroxyl groups. This split personality of the molecule permits it to interact at the same time with both an organic phase and a water phase by concentrating at the surface between the two. The general name for such molecules is *surfactant*.

As illustrated in the lower part of Figure 3.7, detergents work by agglomerating at the interface between oil-soluble dirt particles and water. They surround these particles, with their hydrophobic parts sticking in and their hydrophilic parts sticking out. Such an agglomeration is called a *micelle*. These micelles float freely in the water and are prevented from aggregating with one another by the mutual repulsions of the polar hydrophilic head groups.

As shown in the first part of Figure 3.8, detergents are derived from both natural and synthetic sources. A natural soap is simply a sodium salt of a fatty acid obtained from the hydrolysis of animal fat. Also shown are synthetic detergents such as sodium alkylbenzene sulfonate, which came into widespread use

---

Sources

a. Natural soaps—derived from animal fats
   Example:

$$C_{17}H_{35}-C\underset{O^{-}Na^{+}}{\overset{O}{\diagup}}$$

   Sodium stearate

b. Synthetic detergents
   Example:

$$C_{12}H_{25}-\!\!\left\langle\!\!\bigcirc\!\!\right\rangle\!\!-SO_3^{-}\,Na^{+}$$

   Sodium alkylbenzene sulfonate

Precipitation of Detergents in Hard Water

$$2C_{12}H_{25}-\!\!\left\langle\!\!\bigcirc\!\!\right\rangle\!\!-SO_3^{-} + M^{2+} \longrightarrow (C_{12}H_{25}-\!\!\left\langle\!\!\bigcirc\!\!\right\rangle\!\!-SO_3^{-})_2\,M^{2+}\downarrow$$

Precipitate

M^{2+} is mostly Ca^{2+}, some Mg^{2+}, and small amounts of Sr^{2+}, Fe^{2+}, and Mn^{2+}.

Figure 3.8 Sources of Detergents and Effect of Hard Water after World War II. They were found by detergent manufacturers to be cheaper and more effective than natural soaps. As shown in the lower part of Figure 3.8, all surfactants with a negative charge, whether natural or synthetic, share the same problem: They are precipitated by doubly charged positive ions such as calcium. They are then unavailable for solubilizing dirt and, moreover, the precipitates tend to be scummy and stick to the items being washed.

Consequently, detergent formulations contain other agents called *builders,* which are intended to eliminate precipitation by the positive ions. They can do this by tying the ions up, either in a soluble form or in a precipitate that can settle easily. Chemicals that tie up the ions in soluble form are called *chelating agents.* As illustrated in the upper part of Figure 3.9, these are molecules with several polar sites that can bind the ions through multiple points of attachment. The chelating agent in common use in commercial detergents is sodium tripolyphosphate (STP), which is shown bound to a Ca^{2+} ion at the top of the figure. This compound is relatively cheap and has the advantage that it rapidly breaks down in the environment to sodium phosphate, which is a naturally occurring mineral. Indeed, phosphate is a nutrient for plants, and it is for this reason that environmental groups have objected to its use in detergents on the grounds that natural bodies of water are being overfertilized as a result. Consequently, consumption of phosphate in detergents has decreased by 67% over the past ten years in the United States.

A variety of substitutes for STP have been explored, but none has been found to be fully satisfactory so far. One chelating agent, sodium nitrilotriacetate (NTA), whose structural formula is shown in Figure 3.9, has considerable promise, but there is concern that NTA can bind not only calcium but also heavy metals and could mobilize these toxic elements in the environment. NTA does not break down as readily as does STP and is, therefore, a more potent carrier of metals. Also, there is some evidence that its breakdown products may themselves be carcinogenic.

In the areas of the country where phosphates have been banned from detergent formulations, the substitutes have generally been sodium carbonate or sodium silicate. As shown in the lower part of Figure 3.9, these precipitate Ca^{2+} ions before they can precipitate the detergent. But the $CaCO_3$ or $CaSiO_3$ precipitates produce a scummy residue and are apparently detrimental to the operation of automatic washing machines. Moreover, there is a safety problem associated with these formulations because of the high alkalinity of sodium carbonate and sodium silicate. Both carbonate and silicate can form hydroxide ions in water as shown in equation 5 of Figure 3.9. The alkalinity may be dangerous if the material is accidentally lodged in the eyes or swallowed. A promising new candidate for detergent builders is zeolite, an aluminosilicate mineral, which, as indicated in equation 6 of Figure 3.9, can trap Ca^{2+} ions by exchanging them for its own Na^+ ions. Suspensions of zeolite are not alkaline.

Chelating Agents: Chemicals That Tie Up Positive Ions in Solution So They Can No Longer React with Detergents

1. Sodium tripolyphosphate (STP): $Na_5P_3O_{10}$

Ca^{2+} + STP →

Ca^{2+} tied up in solution;
no further reaction with surfactant

2. Sodium nitrilotriacetate (NTA): $N(C_2H_2O_2)_3Na_3$

Ca^{2+} + NTA →

Precipitating Agents

3. Sodium carbonate: Na_2CO_3

$$Ca^{2+} + CO_3^- \longrightarrow CaCO_3 \downarrow$$

4. Sodium metasilicate: Na_2SiO_3

$$Ca^{2+} + SiO_3^{2-} \longrightarrow CaSiO_3 \downarrow$$

5. Hydrolysis of excess Na_2CO_3 or Na_2SiO_3 causes alkaline solution:

$$CO_3^{2-} + H_2O \longrightarrow HCO_3^- + OH_-$$
$$SiO_3^{2-} + H_2O \longrightarrow HSiO_3^- + OH^-$$

Strongly basic solution,
dangerous irritant

6. Zeolite exchange:

$$Ca^{2+} + Na_2 \cdot Al_2O_3 \cdot 2SiO_2 \cdot 4.5H_2O \rightarrow CaAl_2O_3 \cdot 2SiO_2 \cdot 4.5H_2O + 2Na^+$$

Zeolite   Suspension

Figure 3.9 Builders to Prevent Precipitation of Detergents in Hard Water

4 | Eutrophication

Overnutrition of bodies of water caused by inputs of phosphates or other nutrients is commonly called *eutrophication*. Technically, eutrophication is sim-

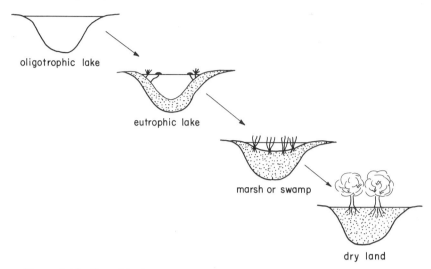

oligotrophic lake

eutrophic lake

marsh or swamp

dry land

Figure 3.10 Eutrophication and the Aging of a Lake by Accumulation of Sediment

ply the natural process of providing a body of water with the nutrients for the aquatic life it supports. As diagrammed in Figure 3.10, the process leads to filling in of lakes with sediment. A lake starts its life cycle as a clear body of water, which is described as *oligotrophic*. Then, as nutrients enter the lake through land runoff and as aquatic life grows and dies, the water acquires a high content of organic debris. At this stage the lake is described as *eutrophic*. Eventually it fills in completely, forming a marsh and then dry land.

As illustrated at the top of Figure 3.11, the natural aging process in lakes and coastal areas is slow because algae and other phytoplankton depend on sunlight and are productive only in the surface layer, called the *euphotic zone*. Nutrients are lost as dead biomass and other organic debris sink into the deeper waters, where sunshine cannot penetrate. Growth is limited by the nutrient balance between surface inputs and losses to the deeper layers. The physical mixing of the deeper layers with the surface is prevented by thermal stratification, since the surface is warmed by the sunlight. As shown at the right side of the first diagram of Figure 3.11, the temperature decreases sharply near the bottom of the euphotic zone. Since warm water is less dense than cold water, this stratification is stable and there is little mixing.

In temperate zones the layers mix in the winter, as diagrammed in the second part of Figure 3.11. When the surface cools down, the temperature and hence the density become uniform. Wind and waves easily induce mixing, which brings nutrient-rich waters to the surface. Productivity is now limited, however, by the low solar intensity in winter.

Of current concern is the enormous acceleration of the eutrophication process

EZ = euphotic zone
stipple represents phytoplankton growth
N → signifies direction of nutrient flow
enclosed arrows indicate circulation of waters

Figure 3.11 Natural Cycling of Nutrients for Controlled Growth of Aquatic Life in Lakes and Coastal Areas

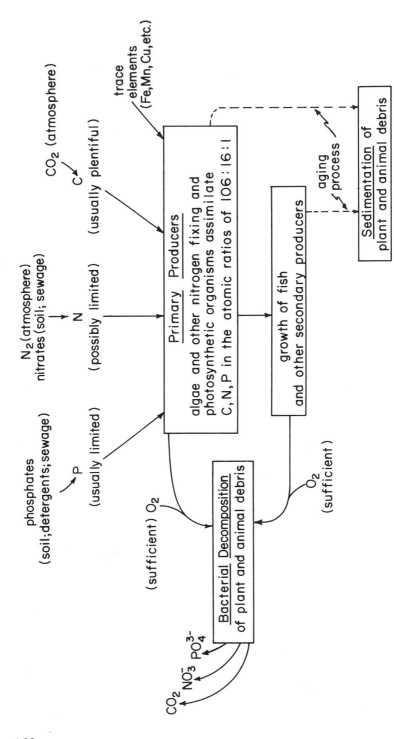

Figure 3.12 Factors That Affect Aquatic Production, Decomposition, and Sedimentation

in lakes and estuaries brought about by the year-round injection of large quantities of phosphates and other nutrients from human sources, thus upsetting the natural balance of the nutrient cycle.

As shown schematically in Figure 3.12, the rate of eutrophication establishes the balance between the production of aquatic life and its destruction by bacterial decomposition. Under natural conditions the rate of decomposition is nearly equal to the rate of production, and little sedimentation occurs. Where there are large inputs of nutrients from human sources, bacterial decomposition cannot keep pace with productivity and sedimentation increases.

As is also shown in Figure 3.12, the primary producers in a lake require specific proportions of various nutrients for growth. They require sources of carbon, nitrogen, and phorphorus in the atomic ratios of 106:16:1 and a large number of other elements in relatively small amounts. These minor elements are usually available at sufficient concentration in the natural environment to provide for the needs of aquatic organisms, although in particular cases the deficiency of one or more of these trace elements may limit growth and determine the nature of the organisms present.

With respect to the major nutrient elements, carbon, nitrogen, and phosphorus, there has been considerable debate about which one limits growth. The nutrient that is present in lowest quantity in relation to the proportions required by the organisms is the one that determines and limits the growth rate.

Carbon is the element required in the largest amounts. Carbon dioxide from the atmosphere is utilized directly by algae and aquatic plants, and bacterial decomposition of organic matter produces more carbon dioxide. Only dissolved carbon dioxide can be used directly by algae. Under conditions of very rapid growth, as may occur in algal blooms, it is possible that the concentration of dissolved carbon dioxide might fall low enough to limit growth. Under normal growing conditions, however, it appears that ample carbon dioxide is available from the atmosphere to prevent carbon from being the limiting nutrient.

Nitrogen is needed by plants to synthesize protein and a variety of other essential constituents. It is available as nitrate, which enters the water in runoff and sewage. Also, a number of species of algae are able to use atmospheric nitrogen directly, thereby providing a sufficient supply of nitrogen to the local water environment. If these algae are absent and nitrate levels are very low, nitrogen can become the limiting nutrient.

Phosphorus is required by all organisms in substantial quantities. It is the only one of the major nutrient elements that does not have any atmospheric source; that is, there is no gaseous form of phosphorus that occurs naturally and forms a part of the biological cycle. Phosphorus has to be obtained from soluble phosphate compounds that enter the water from runoff and sewage. While much of the phosphorus injected into lakes and streams from land runoff is in an insoluble form, detergent phosphates are very soluble and, hence, are readily available for

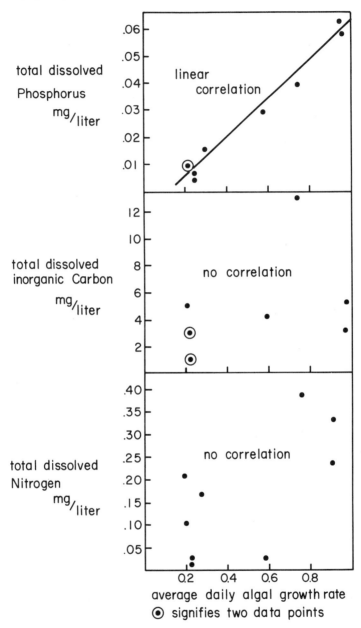

Figure 3.13 Evidence for Phosphorus As the Limiting Nutrient in Algal Growth: An Analysis of Nine Oregon Lakes

Source: G. E. Likens, ed., "Nutrients and Eutrophication, the Limiting-Nutrient Controversy," Proceedings of the Symposium on Nutrients and Eutrophication, Michigan State University, 1971, p. 139.

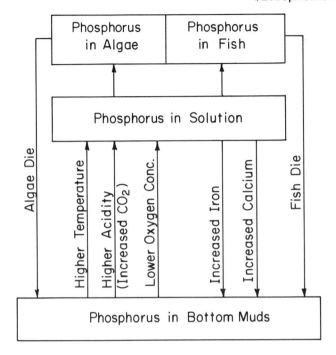

Figure 3.14   Chemical Factors That Affect Phosphorus Equilibria in Lakes

Source: H. R. Jones, *Detergents and Pollution, Problems and Technical Solutions* (Park Ridge, N.J.: Noyes Data Corporation, 1972), p. 8.

biological assimilation. Presently, in regions of the United States that do not have a detergent phosphate ban in effect, approximately one-third of the phosphorus in domestic wastewater is derived from detergents. Due to increasingly strict regulations, this amount has been decreasing steadily since the early 1970s, when half the phosphorus in sewage effluent stemmed from detergent use. There is substantial evidence that for relatively unpolluted bodies of water, phosphorus is indeed the limiting nutrient. As is shown in Figure 3.13, for nine lakes in Oregon, the biological productivity correlates quite well with the phosphorus levels in the water but not with the nitrogen or carbon levels.

The availability of phosphorus for biological growth in oceans and lakes depends both on the inputs of external sources and on the rate of mobilization of phosphorus from bottom sediments. In the temperate zone, the winter overturn diagrammed in Figure 3.11 brings to the surface the phosphorus dissolved in the deep layers. Figure 3.14 shows schematically that the cycling of phosphorus between the sediments and the water above is controlled by chemical factors. Fish and algae die and settle into the sediment, carrying an appreciable part of their phosphorus with them. Also metal ions, particularly calcium and iron, form

Removal by lime:

$$5Ca^{2+} + 4OH^- + 3HPO_4^{2-} \longrightarrow Ca_5(PO_4)_3(OH) \downarrow + 3H_2O$$
Hydroxyapatite

Removal by alum:

$$Al_2(SO_4)_3 + 2PO_4^{3-} \longrightarrow 2AlPO_4 \downarrow + 3SO_4^{2-}$$

Removal by ferric chloride:

$$FeCl_3 + PO_4^{3-} \longrightarrow FePO_4 \downarrow + 3Cl^-$$

Figure 3.15 Precipitation of Phosphate by Lime, Alum, or Ferric Chloride

insoluble phosphates, which settle to the bottom. The solubility of these sedimentary phosphate deposits depends on the conditions in the bottom water. The solubility increases with increasing temperature and also with decreasing pH, since hydrogen ions form soluble complexes with phosphate. The amount of dissolved oxygen is also important because under oxygen-free conditions, tripositive iron ions, called *ferric ions,* are reduced to dipositive iron ions, called *ferrous ions,* and it appears that ferrous phosphates are substantially more soluble than ferric phosphates.

This chemistry makes a quantitative evaluation of the dependence of biological growth rates on phosphorus inputs difficult, and modeling of this complex process is an active area of current research. It seems that a number of lakes and streams in the United States are sufficiently polluted already so that eliminating phosphorus in detergents would have relatively little effect on the biological productivity. Growth in these lakes is no longer limited by phosphorus. It will take a long time and substantial control measures to restore them to the conditions of relative purity required for phosphorus limitation. Removing phosphorus from detergents would be a contribution toward this end, however.

An alternative approach is to introduce phosphate removal at the sewage treatment plant. This can be done fairly simply by adding lime, calcium oxide, alum (aluminum sulfate), or ferric chloride to the sewage. The calcium, aluminum, or ferric ions precipitate the phosphate quite effectively via the reactions shown in Figure 3.15. This procedure has the advantage that all phosphates from human waste as well as from detergents are removed and prevented from entering the hydrosphere.

5 | The Oceans

In addition to the problem of overnutrition of bodies of water, an area of increasing concern is pollution of the world's water systems by toxic materials, and the subsequent lethal effects on plant and animal life. Figure 3.16 shows the pattern of distribution for the primary production of photosynthetic organisms in

Figure 3.16 Distribution of Annual Production of Plant Biomass (Primary Production) in the World's Oceans

Source: *Productivity of World Ecosystems* (Washington, D.C.: National Academy of Sciences, 1975), p. 22. Reproduced with the permission of the National Academy of Sciences.

the world's oceans. The pattern for secondary production, that is, the animals and fish that feed on the primary producers, corresponds closely to that for primary production. One can see that the regions of greatest marine productivity, the estuaries, upwellings, coral reefs, and continental shelf areas, which provide most of the fish we eat, lie close to the continental areas. Large quantities of hazardous wastes can be injected directly into these high-productivity areas by river flow, runoff from the land, or direct discharge. The concern is that these toxic inputs will have serious effects on the entire marine ecosystem and on the fish population that it supports.

Some effects on the oceans have already been observed. One of the more notorious examples of pollution is the New York Bight, a 50,000-km^2 area of the ocean not far from New York City where an enormous amount of municipal sewage sludge and industrial wastes has been dumped continuously. The high concentrations of nutrients actually support a level of aquatic productivity that is higher than average for ocean coastal regions, but there has been a noticeably adverse effect on fish life. High percentages of dead and abnormal fish eggs have been found in particular areas of the Bight, and the winter flounders have an uncommonly high incidence of fin rot. These effects are thought to be linked to the elevated levels of chlorinated organics and heavy metals (lead, silver, cadmium, and chromium) that have been found in the Bight.

Another aspect of ocean pollution is contamination by petroleum. Table 3.3 shows a projection of the sources and annual amounts of petroleum inputs in the early 1980s. Although spectacular oil spills have been highly publicized over the years, the smaller day-to-day inputs in the coastal waters and harbors of the world produce chronic pollution that is much larger in total volume. Municipal and industrial effluents as well as runoff from the land and rivers all contribute

Table 3.3 Estimated Inputs of Petroleum Hydrocarbons in the Oceans during the Early 1980s

Input Source	Millions of Metric Tons Per Year
Natural seeps	0.60
Offshore production	0.20
Transportation	
Accidental spills	0.25
Losses during normal operation	0.55
(bilges bunkering, tanker washings, etc.)	
Coastal refineries	0.02
Atmosphere	0.60
Municipal and industrial	0.45
Urban runoff	0.30
River runoff	1.60
Total	4.57

Source: *Petroleum in the Marine Environment* (Washington, D.C.: National Academy of Sciences, 1975), p. 14.

significantly. Offshore oil drilling will be increasingly important as the search for oil in the continental shelf areas intensifies.

Crude oil and petroleum products contain many substances that are poisonous to marine life. There are, however, natural mechanisms for the degradation of oil at sea. The most important of these is bacterial decomposition, which, unfortunately, is least effective for the most poisonous compounds in oil.

Our understanding of the effects of petroleum pollution on the marine ecosystem stems largely from studies on oil spills in which relatively high concentrations have been injected into small areas. These effects have been the subject of controversy, but it is well documented that under certain conditions even a relatively small oil spill can devastate the local marine ecosystem. For example, shellfishing was still forbidden in Buzzard's Bay, Massachusetts, in 1978, nine years after 700 tons of oil had been washed up into the salt marshes and pounded into the sediment of the shallow bay by storm waves. A really large oil spill can release as much as 100,000 tons of oil.

The impact of an oil spill depends on many factors. It is ameliorated if winds or currents push the oil out into the high seas. Another determinant is the amount of clay suspended in the seawater. The clay tends to adsorb onto the spilled oil, making it heavier and causing it to sink and concentrate in the sediment before it is dispersed in the ocean.

We are just beginning to learn about the effects of petroleum on marine ecology, especially chronic exposure to low-level concentrations. A reliable assessment will require studies of the effects on the lower organisms in the food chain as well as on fish.

6 | Sewage Treatment

Abatement of water pollution from overnutrition or toxic chemicals depends largely on the efficacy of wastewater treatment. It is becoming increasingly apparent that the treatment of hazardous industrial wastes should be separated from that of nonhazardous organic wastes from domestic sewage. Let us now take a closer look at how sewage wastewater can be purified.

$$(C, H, O, N, S)^* + O_2 \xrightarrow[\text{bacteria}]{\text{aerobic}} CO_2 + H_2O + H_2SO_4 + NH_4^+ + NO_3^-{}^\dagger$$

Figure 3.17   Bacterial Action in Water Containing Organic Wastes

*(C, H, O, N, S) are the major elements in wastewater.
†Bacteria needed to oxidize NH_4^+ to NO_3^- grow slowly in wastewater and generally do not compete well with carbon-feeding bacteria.

Domestic sewage treatment

Conventional sewage treatment plants have been designed to deal solely with nontoxic organic wastes by utilizing bacteria to decompose them, as shown in the reaction of Figure 3.17. The key feature of the process is an abundance of oxygen, a condition called *aerobic*. The solubility of gaseous oxygen in water is not very high—about 9 mg/l at 20° C and less at higher temperatures. The oxidation of 1 mg of carbon requires 2.67 mg of dissolved oxygen. Organic hydrogen, sulfur, and nitrogen are also oxidized and use up additional oxygen.

Thus, the purity of water depends primarily on the rate of transport of oxygen by aeration and on the total load of organic material that must be oxidized. As shown in the upper part of Figure 3.18, this load is expressed as the biological

Definition

(solubility of O_2 in water = 9 mg / liter)

BOD = milligrams of oxygen which must be removed from the water to decompose the organic material contained in one liter of wastewater.

Typical BOD's for Various Processes[*]

type	BOD (mg O_2/ liter waste water)
Domestic sewage	165
All manufacturing	~200
Chemicals and allied products	314
Paper	372
Food	747
Metals	13

Figure 3.18   Biological Oxygen Demand (BOD)

Source of lower table: "Intermedia Aspects of Air and Water Pollution Control," U.S. Environmental Protection Agency (600/5-73-003), August 1973, p. 76.

oxygen demand (BOD), the number of milligrams of oxygen needed to carry out the overall oxidation reaction in one liter of water. This biological oxygen demand is very high for sewage and the waste products of various industries, as seen by the numbers in the second part of Figure 3.18. Domestic sewage on the average requires 165 mg of oxygen per liter and manufacturing wastewater requires about 200 mg/l. Obviously, this load would overwhelm the capacity of most natural bodies of water, so sewage treatment is necessary to maintain water quality.

Figure 3.19 is a diagram of the processes that are most commonly used today for domestic sewage. Primary treatment consists of removing solid wastes from the water by screening, scum removal, and settling of sludge. The remaining liquid is then subjected to secondary treatment, which is a method of greatly accelerating natural biological respiration. The medium for doing that is called *activated sludge,* which is essentially a bed of microbes that are allowed to grow rapidly and feed on the organic solutes in the wastewater under well-aerated conditions. The effluent from such a tank has a much lower biological oxygen demand due to the action of the microbes in the sludge. As the volume of the sludge increases through growth of the microbes, excess sludge is removed and thickened for disposal along with the primary sludge. Most sewage treatment, then, consists of removal of solids and then biological oxidation of soluble organic materials.

Sludge disposal is one of the major problems of sewage treatment. The sludge can be spread on soil or landfills, although available land for this method of disposal is becoming scarce. For communities that are close to the shore, the sludge commonly has been dumped into the ocean. Because of the fragility of the ocean's ecosystem, however, all ocean dumping will be stopped in the United States in the 1980s.

In principle, sludge could be used as fertilizer on crop lands, and some experiments in this are being carried out. However, the problem of toxic materials in the sludge is again the major stumbling block, and methods need to be developed for their removal. The incineration or pyrolysis of sludge is being considered in many areas. This method also suffers from the presence of toxic pollutants in the sludge, which can be emitted into the atmosphere. An alternative is to use the sludge in the production of methane gas using anaerobic digestion, as mentioned in the first part of this book.

The liquid effluent from secondary treatment plants has a considerably reduced biological oxygen demand. After being treated by chlorination to kill pathogenic microorganisms, it is often mixed directly into lakes and streams. Figure 3.19 shows the composition of typical secondary effluent—a BOD of 25 mg/l, an ammonium concentration of 20 mg/l, and a phosphate concentration of 25 mg/l. For clear lakes, these concentrations can enhance the rate of eutrophication. Removal of the dissolved materials requires further steps, which come under the heading of tertiary treatment. A flow diagram for one type of tertiary treatment

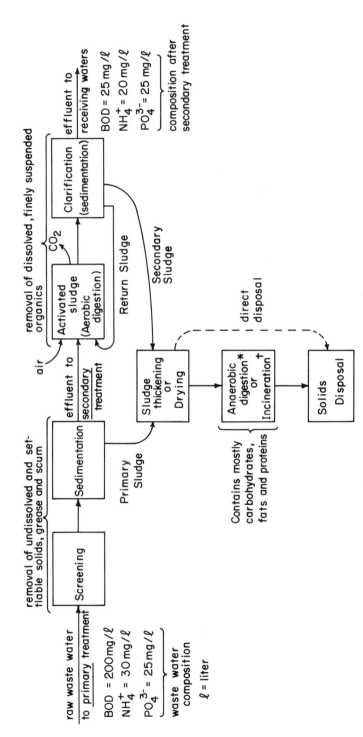

Figure 3.19 Primary and Secondary Treatment of Municipal Wastewater

*Typically, 50% of the sludge can be digested anaerobically to produce methane gas by a method similar to that shown in Figure 28.
†Dried sludge can be burned as low-quality fuel with a typical heat value of about 3,200 calories/g.
Source: Adapted from *Cleaning Our Environment, the Chemical Basis for Action* (Washington, D.C.: American Chemical Society, 1969), p. 107.

150

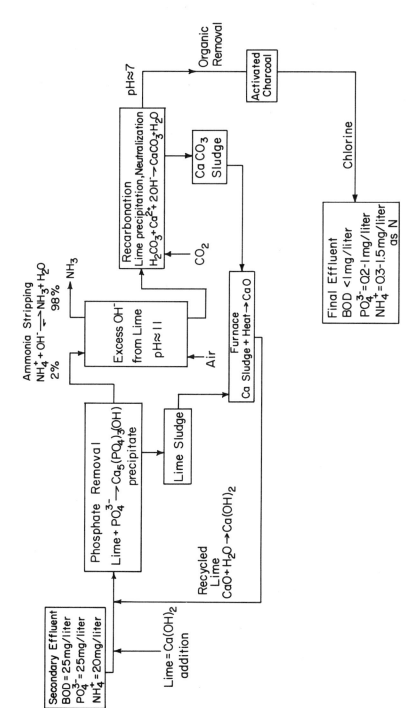

Figure 3.20 Tertiary Treatment of Municipal Wastewater

Secondary Effluent
BOD = 25 mg/liter
PO_4^{3-} = 25 mg/liter
NH_4^+ = 20 mg/liter

Lime = $Ca(OH)_2$
addition

Phosphate Removal
Lime + $PO_4^{3-} \rightarrow Ca_5(PO_4)_3(OH)$
precipitate

Lime Sludge

Recycled Lime
$CaO + H_2O \rightarrow Ca(OH)_2$

Furnace
Ca Sludge + Heat $\rightarrow$ CaO

Air

Ammonia Stripping
$NH_4^+ + OH^- \rightleftharpoons NH_3 + H_2O$
2%   98%

NH_3

Excess OH^-
from Lime
pH $\approx$ 11

Recarbonation
Lime precipitation, Neutralization
$H_2CO_3 + Ca^{2+} + 2OH^- \rightarrow CaCO_3 + H_2O$

CO_2

$CaCO_3$ Sludge

pH $\approx$ 7

Organic Removal

Activated Charcoal

Chlorine

Final Effluent
BOD <1 mg/liter
PO_4^{3-} = 0.2–1 mg/liter
NH_4^+ = 0.3–1.5 mg/liter
as N

151

plant, originally designed to maintain the purity of Lake Tahoe, California, is shown in Figure 3.20.

Secondary effluent enters a flocculation tank where lime, calcium hydroxide, is added to remove phosphates as calcium phosphate. From there the water moves to an ammonia stripping tower. The nitrogen present in the wastewater exists mainly as ammonium ions, which are converted to gaseous ammonia at the high pH values produced by the addition of the lime. Finally, the remaining organic materials are removed by adsorption on activated carbon, and chlorine is added as a disinfectant. The levels of nitrogen, phosphorus, and dissolved organic carbon are quite low following the tertiary treatment.

Phosphorus and nitrogen removal are not practiced presently on a wide scale because of the added cost of the required tertiary treatment facilities. Such plants are expensive to run as well as build, because of their high energy requirements.

The data in Table 3.4 show the relative energy requirements of the various steps indicated in the tertiary treatment process diagrammed in Figure 3.20. The combination of lime treatment and ammonia stripping requires substantially more

Table 3.4 Energy Requirements for Secondary and Advanced Wastewater Treatment Processes (100 million gallons per day plant)

Process		Energy Requirement (kwh/day)
Secondary treatment		154,282*
Lime treatment		
Lime addition		5,613
Recalcining		182,860
Recarbonation		29,133†
	Total	217,606
Ammonia stripping		186,587
Nitrification/denitrification		
Nitrification		60,259
Denitrification		1,020
Purification and transport of methanol		35,826
	Total	97,105
Activated carbon		
Operation		23,773
Regeneration		31,620‡
	Total	55,393
Chlorination		607

*Of this, 61,000 kwh/day can be recovered as methane through sludge digestion.

†Does not include energy for carbon dioxide production and transportation.

‡Does not include energy for carbon production and transportation needed to replace carbon lost in regeneration.

Source: Data extracted from R. M. Hagan and E. B. Roberts, *Water Sewage Works* 123, No. 12 (1976): 52; and D. G. Argo and G. M. Wesner, *Water Wastes Eng.* 13, No. 5 (1976): 24.

energy than does secondary treatment. The main energy costs are for recycling the calcium oxide via heating and running the ammonia stripping tower. An additional disadvantage of ammonia stripping is that its efficiency decreases markedly at low temperatures, and ceases to work at all at temperatures below freezing.

An alternative method for nitrogen removal is conversion to N_2, using a combination of nitrifying and denitrifying bacteria. The former use NH_4^+ as an energy source, metabolizing it to NO_2^- and then to NO_3^-, in an aerobic environment. Denitrifying bacteria, on the other hand, use NO_3^- as an oxidant to metabolize organic carbon. The overall products are N_2 and CO_2. The energy requirement for this process is only half that for ammonia stripping, although care must be taken to maintain the right growth conditions for the bacteria.

Another concept for tertiary wastewater treatment that consumes minimal energy is to use the land as a natural filter. Soil particles efficiently absorb phosphate ions and, to a lesser extent, ammonium and nitrate ions. The soil also harbors microbes that can biologically oxidize carbon and nitrogen. One concept

☐ waste water

▨ recharged water

Figure 3.21 Tertiary Treatment by Spraying the Effluent from Secondary Treatment on Forest and Crop Land

Source: "Renovation of Secondary Effluent for Reuse As a Water Resource," U.S. Environmental Protection Agency (660/2-74-016), February 1974, p. 8.

is to spread effluents on the ground itself. In this case, the filtering capacity of the soil is the crucial variable. Another possibility, shown in Figure 3.21, is to spray secondary effluents onto forest or crop land. An experiment of this type has been carried on for a number of years at the Pennsylvania State University, where the effluent from the sewage treatment plant that serves the town of University Park has been sprayed onto agricultural and forest land. The results have shown essentially complete removal of phosphorus and nitrogen from the water before it enters the water table. At the same time, crop and forest productivity has increased. Methods of this type obviously depend on the availability of sufficient land and on the absence from the effluent of toxic materials and pathogenic microorganisms.

The complexity of the problem of toxic materials arises from the multiplicity of sources of the sewage treated by municipal treatment plants. These include households and offices but also hospitals and a variety of industries. Runoff from the city streets or adjacent agricultural areas is also carried to the treatment plants, as storm drains and sewer lines are usually interconnected. Under increasingly strict government regulations, large industries have installed their own waste treatment facilities, and recycling of the wastewater is increasing. Never-

---

Filtering Industrial Wastes by Activated Charcoal

Effectiveness of Activated Charcoal in the Removal of Some Toxic Chlorinated Organics

Compound	Initial Concentration (μg/l)	Concentration after Carbon Treatment (μg/l)	Orgaic Reduction (%)
Aldrin	48	<1.0	99+
Dieldrin	19	0.05	99+
Endrin	62	0.05	99+
DDT	41	0.1	99+
Arochlor 1242 (PCB)	45	<0.5	99+

Source of lower table: D. G. Hager, *Chem. Eng. Prog.* 72, No. 10 (1976): 57.

Figure 3.22 Activated Charcoal Filtration

theless, industrial effluents form a substantial fraction of the wastewater treated by municipal plants. As a result, these plants must often deal with toxic materials that they are not designed to handle. Clearly the ultimate solution to the toxic waste problem is separate treatment for each type of waste product at the point where it is produced.

Industrial wastewater treatment

There are two basic methods for purifying wastewater of toxic, nonbiodegradable chemicals: filtration and membrane techniques. Figure 3.22 shows that activated charcoal, which has a large surface area and readily adsorbs organic molecules, is an effective filter medium. The table gives data that show more than 99% reduction in the concentration of several chlorinated hydrocarbons in the effluent stream. As illustrated in Figure 3.23, synthetic resins are also being used for filtering. The figure shows a styrene-divinylbenzene copolymer that is also effective in removing chlorinated pesticides by adsorption to its surface. Also shown are cationic and anionic ion-exchange resins that have successfully removed ionic dyes from the wastewater from textile manufacturing.

(i)

Styrene -divinylbenzene Matrix

$$- H_2C - CH -$$

$$- CH - CH_2 - CH - CH_2 -$$

for removal of chlorinated pesticides by adsorption

(ii)

Secondary Amine Group
Anion Exchanger

Carboxyl Group
Cation Exchanger

$$\overset{\underset{\mid}{CH_2}}{\underset{\mid}{\underset{H}{N}}} H^+ Cl^- + A^- \longrightarrow \overset{\underset{\mid}{CH_2}}{\underset{\mid}{\underset{H}{N}}} H^+ A^- + Cl^-$$

$$- COO^- H^+ + M^+ \longrightarrow - COO^- M^+ + H^+$$

for removal of anionic and cationic chemicals (e.g. dyes)
by ion exchange

Figure 3.23   Filtering Industrial Wastes by Synthetic Resins

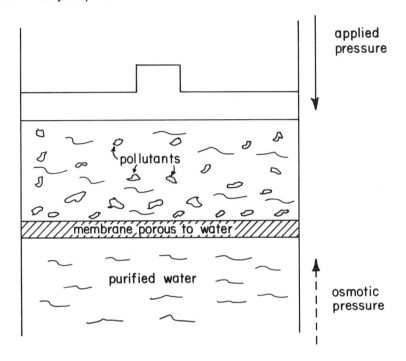

range of pore size
ultrafiltration : 2 to 10,000 nanometers
reverse osmosis : 0.04 to 600 nanometers

Figure 3.24 Industrial Wastewater Purification by the Membrane Technique of Ultrafiltration or Reverse Osmosis

Figure 3.24 illustrates a major membrane technique for toxic waste removal by ultrafiltration or reverse osmosis. In ultrafiltration the solution is forced through a membrane that contains pores of controlled size. These can be anywhere from 2 to 10,000 nm (20–10^5 Å). Molecules that are too big to pass through the pores are held back. The effluent is free of molecules of this size, and the concentrated solution behind the membrane can be led off to another filtration stage for further concentration and finally for disposal. Reverse osmosis is essentially the same technique (*osmosis* is the thermodynamically driven passage of solvent through a semipermeable membrane from a less to a more concentrated solution), except that the pore sizes of the membrane are generally smaller, from about 0.04 to 600 nm. Also, charged groups on the pore surface impede the passage of ions. Table 3.5 contains a list of current applications of these techniques.

Another membrane technology, electrodialysis, is appropriate for the concen-

Table 3.5   Applications of Reverse Osmosis and Ultrafiltration

Metal Industry
Recovery of gold, silver, platinum, nickel, chrome, zinc, aluminium, and cadmium from plating wastes
Reuse of rinse waters
Recovery of metal salts: nickel sulfamate, copper sulfate, copper pyrophosphate, zinc chloride
Recovery of detergent for reuse in cleaning operations in metal phosphating; oil concentration
Removal of sulfates from acid mine drainage
Textile Industry
Recovery of polyvinyl alcohols and mineral oils
Removal of dyes
Paper and Pulp
Color removal
Solids concentration from white liquor
Cleaning of water from black liquor
Food Industry
Concentration of whey from dairy wastes
Sugar recovery in candy manufacture
Miscellaneous
Desalting
Chromate removal from cooling tower blowdowns
Concentration of radioactive wastes
Removal of emulsified oils

Source: Adapted from T. J. Mulligan and R. D. Fox, _Chem. Eng._ 83, no. 22 (1976): 49.

tration of ions. The process is depicted in Figure 3.25. An applied voltage causes anions to migrate toward the anode (positive electrode) on the right, and cations to migrate toward the cathode (negative electrode) on the left. The cell contains membranes with fixed charges that are either negative or positive and that render the membranes impermeable to either anions or cations. These are arranged alternately, so that every other compartment gradually becomes more concentrated in electrolyte (sodium chloride in this illustration), while the remaining compartments become less concentrated. After a time the freshwater can be separated from the brine and the entire operation can be run continuously. The method can be used to obtain freshwater in arid coastal regions. Japan obtains its entire salt supply by electrodialysis of seawater. In the United States electrodialysis is widely used for desalting cheese whey, which is a major additive in processed food. Other anticipated uses are for the treatment of industrial discharges from metal plating, battery manufacture, glass etching, and wood pulp washing, and of saline effluents generally.

Although the removal of toxic chemicals from the wastewater from industrial facilities is expensive and energy-consuming, many of the trapped chemicals can be recycled or used in other processes. The purified water may also be suitable for further use in manufacturing. Both of these factors cut down the overall cleanup cost.

C = cation permeable
membrane

A = anion permeable
membrane

Figure 3.25 The Electrodialysis Process

7 | Drinking Water Supplies

Thus far we have dealt with the purification of sewage and industrial wastewater. Drinking water supplies must also be treated to ensure public safety. Potable water treatment plants are generally simpler than sewage treatment plants. The biological oxygen demand is very low and no bacteria digesters are needed. The major steps involve disinfection and, where necessary, the removal of unpleasant physical characteristics such as turbidity, color, and bad taste.

Small particles that cause turbidity and discoloration can be removed by coagulating them into larger particles that are heavy enough to precipitate out. The coagulating agents commonly used are aluminum sulfate, or alum, and iron chloride. These are the same chemicals used to precipitate soluble phosphates from sewage effluents, as was shown in the reactions in Figure 3.15.

Disinfection is carried out in the United States by chlorination. Other countries such as France and Switzerland use ozone to kill bacteria. Chlorination is less expensive in terms of energy use, since ozone is produced in an electric discharge. Also, ozone is unstable and rapidly converts to oxygen, so chlorine is a longer-lasting disinfectant. The usefulness of chlorination was unquestioned for

$$(---\overset{\displaystyle H}{\underset{\displaystyle H}{C}} - \overset{\displaystyle H}{\underset{\displaystyle H}{C}} - \overset{\displaystyle H}{\underset{\displaystyle H}{C}} - \overset{\displaystyle H}{\underset{\displaystyle H}{C}} ---) \quad + \quad Cl_2 \quad \longrightarrow \quad CHCl_3 \quad + \quad (C, H, Cl)$$

dissolved organics,   from chlorine   chloroform   chlorinated
humus, etc.   treatment   organics

Figure 3.26 Generation of Chlorinated Hydrocarbons in Drinking Water by Reaction of Chlorine with Natural Organics

decades until recently. As shown in Figure 3.26, it has been discovered that chlorine plays a role in generating toxic chlorinated compounds by reacting with organic material that is naturally present in the water.

Virtually every water system investigated in a nationwide survey by the U.S. Environmental Protection Agency showed trace levels of chloroform contamination. As a result, the EPA has proposed regulations that would limit chloroform concentration in drinking water to 100 parts per billion. The most effective way to meet this standard is to install activated carbon treatment as shown in Figure 3.22 as a final step after chlorination. Not only chloroform but also other halogenated organics from various industrial and agricultural sources can be removed simultaneously.

8 | Agricultural Pollution

While much attention is focused on municipal and industrial water supplies, problems associated with agricultural water pollution are increasingly coming to the fore. Table 3.6 tabulates the four main sources: erosion of crop land, animal wastes, commercial fertilizers that contain nitrates and phosphates, and pesticides.

Erosion leads to the silting of waterways and the loss of good topsoil. In the United States, the Agriculture Department's Soil Conservation Service estimates that 3 billion tons of topsoil are lost every year. One major abatement strategy involves the planting of a legume such as alfalfa or clover in late summer to serve as a cover crop for winter when wind and rain cause the most severe soil losses. As we will see in the next section, this technique has the added advantage of supplying nitrogen to the soil, which can be plowed under in the spring. There are severe erosion problems when sloped land is cultivated as it often is in poor, overpopulated countries where arable land is scarce. In such cases erosion can be reduced by terracing the land or building diversion ditches to slow down the runoff that carries suspended soil particles.

Erosion is becoming an increasingly severe worldwide problem as arable land

Table 3.6 Water Pollution from Agriculture

Source	Soil Erosion	Feedlot Animal Wastes	Fertilizers	Pesticides
Effect on Water Quality	Silting of waterways	Leaching of nitrates into groundwater; increasing biological oxygen demand	Leaching of nitrates into groundwater; runoff of nitrates and phosphates into river flow	Leaching into groundwater; runoff into natural bodies of water
Abatement Strategy	Cover cropping; terracing of sloped land; abundance of freshwater supplies	Production of methane gas by bacterial action	More conservative application; more use of legumes, manure, and mulch	Biodegradable substitutes; alternative techniques

dries up when irrigation water is diverted to supply growing needs for water in cities. Furthermore, as water supplies become more scarce, groundwater with high salt content will be used increasingly for irrigation. With time the soil becomes salty and unfit for agricultural purposes. When the land is abandoned, it is especially vulnerable to the ravages of wind erosion.

With respect to pollution from animal wastes, it has been estimated that farm animals in the United States produce about 20 times more wastes than does the human population. As long as this is spread over the land as fertilizer, it constitutes a resource rather than pollution, but increasingly the production of animals is being concentrated in feedlots and poultry farms, and the animal wastes are concentrated along with them. The biological oxygen demand of the wastewater from a feedlot with 10,000 cattle is equivalent to that of the sewage from a city of about 45,000 people. As mentioned early in this book, this animal waste could be converted into an energy source by methane digestion.

Of particular concern is the seepage of nitrate through the soil and into water tables. Nitrate is produced by microbial oxidation of ammonia associated with animal wastes. The problem is even more acute in farming areas that rely on heavy use of commercial fertilizer, which is essentially ammonium nitrate. Plants often cannot absorb the applied nitrogen fast enough, and nitrates tend to be washed through the soil to aquifers or carried away in runoff. As a result, drinking water in many agricultural areas has increasingly high levels of nitrate. While nitrate itself is relatively innocuous, biologically speaking, it can be reduced to nitrite by microbes in the human intestines, particularly in the intestines of small children. There has been concern that nitrites can react with amines in the digestive system to produce nitrosamines, which are known to be carcinogenic, a subject we will examine more closely in the next section.

Pesticide pollution in our water systems has created much concern. Strategies for reducing this problem also will be discussed in detail in the next section.

9 | Summary

The chemistry of the hydrosphere is dominated by dissolved oxygen and dissolved ions, including hydrogen ions, metal ions, and negatively charged ions such as carbonate, nitrate, and phosphate. Together, they determine the nature and level of the biological activity in water. The problem of water pollution is largely one of misplaced resources. The wastes that are flushed into streams, lakes, and oceans can easily overwhelm the biological capacities of the receiving waters. The same wastes applied to the land, with its much higher level of aeration, could significantly increase biological productivity. The main obstacle is the presence in wastes of toxic chemicals and pathogens, which have to be removed, preferably close to the source.

Problem Set

1. Given that the concentration of O_2 in water is only 9 milligrams per liter, why should water be a last resort for dumping of organic wastes and biodegradable chemicals? Why is the soil a more efficient medium?

2. Why is a soap micelle an effective cleansing agent for hydrophobic substances such as grease and oil? How does a builder foster micelle growth?

3. Assume algae need carbon, nitrogen, and phosphorus in the atomic ratios 106:16:1. What is the limiting nutrient in a lake that contains the following concentrations: total C = 20 mg/l, total N = 0.80 mg/l, and total P = 0.16 mg/l? If it is known that half the phosphorus in the lake originates from the use of phosphate detergents, will banning phosphate builders slow down eutrophication?

4. Five hundred kilograms of n-propanol ($CH_3CH_2CH_2OH$) is accidentally discharged into a body of water containing 10^8 l. By how much is the BOD (in milligrams per liter) of this water increased? Assume the following reaction:

$$C_3H_8O + \tfrac{9}{2}O_2 \rightarrow 3CO_2 + 4H_2O$$

5. A 10-ml sample of wastewater is diluted to 500 ml. The initial concentration of dissolved oxygen in the dilute sample is found to be present at 7.3 mg/l. The sample is then treated with bacteria and incubated for five days. The oxygen concentration after that time is 1.8 mg/l. What is the BOD of the original sample after five days? (Such a measurement is called BOD_5, which is a common parameter in wastewater engineering.)

6. The density difference between water at 30° C and at 29° C is 0.000298 g/ml, and the density difference between water at 5° C and at 4° C is 0.000008 g/ml. Using this information, can you explain why the wind circulates nutrients in lake water most readily in early spring and autumn when the temperature of the water is around 4° C, rather than in summer when the surface temperature is generally higher than 20° C?

7. a) A lake with a cross sectional area of 1 km² and a depth of 50 m has a euphotic zone that extends 15 m below the surface. What is the maximum weight of the biomass (in grams of carbon) that can be decomposed by aerobic bacteria in the region of the lake below the euphotic zone during the summer when there is no circulation with the upper layer? The reaction is:

$$(CH_2O)_n + nO_2 \xrightarrow{\text{bacteria}} nCO_2 + nH_2O$$

The solubility of oxygen in pure water saturated with air is 8.9 mg/l; 1 m³ = 1,000 l.

b) Sugarcane, one of the most efficient converters of photosynthetic energy, yields about 3,600 g carbon/m² per year. If the lake had the same level of productivity, how deep would it have to be to completely digest the biomass aerobically?

8. a) Assume that an electrodialysis plant for desalting seawater removes 60% of the salt each time the water is passed through an electrodialysis stack (see Figure 3.25 for

a schematic). The electrical energy requirement in kilowatt-hours per cubic meter of product water for a single pass through the stack is

$$E = \frac{I \times V}{1,000 \times W}$$

where I (current) = 74 a, V (voltage) = 1,000 v, and W is the product flow rate = 30 m^3/hour. Since seawater contains about 35,000 ppm of total dissolved salts, through how many stacks must the water be passed to obtain water that contains 1,000 ppm—the maximum salinity permissible for human consumption? How many kilowatt-hours of energy are needed per cubic meter of potable water?
b) What is the efficiency of the process if the theoretical minimum energy expenditure for potable water is 0.71 kwh/m^3?

9. A wastewater effluent contains dust, bacteria, viruses, glucose, and proteins. Using membrane filter technology, devise a way to separate the glucose and proteins from the rest of the material. The diameter of dust particles is on the order of 1 μm, the bacteria is 5 μm, viruses are 20 nm, glucose is 0.5 nm, proteins are 5 nm, and water is 0.2 nm.

10. Estimate the average height by which the oceans would be raised if half the ice caps and glaciers in the world melted. The total surface area of the oceans is 3.61×10^8 km^2; the total volume of water in the oceans is $1,320 \times 10^{18}$ l; and the amount trapped in glaciers and ice caps is $29,148 \times 10^{15}$ l (melted volume).

11. A 100 million gallon per day sewage treatment plant serves a population of 500,000. The energy needed to run the plant is 200,000 kwh/day. During sludge digestion methane gas is produced in a quantity equal to 150,000 calories per capita per day. What percentage of the energy needs of the treatment plant is provided by methane gas production?

12. a) Phosphate removal for a 100 million gallon per day sewage treatment plant requires 217,606 kwh/day of energy. Typically, 6,000 lb of phosphorus is removed per day. Compare this with the amount of sulfur emitted as sulfur dioxide by a coal-burning power plant that supplies the extra energy needed for phosphorus removal. Assume that this plant, which uses bituminous coal, produces 3,260 kwh of electrical energy per ton of coal burned. Further assume the coal contains 2% sulfur and that half the sulfur is emitted as sulfur dioxide. How many pounds of pollutants are produced by the plant if the cumulative weight of other air pollutants (i.e., fly ash, nitrogen oxides, unburned hydrocarbons, and carbon monoxide) equals that of sulfur dioxide?
b) Since phosphorus is an essential plant nutrient, whereas sulfur dioxide and other air pollutants are dangerous to public health, under what conditions could you justify the removal of phosphorus from sewage wastewater?

13. Raw river water used for a public drinking supply was found to contain no Cl$_2$ and 0.9 μg/l (ppb) of chloroform (CHCl$_3$), a suspected carcinogen. Upon treatment with chlorine, the water contained 6 ppm Cl$_2$ and 22.1 μg/l of CHCl$_3$. After the water settled for three days, it contained 2 ppm of Cl$_2$ and 60.8 μg/l of CHCl$_3$. Give a possible explanation for these observations. Cite at least two ways in which chlori-

nated hydrocarbon can be eliminated from finished drinking water supplies. [Data from T. A. Bellar, J. J. Lichtenberg, and R. C. Kroner, "The Occurrence of Organohalides in Chlorinated Drinking Waters," *Am. Water Works Assoc. J.* 66 (1974):703.]

14. If the concentration of carbon dioxide in the atmosphere doubles as a result of burning fossil fuels, what is the predicted *change* in the pH of (unpolluted) rainwater?

15. Describe how deforestation, conversion of forest land for agricultural use, and diversion of water supplies for growing cities and industries can lead eventually to desert conditions without proper water and land management.

Suggestions for Further Reading

Aqueous Solutions

Eisenberg, D., and Kauzmann, W. *The Structure and Properties of Water.* New York: Oxford University Press, 1969.

Frank, H. S. "The Structure of Ordinary Water." *Science* 169 (1970):635.

Frank, H. S., and Wen, W. Y. "Ion-Solvent Interactions: Structural Aspects of Ion-Solvent Interactions in Aqueous Solutions—A Suggested Picture of Water Structure." *Discus. Faraday Soc.* 24 (1957):133.

Meites, L., Pode, J., and Thomas, H. C. "Are Solubilities and Solubility Products Related?" *J. Chem. Educ.* 43 (1966):667.

Hydrophobic Bonding in Micelles and Biological Systems

Kauzmann, W. "Some Factors in the Interpretation of Protein Denaturation." *Adv. Protein Chem.* 14 (1959):1.

Tanford, C. "Micelle Shape and Size." *J. Phys. Chem.* 76 (1972):3020.

Tanford, C. *The Hydrophobic Effect: Formation of Micelles and Biological Membranes.* New York: J. Wiley & Sons, Inc. 1973.

Lehninger, A. L. *Biochemistry,* 2nd ed. New York: Worth Publishers, 1975, pp. 287–307.

Acid Rain

Likens, G., Wright, R., Galloway, J., and Butler, T. "Acid Rain." *Sci. Am.* 241 (October 1979):43.

Likens, G. "Acid Precipitation." *Chem. Eng. News,* November 22, 1976, p. 29.

Vermeuler, A. "Acid Precipitation in the Netherlands." *Environ. Sci. Technol.* 12 (September 1978):1016.

Johnson, N. "Acid Rain: Neutralization within the Hubbard Brook Ecosystem and Regional Implications." *Science* 204 (1979):497.

Lakes and Oceans

Ruttner, F. *Fundamentals of Limnology,* 3rd ed. Toronto: University of Toronto Press, 1963.

Russell-Hunter, W. D. *Aquatic Productivity.* New York: Macmillan Publishing Co., Inc., 1970.

Cole, G. A. *Textbook of Limnology.* St. Louis: The C. V. Mosby Company, 1975.

Beeton, A. M. "Eutrophication of the St. Lawrence Great Lakes." *Limnol. Oceanogr.* 10 (1965):240.

Rogatzkie, R. A. "The Great Lakes Rediscovered." *Am. Sci.* 62 (July–August 1974):454.

Hutchinson, G. E. "Eutrophication." *Am. Sci.* 61 (May–June 1973):269.

Lee, G., Rast, W., and Jones, R. "Eutrophication of Water Bodies: Insights for an Age-Old Problem." *Environ. Sci. Technol.* 12 (August 1978):900.

MacIntyre, F. "Why the Sea Is Salt." *Sci. Am.* 223 (November 1970):104.

Herring, P. J., and Clarke, M. R., eds. *Deep Oceans.* New York: Praeger Publishers, Inc., 1971.

Mueller, J. A., Anderson, A. R., and Jeris, J. S. "Contaminants in the New York Bight." *J. Water Pollut. Control Fed.* 48 (1976):2309.

Dewling, R. T., and Anderson, P. W. "New York Bight I: Ocean Dumping Policies." *Oceanus* 19, no. 4 (1976):2.

Gross, M. G. "New York Bight II: Problems of Research." *Oceanus* 19, no. 4 (1976):12.

Olexsey, R. A. "After Ocean Disposal, What?" *Water Wastes Eng.* 13, no. 9 (1976):59.

Travers, W. B., and Tuney, P. R. "Drilling, Tankers, and Oil Spills on the Atlantic Outer Continental Shelf." *Science* 194 (1976):791.

Harwood, M. "Oil and Water: In the Wake of the Argo Merchant." *Harper's,* September 1978:43.

"Petroleum in the Environment." Washington, D.C.: National Academy of Sciences, 1975.

Wastewater Treatment

Keith, L. H., and Telliard, W. A. "Priority Pollutants—A Perspective View." *Environ. Sci. Technol.* 13 (April 1979):416.

Westman, W. E. "Problems in Implementing U.S. Water Quality Goals." *Am. Sci.* 65 (March–April 1977):197.

Argo, D. G., and Wesner, G. M. "Advanced Waste Treatment: Energy Needs a Prime Concern." *Water Wastes Eng.* 13, no. 5 (1976):24.

Hagan, R. M., and Roberts, E. B. "Energy Requirements for Waste-water Treatment." *Water Sewage Works* 123, no. 12 (1976):52.

Dean, R. B., and Forsythe, S. L. "Estimating the Reliability of Advanced Waste Treatment." *Water Sewage Works* 123, no. 6 (1976):87.

Mulligan, T. J., and Fox, R. D. "Treatment of Industrial Wastewaters." *Chem. Eng.* 83 (October 18, 1976):49.

Bush, K. E. "Refinery Wastewater Treatment and Reuse." *Chem. Eng.* 83 (April 12, 1976):113.

Behrman, B. W. "Nitrogen Removal Depends on Form Nutrient Takes." *Water Wastes Eng.* 13, no. 2 (1976):27.

Stover, E. L., and Kincannon, D. F. "One- Versus Two-Stage Nitrification in the Activated Sludge Process." *J. Water Pollut. Control Fed.* 48 (1976):645.

Hayes, D. G. "Waste Water Treatment Via Activated Carbon." *Chem. Eng. Prog.* 72, no. 10 (1976):57.

Suffet, I., McGuire, M., Josephson, J., and Ember, L. "Activated Carbon Cleanup: That Old Black Magic Works Again!" *Environ. Sci. Technol.* 12 (October 1978):1138.

Kim, B. R., Snoeyink, V. L., and Saunders, F. M. "Adsorption of Organic Compounds by Synthetic Resins." *J. Water Pollut. Control Fed.* 48 (1976):120.

Fisher, S. A., and McGarvey, F. X. "Ion Exchange for Water Recycle." *Ind. Water Eng.* 13, no. 2 (1976):14.

Sammon, D. C., and Stringer, B. "Application of Membrane Processes in the Treatment of Sewage." *Process. Biochem.* 10 (March 1975):4.

Leitz, F. B. "Electrodialysis for Industrial Water Cleanup." *Environ. Sci. Technol.* 10 (1976):136.

Westbrook, G. T., and Wirth, L. F. "Water Reuse—By Electrodialysis." *Ind. Water Eng.* 13, no. 2 (1976):8.

Stover, R. C., Sommers, L. E., and Silviera, D. J. "Evaluation of Metals in Wastewater Sludge." *J. Water Pollut. Control Fed.* 48 (1976):2165.

"Application of Sewage Sludge to Cropland: Appraisal of Potential Hazards of the Heavy Metals to Plants and Animals." Council for Agricultural Science and Technology (CAST), Report No. 54. Ames, Iowa, 1976.

Hyde, H. C. "Utilization of Wastewater Sludge for Agricultural Soil Enrichment." *J. Water Pollut. Control Fed.* 48 (1976):77.

Varanka, M. W., Zablocki, Z. M., and Hinesly, T. D. "The Effect of Digested Sludge on Soil Biological Activity." *J. Water Pollut. Control Fed.* 48 (1976):1728.

Crites, R. W., and Pound, C. E. "Land Treatment of Municipal Wastewater." *Environ. Sci. Technol.* 10 (1976):548.

Harvey, W. B. "Spray Irrigation Solves Disposal Problem." *Water Wastes Eng.* 13, no. 10 (1976):31.

Woodwell, G. W. "Recycling Sewage through Plant Communities." *Am. Sci.* 65 (September–October 1977):556.

Rehlberger, G. W. "Chlorination: The Current Dilemma." *Water Sewage Works* 122, no. 11 (1975):62.

Hoehn, R. C. "Comparative Disinfection Methods." *J. Am. Water Works Assoc.* 68 (1976):302.

Furr, A. K., et al. "Multielement and Chlorinated Hydrocarbon Analysis of Municipal Sewage Sludges of American Cities." *Environ. Sci. Technol.* 10 (1976):683.

Drinking Water, Conservation, and Water Resources

Agino, E., Wixson, B., and Smith, I. "Drinking Water Quality and Chronic Disease." *Environ. Sci. Technol.* 11 (July 1977):660.

Shoji, K. "Drip Irrigation." *Sci. Am.* 237 (November 1977):62.

Ambroggi, R. P. "Underground Reservoirs to Control the Water Cycle." *Sci. Am.* 236 (May 1977):21.

Eckholm, E., and Brown, L. "Spreading Deserts—The Hand of Man." *Bull. Atom. Sci.* 34 (January 1978):10.

PART IV | BIOSPHERE

1 | Nitrogen and Food Production

The final part of this book concerns the biosphere—the realm of living organisms and their interactions. We have already touched on several aspects of the biological world in connection with energy flows and air and water chemistry, but we now focus more directly on biological processes, particularly as they affect human welfare.

The first topic we will consider is food production and the important role of the nitrogen cycle. The main process in the production of biological energy is the carbon cycle. However, as we saw in the preceding section, organisms need more carbon dioxide and water as nutrients. They also require nitrogen, phosphorus, and several other elements in smaller amounts. Most of these elements are available in the soil in sufficient quantities to support plant growth, although some of them may need to be supplemented for intensive agriculture. The main limitation to plant productivity is the supply of nitrogen. While 80% of the atmosphere consists of molecular nitrogen, it is in an extremely stable and unreactive form, as observed in our discussion of atmospheric chemistry. In order to participate in biological reactions, nitrogen must be fixed; that is, it must be combined with other elements.

The upper part of Figure 4.1 contains a schematic diagram of the nitrogen cycle. We have already seen that at sufficiently high temperatures, such as in combustion or during lightning, nitrogen and oxygen can combine to form nitrogen oxides. These eventually are converted to nitric acid, which is washed out by rain. Nitric acid is a strong acid and readily dissociates in water to hydrogen ion and nitrate ion.

Plants, but not animals, can utilize nitrate in the production of protein as well as other essential organic nitrogen compounds. But the pathway through nitrogen oxides and nitrate is insufficient to support the abundant plant life we know. Most nitrogen fixation goes via the pathway shown on the left-hand side of the figure, in which certain bacteria and algae combine molecular nitrogen with hydrogen to produce ammonia, NH_3, or its acid form, ammonium ion, NH_4^+. This unique class of organisms possesses a specialized biochemical apparatus

The Nitrogen Cycle

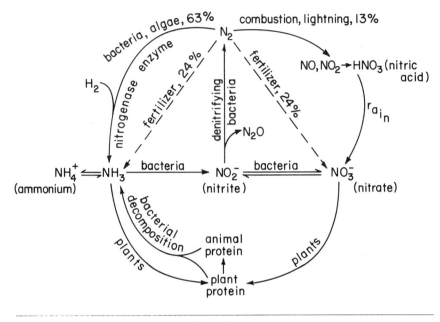

Fertilizer Production

1. $3H_2 + N_2 \xrightarrow[\text{high}\begin{cases}\text{temperature}\\\text{pressure}\end{cases}]{\text{Fe}} 2NH_3$ (Haber process)

2. $NH_3 + 2O_2 \xrightarrow[\text{high temperature}]{\text{catalyst}} HNO_3 + H_2O$

3. $NH_3 + HNO_3 \longrightarrow NH_4NO_3$ (fertilizer)

4. $2CH_4 + \text{air} + H_2O \longrightarrow 5H_2 + 2N_2 + 2CO$ (hydrogen production)
   Methane

Figure 4.1

called the *nitrogenase enzyme system,* which can form ammonia rapidly at ambient temperatures. Plants can use ammonia directly for their nitrogen source. When plants and animals die, their protein is decomposed by another type of bacteria to produce ammonia again.

In the middle of the diagram we find nitrite ion, NO_2^-, which represents an oxidation level of nitrogen intermediate between ammonia and nitrate. Some kinds of bacteria oxidize ammonia to nitrite and then nitrite to nitrate. Still other bacteria, called *denitrifying bacteria,* can convert nitrite back to molecular nitrogen, thus completing the nitrogen cycle. A by-product of this denitrification reaction, accounting for an estimated 5–10% of the total, is nitrous oxide, N_2O. As we saw in our consideration of the ozone layer, this gas is important in the ozone balance. It is inert in the lower atmosphere but can be converted to nitric oxide in the stratosphere, thereby accelerating the destruction of ozone. There is some concern currently that the rate of production of nitrous oxide might be increasing as a result of the use of artificial fertilizers, but we do not yet know enough about the quantitative aspects of the denitrification reaction to tell whether this is a serious problem.

The main natural sources of nitrogen for agriculture are the nitrogenase-containing bacteria, which grow in symbiosis with a limited variety of food plants, most notably those of the legume family. The nodules of legumes, such as beans, peas, alfalfa, and clover, contain these bacteria. When the plants die, nitrogen is returned to the soil in fixed form, where it is available for other kinds of plants, except for the fraction that is returned to the atmosphere via the denitrification reaction. For this reason, crop rotation, in which legumes are planted alternately with cereals, grains, and other vegetables, is an ancient agricultural practice designed to maintain the productivity of the nonlegume plants. In the absence of crop rotation, plants that do not fix nitrogen quickly deplete the soil of its nitrogen stores, unless they are replaced by the addition of fertilizer. Animal manure can be used for this purpose, but in recent years it has been increasingly supplanted by artificial fertilizers produced industrially.

This industrial supplementation of nature's nitrogen fixation is indicated by the dashed lines in the first part of Figure 4.1. The commercial production of fertilizer is shown by the four reactions in the lower part of Figure 4.1. The first step is the Haber process, in which nitrogen is combined directly with molecular hydrogen to form ammonia. This reaction releases energy and therefore should occur spontaneously, but because of the very strong bond that connects the two nitrogen atoms, the reaction is extremely slow except at very high temperatures, unless a catalyst is used to lower the activation energy. In the Haber process, iron is used as a catalyst, and the reaction runs efficiently at 500° C and 100 atm pressure. As shown in reactions 2 and 3, the ammonia is then partially oxidized to ammonium nitrate, which is the main form of nitrogen in commercial fertilizer. As we have seen, plants use both ammonia and nitrate. The Haber process requires hydrogen gas. Currently, the most economic process for obtaining hydrogen is the partial oxidation of methane, shown in reaction 4 of Figure 4.1.

Table 4.1 summarizes present estimates of worldwide nitrogen fixation through the natural pathways and by industrial production. Industry now accounts for about one-quarter of the total production of fixed nitrogen, and its contribution is increasing rapidly.

The application of fertilizer can dramatically improve agricultural yields. The graphs in Figure 4.2 demonstrate the correlation between increased fertilizer use and increased crop yields in the Iowa cornbelt over the past few decades. The

Table 4.1   Estimates of Total Nitrogen Fixation for 1974

	Nitrogen Fixed	
Mechanism of Fixation	MT/year	Percent of Total
Bacteria and algae	150	63.3%
Lightning	10	4.2
Combustion	20	8.4
Industrial ammonia production	57	24.1
Total	237	100.0%

Source: "Effect of Increased Nitrogen Fixation on Stratospheric Ozone," Council for Agricultural Science and Technology, Report No. 53, January 19, 1976, p. 13.

tripling of yields for corn and certain other grains between 1940 and 1975 has made the U.S. and Canadian Midwest the breadbasket of much of the world.

When sufficient fertilizer has been added to support plant growth at its maximum rate, then further additions either have no effect or actually inhibit growth. The curve of diminishing returns for corn is shown in Figure 4.3. The dashed curve shows that the total yield of corn begins to decrease after about 200 pounds of nitrogen per acre is added. The solid curve is the ratio of the energy contained in the corn produced per unit of energy required to grow it in the United States. This curve peaks between 100 and 120 pounds of nitrogen per acre.

Fertilizer is the highest energy consumer in U.S. corn production, accounting for nearly one-third of the total energy used. The main reason for the high energy cost is that, as we saw in reaction 4 of Figure 4.1, methane gas must be utilized to produce hydrogen. The Haber process is quite efficient, but the hydrogen required to reduce nitrogen is high-quality stored energy. The cost of ammonia production is therefore tied directly to the price of natural gas, which has been escalating steeply since the fuel crunch of 1973. Hydrogen can also be produced from coal, or by any of the other energy sources discussed in the first part of this book. The cost of any of these alternative sources is higher than that of natural gas, even at today's prices, but that situation may change in the future. The low price of fossil fuels until 1973 was a major factor in the rapid increase in fertilizer use during the preceding 30 years.

The vertical lines in Figure 4.3 show the rates of current fertilizer application for U.S. cornfields. This range corresponds to a region of the productivity curve where the total yield is still increasing but the energy output/input ratio has leveled off. No doubt increasing prices will provide an incentive to conserve fertilizer and in some measure to reintroduce traditional agricultural practices such as crop rotation and the use of animal manure. This economic incentive reinforces recent interest in organic farming, whose proponents claim that the use

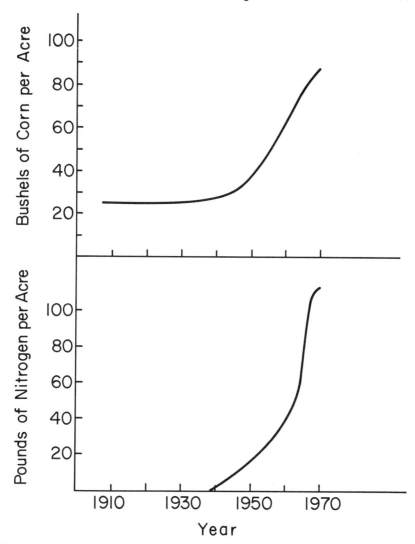

Figure 4.2 Effect of Fertilizer Use on Corn Yields in the United States

Source: Adapted from D. Pimentel, L. E. Hurd, A. C. Bellotti, M. J. Forster, I. N. Oka, O. D. Sholes, and R. J. Whitman, *Science* 182 (1973):445.

of natural fertilizers, as opposed to ammonium nitrate, helps to build up the humus of the soil and maintain it in a more productive state.

Increased fertilizer prices are more critical for poor countries, which are trying hard to expand their agricultural production to meet the hunger of their growing and ill-fed populations. Considerable progress in this very difficult task was

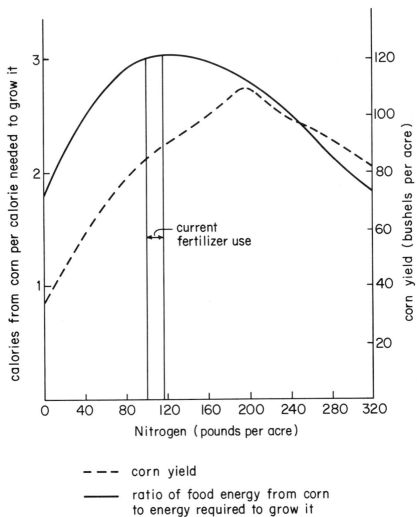

Figure 4.3 Corn Yield and Energy Return Versus Fertilizer Use

Source: D. Pimentel, et al., *Science* 182 (1973):445.

achieved in the 1960s through what has become known as the Green Revolution. This involved the development by plant scientists, working in research institutes in Mexico and the Philippines, of new strains of wheat and rice that produce high yields when fertilized. As shown in Figure 4.4, traditional varieties of grain indigenous to tropical and subtropical countries do not respond well to fertilizer. They grow too tall and fall over in winds and heavy rain. The new strains are

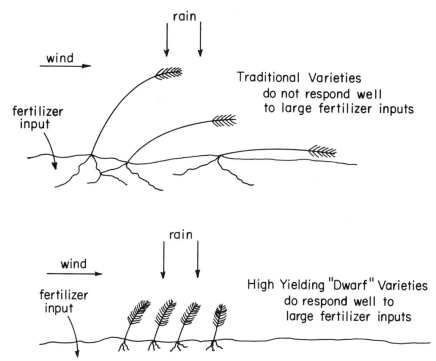

Figure 4.4 The Green Revolution: High-Yielding Variety Grains for Use in the Developing World

dwarf plants, with stalks that remain short while the grain matures. A larger number of plants can be sown per unit area for the dwarf varieties than for the less compact traditional varieties, which have large leaves and extended root networks to absorb the small amounts of nutrients and water often found in tropical soil.

During the six years between 1965 and 1972, the developing countries increased their food production by 23%, as more than 70 million acres in Asia and North Africa were planted with high-yielding varieties of grain. The years 1972 and 1974 produced a severe setback to the Green Revolution, however, with significant production declines and widespread famine. The main causes were bad weather and the petroleum crisis. Not only was industrial fertilizer too expensive for third-world farmers, but so was the fuel for operating irrigation pumps. Many farmers elected to return to the traditional plant varieties, which are hardier and more resistant to drought than the high-yielding varieties.

This experience produced much discouragement about the concept of the Green Revolution, but the real problem appears to be overreliance of the world

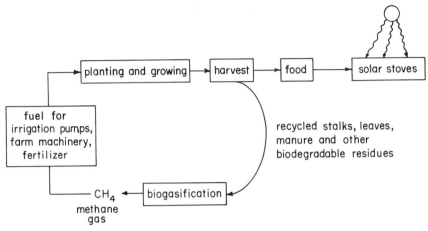

Figure 4.5 Appropriate Technology for Achieving Energy Self-Sufficiency in Agriculture in the Developing World

agricultural system on petroleum and natural gas deposits. For poor countries in particular, the development of alternative, domestically available energy sources is a critical need. One plan for achieving energy self-sufficiency in agriculture is shown in Figure 4.5. A number of sources that seem relatively insignificant in the context of the U.S. energy supply could make an important contribution in developing countries. A good example is biogasification, the process shown earlier in Figure 1.28, by which farm wastes, nonwoody plants, and sewage can be converted to methane in simple microbial digesters. Even in the United States, it has been estimated that enough energy is available from this resource, at a conversion efficiency of 40%, to supply all farm energy needs, including fuel, electricity, fertilizer production, and irrigation. Since agriculture is much less energy-intensive in most developing countries, a much lower conversion efficiency would still allow the fulfillment of energy needs. Community-sized biogasification plants could produce methane for making fertilizer, driving irrigation pumps, and running simple farm machinery. Engines that now operate on liquid fuels could readily be adapted to run on gaseous fuel.

Direct solar energy could also be an important resource for poor countries in tropical areas that have abundant sunshine. The widespread adoption of solar stoves for cooking would be particularly desirable. At present, wood and cow dung are used as cooking fuels in most rural areas of poor countries. These fuels are inefficient and in short supply, however. Cooking with them expends as much energy as is required to grow the food being cooked. Cow dung would be better utilized as fertilizer or in the production of methane gas, and the use of wood for fuel has produced serious deforestation in many tropical areas, with attendant erosion and loss of arable land. Solar stoves have been developed that are surprisingly effective. One model with a parabolic collector is capable of cooking a kilogram of rice in 15 minutes, a rate comparable to that of a small coal stove.

Much current agricultural research is aimed at improving the rates of natural nitrogen fixation as well as photosynthesis. One avenue of investigation involves experiments in plant breeding designed to produce symbiotic association between nitrogen-fixing bacteria and cereal plants such as wheat and rice. If this work is successful, it opens the door to freeing the production of important cereal crops from the current dependence on nitrogen supplementation.

2 | Nutrition

Having looked at the essential energy and nitrogen requirements for plant growth, let us turn our attention to the biochemical pathways whereby the food we eat keeps us functioning. This is the chemistry of biological metabolism.

The major nutritional categories are carbohydrates, fats, and protein. As shown in the upper part of Figure 4.6, carbohydrates are sugar molecules linked together in a long chain. Fats are triglycerides of fatty acids, which have long hydrocarbon chains, designated by R in the figure, bonded to a glycerol unit. Proteins are composed of amino acids strung together like beads and joined by peptide bonds. Each amino acid contains a characteristic side chain, designated by R in the figure.

The lower part of Figure 4.6 gives a simplified flow chart for the main biochemical processes. We have already seen that carbohydrates are the immediate product of photosynthesis and also the immediate source of biological energy in the process of respiration. Most of the energy that we need to keep our various bodily functions going is obtained from the oxidation of carbohydrates.

Fats represent a form of biological energy storage. In comparison with carbohydrates, fats contain less oxygen and more carbon and hydrogen, whose oxidation is the source of our energy. The energy content of fats is 9 calories/g, compared with 4 calories/g for carbohydrates. Also, fats are immiscible with water, whereas carbohydrates are hydrophilic. Carbohydrates are usually found in association with a quantity of water that is approximately four times their weight. Consequently, the conversion of carbohydrates to fats represents a concentration of energy in lightweight portable form. A person who weighs 70 kg, which is about 154 pounds, contains about 16% fat. This represents enough energy for bodily requirements for 30 days. If this amount of excess energy were stored as carbohydrate with its associated water, the body weight would have to be 160 kg, or 350 pounds. When we eat more food than we require for our energy needs, the excess calories are stored as fat. The biological oxidation of fat is slower than that of carbohydrates. When we need energy, we burn off our carbohydrate supply first and then call upon the fat stores.

Aside from an energy supply, we need to maintain the biochemical machinery of the body itself. This is the realm of protein chemistry. Proteins make up most

(i)
Chemical Structures

<u>Carbohydrates</u> are sugar polymers

e.g.

<u>Fats</u> are triglycerides of fatty acids

e.g.

$R-\overset{\overset{O}{\|}}{C}-$, etc. are fatty acids
R is a hydrocarbon chain

glycerol unit

<u>Proteins</u> are polypeptides

e.g.

peptide link between two amino acids

R is an amino acid side chain.

one amino acid unit   second amino acid unit

(ii)
Biochemical Functions

plant photosynthesis

fixed N_2

Carbohydrates ⟶ energy for body function

Fats ⟶ energy storage

Proteins ⟶ tissue building, enzymes

CO_2

(starvation)

Figure 4.6 Major Nutritional Categories

General formula

Amino Acid*	R (side chain)
1. Glycine	—H
2. Alanine	—CH_3
3. Serine	—CH_2OH
4. Aspartic acid	—CH_2COOH
5. Glutamic acid	—CH_2CH_2COOH
6. Asparagine	—CH_2CONH_2
7. Glutamine	—$CH_2CH_2CONH_2$
8. Arginine	—$CH_2CH_2CH_2NHC(NH)NH_2$
9. Cysteine	—CH_2SH
10. Tyrosine	
11. Proline	
12. Histidine	

Essential Amino Acids	
13. Valine	—$CH(CH_3)_2$
14. Leucine	—$CH_2CH(CH_3)_2$
15. Isoleucine	—$CH(CH_3)CH_2CH_3$
16. Threonine	—$CH(OH)CH_3$
17. Lysine	—$CH_2CH_2CH_2CH_2NH_2$
18. Methionine	—CH_2CH_2-S-CH_3
19. Phenylalanine	
20. Tryptophan	

Figure 4.7 The 20 Common Amino Acids—The Building Blocks of Protein

*1–12 can be synthesized by the human body if sufficient protein nitrogen is present in the diet. 13–20 cannot be synthesized and must be obtained directly from food.

of the body's structural tissues and also the myriad enzymes, the biological catalysts that carry out the thousands of reactions that are necessary for the maintenance of life. There are 20 different kinds of amino acids, each with a different chemical side chain. Their chemical structures are given in Figure 4.7. Each kind of protein molecule is made up of a fixed sequence of these

Table 4.2 Essential Amino Acid Content in Common Foods

Essential Amino Acid	Average Frequency of Occurrence in Human Protein (out of 100 amino acids)	Out of 100 Amino Acids Number Present in:			
		Cow's Milk	Meat	Beans	Wheat
Tryptophan	0.6	0.5	0.5	0.4	0.6
Phenylalanine	3.1	3.8	2.7	2.8	2.8
Lysine	2.6	3.3	3.4	2.8	1.1
Threonine	2.0	2.0	2.0	1.6	1.3
Methionine	3.5	2.8	3.3	2.2	3.2
Leucine	4.0	4.2	3.3	3.1	3.1
Isoleucine	2.5	2.8	2.3	2.2	1.6
Valine	3.2	3.6	2.7	2.5	2.0

Source: Extracted from data in F. E. Deathrage, *Food for Life* (New York: Plenum Press, 1975), pp. 74, 84; and President's Science Advisory Committee, *The World Food Problem*, Report of the Panel on World Food Supply, Vol. II (Washington, D.C.: 1967), p. 315.

amino acids. Most of the amino acids can be synthesized by the body from a variety of starting materials as long as there is an adequate supply of protein nitrogen in the diet. There are, however, eight amino acids, shown in the box in Figure 4.7, that the body cannot synthesize. They are valine, leucine, isoleucine, threonine, lysine, methionine, phenylalanine and tryptophan. These essential amino acids must be obtained directly from the diet. They occur with different frequencies in different proteins. Table 4.2 shows these frequencies for the average of all protein matter in the body. For example, tryptophan represents 0.6 out of every 100 amino acids, while lysine represents 2.6 out of every 100. We need to maintain a proper balance of the essential amino acids in our diet. The ratio of tryptophan to lysine needs to be 0.6 to 2.6. If this ratio is exceeded, the amount of protein that can be made by the body is limited by the lysine, and the extra tryptophan is simply burned up. The notion of essential amino acid balance is similar to the concept of limiting nutrients that we discussed in connection with the growth of algae in water. Whichever amino acid is present in the lowest amount relative to the frequency with which it is used is the one that limits the total amount of protein produced.

Different food sources contain different amounts of protein; but also the amino acid composition of their protein is variable. As you might expect, animal protein is fairly close to human protein in its amino acid composition. For this reason, milk, eggs, and meat provide us with a rather close approximation to the amino acid balance we need. This is demonstrated in Table 4.2, where we see that the amino acid frequencies for cow's milk and meat are fairly close to the human average. Plant protein, on the other hand, is farther from the human composition, as the table also shows. The cereal plants, particularly wheat, are quite deficient in lysine. The lysine frequency in wheat is less than half that of the human

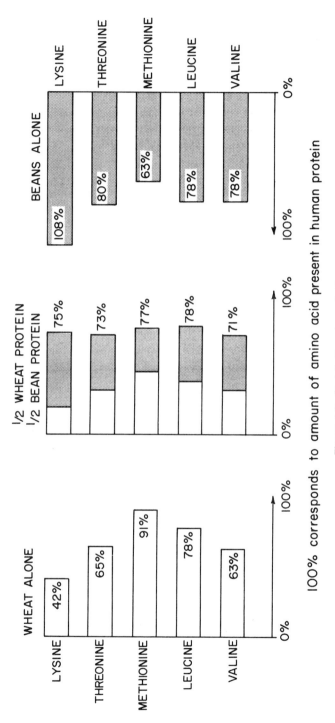

Figure 4.8 Protein Complementarity

100% corresponds to amount of amino acid present in human protein

WHEAT ALONE

LYSINE	42%
THREONINE	65%
METHIONINE	91%
LEUCINE	78%
VALINE	63%

1/2 WHEAT PROTEIN
1/2 BEAN PROTEIN

	75%
	73%
	77%
	78%
	71%

BEANS ALONE

LYSINE	108%
THREONINE	80%
METHIONINE	63%
LEUCINE	78%
VALINE	78%

average. It would take more than twice as much wheat protein as milk protein to supply human needs. Even though the remaining amino acids are closer to the correct proportions, they cannot be utilized without sufficient lysine. For this reason, wheat protein is often referred to as low-quality protein in comparison with the high-quality protein contained in meat, eggs, and milk.

We can also see from Table 4.2 that different plants show different patterns of deviation from the ideal amino acid balance. Thus, whereas wheat is deficient in lysine, beans have lysine in abundance. However, beans are deficient in methionine, which wheat has in abundance. In this respect, wheat and beans are complementary. As shown in Figure 4.8, if we mix the two together, the amino acid balance is greatly improved. It takes less total vegetable protein for the mixture than for either one alone to provide the human requirements. A diet of half wheat protein and half bean protein provides a protein mixture that is only 10% less efficient than milk protein in providing the right balance. It is no accident that beans and rice or wheat products are traditionally eaten together in many parts of the world. In order to be effective complements, the different proteins must be mixed in the same meal, so that they are digested together. Thus, vegetarians must pay close attention to balancing different protein sources.

Although meat is an important component in the diets of relatively prosperous nations, most people in the world cannot afford to eat meat, and it is possible to do without meat altogether and still remain healthy. While it is a high-quality source of protein, meat represents a considerable waste of biological energy, since animals typically store only 10% of the food they consume in the form of meat. It takes 10 g of plant protein to produce 1 g of meat protein. Most countries do not have enough plant protein to spare for meat production on a large scale. If there is sufficient grass to support grazing animals, they can make a net contribution to the human food supply. In recent years in meat producing countries, however, it has become increasingly common to feed animals high-quality plant food, cereals and soybeans, for example, in order to fatten them more quickly.

3 | Insecticides

Another limitation on the human food supply is that we must share plant foods with insects. It has been estimated that the weight of the world's insect population exceeds that of its human inhabitants by a factor of 12. Only a small fraction of the insect species, about 500 species out of the world total of 5 million, actually feed on human crops, but these have the potential of doing enormous damage. Moreover, there are other insect species, such as the mosquito, flea, and tsetse fly, that are carriers of devastating human diseases. Insect invasions, sometimes on a massive scale, have been a recurrent part of human history.

Attempts to combat insect pests were relatively ineffective until the development of modern chemical pesticides. The first of these was DDT, whose chemical structure is shown in Figure 4.9. Introduced as a pesticide for the first time during World War II, DDT saved millions of lives through malaria control programs. It won for its discoverer, the Swiss chemist Paul Müller, the Nobel Peace Prize in 1948. After the war, DDT was the first pesticide to come into widespread agricultural use.

The reason for DDT's effectiveness as a pesticide is still not completely understood. Being oil soluble, it is readily absorbed by the waxy outer coating of insects. Once inside, the chemical quickly paralyzes the insect. Evidently it acts on the nervous system, and it is thought to block specific channels for the flow of the sodium and potassium ions that carry the nerve impulses. The shape of the molecule is quite important. Some chemical changes can be made, as shown for

Figure 4.9   DDT and Analogs

the DDT analogs in Figure 4.9, all of which are effective insecticides. But other chemical substitutions, the replacement of the chlorine atoms at the ends of the molecule by hydrogen, for example, greatly decrease the insecticide activity.

Despite its useful service to humanity, DDT was banned for most applications in the United States because of concern about its long-term health effects. It is not that DDT is known to be directly toxic; substantial quantities of DDT have been consumed by individuals accidentally or in voluntary tests without any observable symptoms. Apparently DDT does not act directly on the human nervous system in the way that it does on insects. The concern is about the possibility of long-term effects that are much more difficult to determine. DDT is a persistent chemical; that is, it breaks down very slowly in the environment. Consequently, the DDT already produced and discharged will circulate in the environment for many years.

Because DDT is oil soluble, it accumulates in fat tissues; moreover, DDT builds up in the food chain. As one animal eats another, it stores the accumulated DDT in its own body fats. This is shown for an aquatic food chain in Figure 4.10. The numbers given for the different organisms are the concentrations of DDT in parts per million in the tissues. Plankton contain 0.04 ppm, but the clams that feed on plankton have ten times as much, while the fish that feed on the clams can have up to 2 ppm and the birds that feed on the fish are found to have up to 75 ppm in their muscles. Similar concentrations occur in the terrestrial food chains that provide us with our meats and milk. As a result, all of us have DDT stored in our bodies. The levels vary from country to country depending on the use of DDT. Residents of the United States and most of Western Europe had about 7 ppm stored in their fat tissues in 1975, whereas residents of India, for example, had levels several times higher.

We do not know whether DDT has adverse effects over the long term. There is at least a possibility that DDT might upset hormone balances. This is because DDT, along with other fat-soluble substances, can induce the body to produce enzymes that convert these substances to water-soluble chemical forms so that they are more readily eliminated. These same enzymes are involved in the transformation of hormones from active to inactive forms, and vice versa. It is known that many species of hunting birds are threatened with extinction because the eggs they lay have shells that are too thin and fragile, probably because of interference with the hormones that control calcium deposition. These birds have high levels of DDT, as we saw in Figure 4.10, and there is strong evidence linking DDT with eggshell fragility, although other pollutants may also be involved. The potential long-term effects of a chemical stored in body fat were enough to persuade the U.S. Environmental Protection Agency that most uses of DDT should be banned. The situation is different elsewhere in the world. Particularly where malaria is still endemic, it would be unreasonable to expect DDT to be banned, since no adequate substitute for mosquito control has been developed.

Although DDT was banned in the United States in 1973, its use had been declining since 1959. The reason for this has nothing to do with its potential health hazards, but rather with the fact that DDT has become much less effective than it originally was. The chemical itself has remained the same but the insects have changed by evolving a resistance to the insecticide. Because individual insects that are relatively resistant to DDT are more likely to survive than those that are susceptible, the new generations that are born have a steadily higher incidence of resistant characteristics. The resistance factor for DDT is an enzyme called *DDTase,* which carries out the chemical transformation shown in Figure 4.11. The product, DDE, has lost a hydrogen atom and a chlorine atom and has a new double bond in the middle. This molecule is no longer toxic to the insect. It is, however, as persistent as DDT in the environment and also builds up in fat tissue. The levels of DDT recorded usually include the contribution of DDE.

Although the level of DDT used has been declining since 1959, the total amount of chemical insecticides in use has been increasing. The DDT has been replaced by other chemicals that have been developed. Figure 4.12 shows some other organochlorine chemicals that are effective pesticides. These share with DDT the characteristic of environmental persistence and they also build up in fat tissues. Moreover, some of them are distinctly more toxic than DDT and cause at least as much concern about health effects. In 1974, the U.S. Environmental Protection Agency stringently regulated the application of aldrin and dieldrin, which had come into widespread use.

Meanwhile, some nonpersistent classes of insecticides have been developed; they degrade quite rapidly in the environment. Figure 4.13 shows representatives of the two major classes, organophosphates and carbamates. The organophosphates all have a phosphorus atom, connected by a double bond to either sulfur or oxygen, and by single bonds to oxygen or sulfur atoms with attached organic groups. Carbamates have a chemical structure in which a carbon atom is connected by a double bond to an oxygen atom and by single bonds to oxygen on one

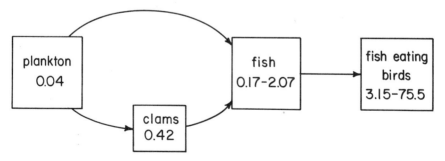

Figure 4.10   Accumulation of DDT in Aquatic Food Chain (ppm)

Source: C. A. Edwards, *Persistent Pesticides in the Environment,* 2nd ed. (Cleveland: CRC Press, 1973), p. 80.

Figure 4.11   Insect Resistance to DDT

side and nitrogen on the other, each with attached organic groups. As shown in Figure 4.14, both organophosphates and carbamates react with oxygen and water to decompose within a few days in the environment. The products are not toxic; they are phosphates and alcohols in the case of the organophosphates, and carbon dioxide, alcohols, and amines in the case of the carbamates. The mechanism of action of these insecticides is that they inhibit a vital enzyme, acetylcholinesterase, as shown in Figure 4.15. Acetylcholine is a neurotransmitter; it serves as the signal for a nerve cell to fire. The space between nerve cells, called a *synapse,* contains both acetylcholine and the enzyme, acetylcholinesterase, which breaks acetylcholine down and stops the nerve cell from firing. As shown in reactions (1a) and (1b) of Figure 4.15, this occurs in two chemical steps. In the first, the enzyme attacks the acetylcholine, forming an intermediate molecule, the acetyl enzyme, and one of the products, choline. In the next step, a water molecule splits off the acetyl group to form acetic acid and regenerate the enzyme. An organic phosphate can mimic acetylcholine and induce the formation of a phosphoryl enzyme, as shown in reaction (2a). The rate of the reaction depends on the ease with which the group X is displaced from the phosphorus atom by the enzyme. The subsequent breakdown of this intermediate, shown in reaction (2b), is much slower than that of the acetyl enzyme shown in reaction (1b). Consequently, the amount of phosphoryl enzyme builds up and the level of active enzyme drops. The acetylcholine is no longer broken down rapidly enough, and the nerve continues to fire uncontrollably. This leads to the rapid death of the organism. Reactions (3a) and (3b) show that the carbamates act in a very similar fashion.

The potency of the organophosphates or carbamates in inhibiting acetylcholinesterase depends on the nature of the chemical substituents in the phosphate or carbamate group. Toxicity can be varied over wide limits by chemical substitutions. At one extreme are the deadly nerve gases, developed during World War II, which are organophosphates with fluorine attached to phosphorus.

Aldrin

Dieldrin

Endrin

Heptachlor

Mirex

Kepone

Figure 4.12   Other Effective Organochlorine Pesticides

Fluorine is an easily displaceable leaving group X in reaction (2a). At the other extreme is malathion shown, in Figure 4.13, a relatively mild insecticide that is safe for home use. The more powerful organophosphates and carbamates are quite toxic, and there have been many fatalities as well as less severe episodes of poisoning since their introduction into agricultural use. The organophosphate and carbamate insecticides, therefore, alleviate one problem, namely, the buildup associated with the organochlorine chemicals, but at the expense of accidental deaths associated with acute poisoning.

Increasingly, the main problem associated with all the general classes of chemical insecticides is that they become decreasingly effective as insect resis-

(i)

Organophosphates

$$RO - \overset{\displaystyle S}{\underset{\displaystyle OR}{\overset{\displaystyle \|}{P}}} - X$$

general formula

X represents an SR′ or an OR′ group
R , R′ are organic groups
P=S is rapidly oxidized to P=O

examples:

$$CH_3CH_2O - \overset{S}{\underset{O}{\overset{\|}{P}}} - O - \langle\ \rangle - NO_2$$
$$\underset{CH_3}{\overset{|}{CH_2}}$$

parathion

$$CH_3O - \overset{S}{\underset{O}{\overset{\|}{P}}} - SCHC\overset{O}{\underset{}{\nearrow}} - OC_2H_5$$
$$\underset{CH_3}{\overset{|}{O}}\quad CH_2C - OC_2H_5$$
$$\underset{O}{\overset{}{\|}}$$

malathion

(ii)

Carbamates

$$RO - \overset{\displaystyle O}{\overset{\displaystyle \|}{C}}NHR′$$

general formula

example :

$$O\overset{O}{\overset{\|}{C}}NHCH_3$$

carbaryl

Figure 4.13 Insecticides That Do Not Persist in the Environment

(i)

Organophosphates

$$RO\!-\!\overset{\overset{\displaystyle S}{\|}}{\underset{\underset{\displaystyle OR}{|}}{P}}\!-\!X \;+\; \text{reaction with } O_2 \text{ and } H_2O \;\longrightarrow\; \underset{\text{phosphates}}{PO_4^{3-}} \;+\; \underset{\text{alcohols}}{ROH}$$

(ii)

Carbamates

$$RO\!-\!\overset{\overset{\displaystyle O}{\|}}{C}\!-\!\overset{\overset{\displaystyle R'}{}}{\underset{\underset{\displaystyle H}{}}{N}} \;+\; \text{reaction with } H_2O \text{ and decomposition} \;\longrightarrow\; CO_2 + \underset{\text{amines}}{NH_2R'} + \underset{\text{alcohols}}{ROH}$$

Figure 4.14 Decomposition of Nonpersistent Insecticides in the Environment

187

Normal mode of action

Inhibition by organophosphate insecticide

Inhibition by carbamate insecticide

Figure 4.15 Acetylcholinesterase Inhibition

tance builds up. Not only DDT but any chemical insecticide provides pressure for the selection of insects that have natural defenses, usually enzymes that quickly detoxify the chemicals. Not only do the chemicals become progressively less effective, but they also sometimes remain more effective against the natural enemies of the target pest, thereby actually making the problem worse than it was at the beginning. This is because the predator species are usually slower to reproduce than the prey, and so it takes longer for resistance to develop among them. A fairly common pattern is that the introduction of a new pesticide causes

(i)

Juvenile hormones : natural insect growth regulators
Ex.

$$CH_3 - \underset{\underset{CH_3}{|}}{\overset{\overset{R}{|}}{C}} - CH_2-CH_2-CH_2- \underset{\underset{CH_3}{|}}{CH} -CH_2-CH=CH -\underset{\underset{CH_3}{|}}{C}=CH-C\overset{O}{\underset{R'}{\diagdown}}$$

general formula

specific formula   controls stages of growth in:

$R = H$, $R' = OCH_2CH_3$ potato aphid, cockroach, grain-eating
                                    beetles

$R = H$, $R' = OCH_2C \equiv CH$ green peach aphid, pea aphid,
                                    citrus mealybug

$R = OCH_3$, $R' = OCH(CH_3)_2$ mosquito , apple maggot, mediterranean
                                    fruit fly

(ii)

Pheromones : natural insect sex attractants
Ex.

mixture of molecules emitted by male
boll weevil as sex attractant

Figure 4.16 Use of Juvenile Hormones and Pheromones in Insect Control
Source: Upper part: C. A. Henrick, W. E. Willy, and G. B. Staal, *J. Agric. Food Chem.* 24 (1976):207.
Lower part: R. D. Henson, D. L. Bull, R. I. Ridgway, and G. W. Ivie, *J. Agric. Food Chem.* 24 (1976):228.

an immediate decline in the population of the pest to be controlled, followed a few years later, however, by a population explosion of a strain of the same pest against which the insecticide is no longer effective.

For this reason, increasing attention has been given to the development of pest control methods that operate more selectively. Research on the biochemistry of insects has led to the discovery of hormones that control their growth and sexual behavior. If applied at the right time, these chemicals can disrupt the insect's life cycle. The upper part of Figure 4.16 shows the chemical structures of some juvenile hormones that regulate growth. If these are applied externally, the synchronization of metamorphosis is disrupted and the insects cannot develop.

Shown in the lower part is the set of chemicals that make up the sex attractant of the boll weevil. Sex attractants come under the general heading of *pheromones*—molecules that act as messengers between insects, guiding them to each other or to their food supply. Application of sex attractants can confuse the insects and prevent them from finding mates. It is also feasible to use pheromones to bait insect traps that contain high concentrations of toxic chemicals and are much more effective in killing the insects than is broad-scale spraying.

Another technique of insect control is to sterilize large numbers of male insects, which are bred for the purpose, using chemicals or radiation. When these sterile insects are released, they mate with the native population but no offspring are produced. The result is a substantial reduction in the total insect population. The Mediterranean fruit fly, for example, has been controlled in this fashion in California. It is also possible to artificially introduce predators to control the population of pests and insects. This solution is dangerous, however, since the predator can become so well adapted that it becomes a bigger pest than the target insect.

These new methods of controlling specific insect species are still under development. They require careful planning and timing and are much more sophisticated than simply spraying a field with chemical insecticide. Because they are effective against only one species at a time, however, they are costlier than applying the broad-spectrum insecticides. Nevertheless, with the increasing environmental costs and decreasing effectiveness of the traditional insecticides, pressure is mounting for their development and use.

4 | Inadvertent Contamination by Toxic Organic Chemicals

Although pesticides may be toxic, their danger to human health can be minimized by judicious application. More dangerous is the inadvertent release of toxic chemicals through accident or lack of foresight. Much publicity was generated, for example, by the discovery that the insecticide kepone had been contaminating Chesapeake Bay as a result of unsafe practices in a small manufacturing plant in Virginia. Kepone washings from the plant's wastewater had killed the bacteria in the digesters of the local municipal sewage system, and the contaminated sewage effluent had been discharged into the river that empties into

Chesapeake Bay. Fish and shellfish in the river and estuary were discovered to have kepone concentrations of about one part per million, exceeding allowable health limits, and commercial and sport fishing was prohibited in the affected areas. Worse effects were suffered by the workers in the plant, who inhaled exceedingly high levels of kepone, up to 3 g/m^3 in air, and experienced a variety of illnesses. These conditions led to the closing of the plant in July 1975, 16 months after it had begun operations.

Worrisome sources of chemical contamination are the dump sites for industrial wastes, many of them abandoned and buried close to developed communities. A notorious example is Love Canal in Niagara Falls, New York, which had been used to hold chemical and municipal wastes during the period 1930–53. In 1953 the site was covered with earth and sold to the City Board of Education, which built an elementary school there. Houses were constructed on the periphery of the site. Over the years the residents complained of bad odors and a variety of health problems. They were found to be subject to a significantly higher incidence of spontaneous abortions and congenital birth defects than would normally be expected. In 1978, state and federal officials, monitoring air samples in the basements of houses adjacent to the former dump site, identified 26 toxic organic compounds, some of which are listed along with the highest levels found in Table 4.3. The total concentration of organic compounds reached 12.9 mg/m^3 in the dining room of one of the homes. This value approaches the limits set for workers in the chemical industry, which vary from about ten to several hundred milligrams per cubic meter, depending on the compound, for a 40-hour workweek. As a result of these findings, the state of New York declared a health emergency in the area and relocated more than 300 families who were potentially affected.

The buildup of the organic chemicals can be traced to the characteristics of the dump site itself, diagrammed in Figure 4.17. The overlying soil is relatively porous, but the stratum under the wastes consists of silt and clay of low permeability, which acts as a barrier to penetration of the waste into deeper ground. When the soil is wet, volatile organics rise to the surface and infiltrate the basements of the surrounding homes.

No one knows how many similar trouble spots exist. The U.S. Environmental Protection Agency has identified 638 chemical dumps that may contain significant quantities of toxic materials, and there are literally thousands of other dump sites in the United States alone that have not yet been examined.

Perhaps the most dramatic recent incident of chemical contamination occurred in the Italian town of Seveso, where a chemical plant accidentally released about 2 kg of the toxic chemical TCDD in a cloud that settled in the surrounding area. Some 250 of the residents were affected by skin disorders of varying severity, and many of the animals in the area died. There was extensive damage to plants, primarily burning and browning of trees. About 1,000 persons were evacuated from two affected areas covering 123 acres.

Table 4.3 Concentrations of Some Toxic Organic Chemicals Found in Houses near Love Canal Dump Site

Chemical	Highest Concentration Observed ($\mu g/m^3$)*
Chloroform	24
Benzene	270
Trichloroethylene	73
Toluene	570
Perchloroethylene	1,140
Chlorobenzene	240
Chlorotoluene	6,700
Xylene (meta + para)	140
Xylene (ortho)	73
1,3,5-Trichlorobenzene	74
Total organics (one sample, dining room)	12,919 (12.9 mg/m³)

*Except as noted for total organics, concentrations were measured in the basements of homes.
Source: "In the Matter of the Love Canal Chemical Waste Landfill Site," Report of the Commissioner of Health of the State of New York, August, 1978; and *Chem. Eng. News.* August 7, 1978, p. 6.

TCDD stands for 2,3,7,8-tetrachlorodibenzo-p-dioxin, and its structure is highlighted in the center of Figure 4.18. As illustrated there, TCDD, a member of the dioxin family of molecules, is produced as a by-product from 2,4,5-trichlorophenol in the manufacture of the herbicide 2,4,5-trichlorophenoxyacetate (usually abbreviated 2,4,5-T) or of the germicide hexachlorophene. A similar chlorinated dioxin, which is also highlighted in the figure, is made as a by-product of pentachlorophenol, a widely used wood preservative.

TCDD is a flat molecule, which fits into a rectangle about 10 Å long and 3 Å wide, as illustrated in Figure 4.19. There are chlorine atoms at each of the four corners of the rectangle. These aspects of molecular structure seem to be the important ones associated with the toxicity of TCDD. If two or more of the chlorine atoms are removed or placed in other positions, or if the molecule is changed so that it is no longer flat, its toxicity decreases markedly. Other molecules with similar shape produce the same kind of toxicity. An example is tetrachlorodibenzofuran, which is also shown in Figure 4.19. It differs from dioxin only in having a direct bond between the two benzene rings replacing one of the dioxin oxygen atoms. Chlorinated dibenzofurans are by-products in the formation of polychlorinated biphenyls (PCBs); an example of a PCB is also shown in the figure. Chlorinated dibenzofurans can also be formed from PCBs on exposure to high temperatures, as in an incinerator. PCBs themselves share some of the toxicity of dibenzofurans and dioxins, since they have a similar molecular shape, as shown in the figure. PCBs have been used widely in a variety of

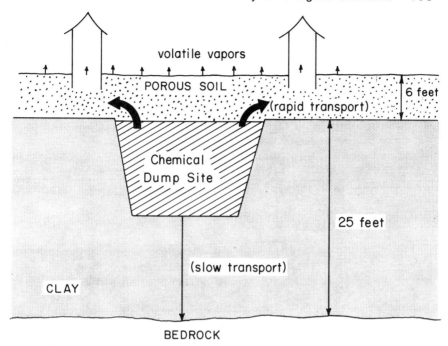

Figure 4.17   Transport of Toxic Organic Chemicals from Love Canal Dump Site into Surrounding Homes

manufacturing processes. Although their application is now restricted to insulating fluids in high-voltage transformers, large quantities have already been dispersed in the environment.

The biochemistry of these compounds is not fully understood at present and is a subject of active research. In laboratory animals, TCDD produces birth defects, cancer, skin disorders, liver damage, suppression of the immune system, and death from undefined causes. Toxic doses are quite low, although different animals vary widely in their sensitivity. Guinea pigs are the most susceptible species, with a dose of 1 μg/kg of body weight being sufficient to kill half the affected animals. Monkeys are 70 times less sensitive, and dogs are less sensitive still. The exact sensitivity of humans is not well defined. There have been a few deaths due to industrial accidents, but symptoms of TCDD exposure have mostly been limited to the skin disorder called *chloracne,* which can sometimes be long-lasting and painful.

At the cellular level, it is now known that TCDD induces the production of a number of enzymes, and this activity is correlated with binding of the TCDD molecule to a specific protein that has been isolated from various kinds of cells. It seems that TCDD acts in the same way that a hormone does. As shown in Figure

Dibenzo-p-dioxin

(commonly named Dioxin)

2,3,7,8-Tetrachlorodibenzo-p-dioxin

(commonly named TCDD)

2,4,5-Trichlorophenol

2,4,5-Trichlorophenoxyacetate

(a herbicide commonly named 2,4,5-T)

Hexachlorophene

(a germicide)

Octachlorodibenzo-p-dioxin

Pentachlorophenol (a wood preservative)

Figure 4.18   The Formation of Chlorinated Dioxins As By-products of Manufactured Chemicals

Source: A. Poland and A. Kende, *Fed. Proc.* 35 (1976):2404.

4.20, many hormones work by binding to a receptor protein in a specific target cell. The receptor becomes activated upon attachment of the hormone and causes genes on the DNA strand to initiate the production of various enzymes. Presumably, the toxic symptoms of TCDD are caused by mimicking hormonal activity that alters the cell's biochemical apparatus for enzyme production. It is likely that

TCDD

2,3,7,8 - Tetrachlorodibenzofuran

by - product of manufacturing
or formed on incineration

3,4',4,5'- Tetrachlorobiphenyl
(a PCB)

$*$ $1\ \text{Å} = 10^{-10}$ meters

Figure 4.19   Structural Similarity Between TCDD and Other Toxic Chlorinated Organics

Source: A. Poland, Department of Pharmacology, University of Wisconsin, private communication, February 1979.

the binding site of the receptor protein imposes the structural requirements that are needed for a molecule to possess TCDD-like toxicity.

The concern about TCDD and similar molecules is not limited to dramatic accidents. Because they are present as by-products in a variety of large-volume industrial chemicals, they are widely distributed in the environment. Moreover they can be formed when the chemicals or products that contain them are burned. Recent studies indicate that effluents from incinerators can spread detectable amounts of dioxins around the countryside. No one knows whether low-level environmental contamination causes a significant hazard to human health. Part of the problem is that toxic doses are so low that we do not have methods sensitive enough to monitor the buildup of these chemicals in human beings at subtoxic levels.

Figure 4.20 Mechanism of Hormone Function

5 | Contamination by Toxic Metals

Another environmental concern is that metallic elements that are toxic to human beings are being spread around increasingly as a result of industrial production and use. We have all read news stories about the problem of lead poisoning, particularly among city children, contamination of fish by mercury, and the possibility that cadmium may be harmful to our health. These elements occur naturally in the earth's crust and humans have been living with them throughout evolutionary history. However, the amounts of them that are being stirred up and spread around have been increasing greatly with the advance of industrialization.

Many metallic elements are essential to life. The amounts of them that we need, however, are highly variable, and in some cases are extremely small. For these trace elements, it has been difficult to establish that they are indeed essential. Moreover, even the essential elements are toxic if the amount is too high. This is indicated in Figure 4.21, which shows a schematic dose-response curve for an essential element. At zero concentration, the organism for which the curve is plotted cannot grow at all. As the concentration increases, growth increases rapidly but then levels off and starts to decline at concentrations where the

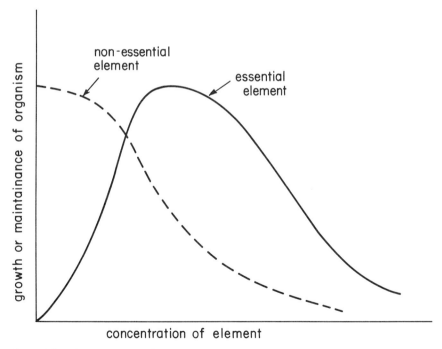

Figure 4.21   Dose-Response Curves for Essential and Nonessential Elements in Metabolic Processes

Table 4.4 Physiological Effects of Lead Poisoning

Symptom	Blood Lead Level (ppm)
1. Interference with heme biosynthesis	
a) Metabolites in urine (δ-aminolevulinic acid)	>0.3
b) Reduced red blood cell production	>0.5
c) Anemia	>0.8
2. Kidney dysfunction	
a) Minimal disorder	>0.5
b) Severe dysfunction	>0.8
3. Permanent nerve and brain damage	>0.8

Source: J. J. Chisholm, *Sci. Am.* 224 (February 1971): 15.

organism can no longer handle the amounts of the element to which it is exposed. The peak of the curve represents the optimum concentration of that element for that particular organism. The dashed curve represents the response of the organism to a nonessential element. Growth declines continuously as the concentration increases from zero. At first the response curve may be fairly flat since the organism may be equipped with mechanisms for eliminating the element in question. But as the machinery for elimination gets overloaded, the toxicity rises and growth diminishes rapidly.

The optimum concentration of the essential elements is highly variable. In the case of iron, for example, the optimum concentration is relatively large. We all carry about 5 g of iron in our body, and it is difficult, although by no means impossible, to take in too much iron. For copper, which is also essential, the optimum level is much lower. We carry only about 80 mg of this element, and copper is quite toxic even at relatively low levels.

For some elements that are known to be toxic, it has only recently been demonstrated that they are also essential. This is true for the element selenium, for example. Selenium has long been known to be poisonous, and cattle that feed on grass that grows in selenium-rich areas become ill. However, it has recently been discovered that selenium provides the body with essential protection against oxidation reactions, and it has been associated with depressed levels of cancer. But the concentrations needed for this protection are very low.

Lead

In the case of lead, we have no indication that the metal fills any essential role in biology and we do know that it is toxic. The physiological effects of lead are outlined in Table 4.4. Lead specifically interferes with the biochemical reactions that lead to the synthesis of the heme group, the iron complex responsible for the binding of oxygen to the transport protein hemoglobin. This interference can be detected at relatively low lead levels, about 0.3 ppm in the blood, because of the buildup of metabolites, substances that are required for the synthesis of heme

Pb bound to EDTA

Pb bound to BAL

Pb bound to d-penicillamine

Lead Removal from Body

$$Ca^{2+}(\text{chelating agent}) + Pb^{2+}$$

body
toxicant

$$Pb^{2+}(\text{chelating agent}) + Ca^{2+}$$

body
nutrient

excreted in
urine

Figure 4.22   Lead Chelating Agents

and cannot be utilized because of the inhibition of key reactions by the lead. The chemical detection of these metabolites, particularly δ-aminolevulinic acid (ALA), provides a sensitive test for lead in the body. At higher levels of lead in the blood, symptoms of anemia can set in due to the deficiency of hemoglobin. More serious is kidney dysfunction, which is also associated with elevated levels of lead. The most serious effects of lead are interferences with nervous tissue. This can lead to brain damage that is permanent unless the lead is quickly removed from the body.

Removal can be accomplished with the help of chelating agents—molecules

Table 4.5 Lead in Urban and Rural Locations
(Manchester, England, 1974)

Type of Locality*	Average Lead Concentration (ppm)
Major roads; moderate/heavy traffic	1,001
Minor roads; light/moderate traffic	888
Streets with very light traffic only	933
Children's playgrounds in urban areas	1,014
Children's playgrounds and parks in rural areas	85

*First four localities are urban areas.
Source: J. P. Day, M. Hart, and M. S. Robinson, *Nature* 253 (January 31, 1975): 343.

with several binding sites for the metal ion. We discussed these agents earlier in connection with the problem of water hardness and detergents. The upper part of Figure 4.22 shows structural diagrams for some chelating agents that have been found to be particularly effective in binding lead. These are fed to the victim of lead poisoning as the calcium chelate. If they were given as the free chelating agent, they would bind calcium in the body and produce calcium depletion. As shown in the lower part of Figure 4.22, lead binds chelating agents more strongly than calcium, and displaces the calcium. The lead chelate is then rapidly excreted in the urine.

At greatest risk from lead poisoning are children in the inner cities. Many older buildings have lead-based paint, which peels from the walls in time. The paint chips are picked up and eaten by infants, particularly those who are undernourished. A good-sized paint chip can provide an infant with a toxic dose of lead. In response to this situation, some communities have set up programs to measure the levels of lead in the blood of ghetto children and to paint over old walls with nonleaded paint.

The problem for city children is not limited to lead-based paints, however. The dust of city streets can sometimes be as rich in lead as are some lead ores. Table 4.5 shows some figures for the industrial city of Manchester, England. High levels of lead were found not only on major roads but on lightly traveled streets as well. Dust in urban playgrounds was found to contain about 1,000 ppm of lead, compared with a concentration of 85 ppm for playgrounds in the country. It is reasonable to expect that children who play in city dust will accumulate substantial amounts of lead. Indeed, a recent study has shown that in some cities 6–8% of preschool children have elevated levels of lead in their blood.

Moonshiners also bear a special risk of lead poisoning. Often backyard stills use old car radiators as condensers, and the hot alcohol vapors gradually dissolve the lead in the solder. Thus, illicit whiskey can contain toxic amounts of lead.

Another source of frequent lead poisoning is pottery that is inadequately fired.

Table 4.6   Respiratory Exposure to Lead and Mean Blood Lead Levels as a Function of Job and Environment

Population	Lead in Air (ppm)	Mean Blood Lead Level (ppm)
Rural United States	0.4	0.16
Urban United States	0.8	0.21
Downtown Philadelphia	1.9	0.24
Cincinnati police officers	1.7	0.25
Cincinnati traffic police	3.0	0.30
Los Angeles traffic police	4.2	0.21
Boston automobile-tunnel employees	5.0	0.30

Source: J. J. Chisholm, *Sci. Am.* 224 (February 1971): 15.

Pottery glaze contains lead compounds to give it the proper flow characteristics. If the glaze is baked on at a high enough temperature in a properly operating kiln, the lead is immobilized and does not easily leach out. If the temperature of the firing is not high enough, however, the lead leaches out into liquids contained in the pottery. Even a hot cup of coffee from a poorly glazed mug can contain significant concentrations of lead. Particularly dangerous are acidic liquids stored in crockery. The acid in fruit juices or soft drinks greatly accelerates the leaching of lead and there have been tragic cases of lead poisoning from this source.

While the dangers of lead poisoning are clear enough, there is controversy about the possible hazards associated with subacute levels of lead. The average concentration of lead in the blood of city dwellers is about 0.2 ppm. This is only a factor of four less than the level at which acute physiological symptoms of lead poisoning can be observed, and to many people a factor of four seems a small margin of safety. Moreover, it is not known whether there may be more subtle effects of chronic exposure to subtoxic amounts of lead. On the other hand, there is no clear evidence that the average lead concentration in blood has been increasing. Table 4.6 shows that there is an association between the amount of lead in blood and exposure to lead in the air. However, the association is fairly weak. The difference in exposure between people who work in the country and those who work in the Boston automobile tunnel is more than a factor of ten, but the difference in the lead levels of blood is only a factor of about two.

The concentration of lead in the blood depends on the rate of excretion as well as on the exposure. Also, lead is deposited in bones, where it replaces calcium. The measured levels of lead in blood do not reflect the amount of lead that is stored in this way. The stored lead can, however, reenter the bloodstream. For example, calcium is mobilized from bone during illnesses that are accompanied by fever. Lead is mobilized along with calcium, and if enough has been stored, lead poisoning can result.

Lead has been spread far and wide in recent years. This is shown graphically in Figure 4.23, which plots the lead content of successive layers of Greenland snow

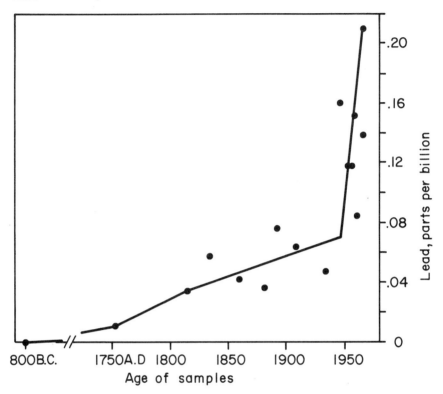

Increase of lead in snow at Camp Century, Greenland, since 800 BC.

Figure 4.23 Lead in the Ecosystem

Source: *Airborne Lead in Perspective* (Washington, D.C.: National Academy of Sciences, 1972), p. 7.

which have been deposited year after year and whose dates are accurately known. There has clearly been a sharp increase in the lead content since 1950. This correlates with the accelerated increase in the lead content of gasoline additives at around the same time. We know that lead emission comes almost entirely from gasoline combustion, as shown in Table 4.7. Therefore, the worldwide spread of airborne lead is quite clearly associated with the use of tetraethyl lead in gasoline. As mentioned earlier, this additive is needed to prevent knocking in gasoline engines. When gasoline is burned, the lead is emitted in fine particles. Most of these settle out rapidly giving city dust its high lead content, but the finest particles travel widely and are also small enough to penetrate the air passages of the lung. As mentioned before, there is considerable pressure to remove lead from gasoline because it poisons the platinum catalysts that are used for the

Table 4.7   Lead Emission in the United States, 1968

Emission Source	Lead Emitted (tons/year)
Gasoline combustion	181,000
Coal combustion	920
Fuel oil combustion	24
Lead alkyl manufacturing	810
Primary lead smelting	174
Secondary lead smelting	811
Brass manufacturing	521
Lead oxide manufacturing	20
Gasoline transfer	36
Total	184,316

Source: *Airborne Lead in Perspective* (Washington, D.C.: National Academy of Sciences, 1972), p. 13.

removal of pollutants in automotive exhausts. The health problems posed by lead provide additional pressures in the same direction.

Mercury

Another toxic metal that has been well publicized is mercury. As indicated in Table 4.8, the toxicity of mercury depends very much on its chemical state. We know elemental mercury as the liquid quicksilver, which is fairly inert and nontoxic if swallowed. The liquid has a significant vapor pressure, however, and the vapor is highly toxic if inhaled. For this reason, liquid mercury should not be handled except in well-ventilated areas, and spills should be quickly cleaned up. The second entry in the table is the mercurous ion, which has two mercury atoms, each with a single positive charge. Mercurous ion forms a rather insoluble compound with chloride ion, and since our stomachs contain a high concentration of chloride, mercurous ion is not very toxic. The mercuric ion, with a double positive charge, is quite toxic. It has a high affinity for sulfur atoms and attaches itself to the sulfur-containing amino acids of proteins. However, it does not move across biological membranes readily and therefore does not easily get inside biological cells. Far more toxic are the organomercury ions, particularly methyl mercury, which are fat soluble and can move across membranes. The diorganomercurials are not themselves toxic, but they can be converted to monoorganomercurials in the envrionment.

The most serious symptom of mercury poisoning is nerve and brain damage, which can easily become irreversible. These symptoms set in at blood levels of about 0.5 ppm for methyl mercury, somewhat lower than the corresponding level for lead. Cases of mercury poisoning have been associated with the consumption of seed grains that have been coated with organomercurial fungicides. If the

Table 4.8   Chemical Forms of Mercury

Molecular Form	Chemical and Biochemical Properties
Hg	Elemental mercury. The liquid is relatively inert and nontoxic. The vapor is highly toxic when inhaled.
Hg_2^{2+}	Mercurous ion. Insoluble as the chloride; low toxicity.
Hg^{2+}	Mercuric ion. Toxic but not easily transported across biological membranes.
RHg^+	Organomercurials. Highly toxic, especially CH_3Hg^+ (methyl mercury); causes irreversible nerve and brain damage; easily transported across biological membranes; stored in fat tissue.
R_2Hg	Diorganomercurials. Low toxicity but can be converted to RHg^+.
HgS	Mercuric sulfide. Highly insoluble and nontoxic. Mercury is trapped in soil in this form.

seeds are planted as they are intended to be, there is no danger of toxicity, since the organomercurial chemicals are broken down in the soil and the mercury is trapped as highly insoluble mercuric sulfide. The danger arises from the misuse of the treated seed grains. In one incident, seed grains shipped from the United States to Iraq were inadvertently diverted to flour mills and baked into bread, leading to many fatalities. In another incident, a New Mexico family fed its pigs treated feed grain. When the slaughtered pig was cooked and eaten by the family, the children suffered brain damage from mercury poisoning. A successful court action brought by the family led to the banning of organomercurials for seed treatment by the U.S. Environmental Protection Agency.

The infamous case of mass mercury poisoning in Minamata, Japan, had a different origin. In this fishing village, a strange disease broke out in the mid-1950s, first among the cats of the village and then among the people. It took some time for the nervous disorders to be traced to mercury poisoning. It was then discovered that the fish in the bay were heavily contaminated with methyl mercury. The Minamata Chemical Company is located on the shore of the bay, and subsequent investigation showed that it was discharging large amounts of mercury but no methyl mercury compounds. The missing link between the discharge of inorganic mercury and the presence in the fish of the organic mercury derivative, methyl mercury, was later filled in by chemical researchers, who discovered that microbes that live in the absence of air and produce methane—the same ones we described earlier in connection with methane digesters—can also convert mercury to methyl mercury. It is the methyl mercury that is passed on up the food chain, as shown in the upper diagram of Figure 4.24. At each level of the aquatic food chain, the mercury concentration builds up strongly, as illustrated in the lower part of the figure. This is true even in uncontaminated waters. Mercury has always been part of our environment, and the biological mercury cycle evolved long before the advent of modern industry. Large fish that were preserved in museums many years ago have been found to contain significant concentrations of mercury. However, mercury pollution markedly increases the concentrations found in each level of the food chain.

The chief sources of mercury pollution have been paper mills and chloralkali plants, which generate chlorine gas by electrolysis using electrodes made of mercury pools. The effluents from these industries leave substantial quantities of mercury in the sediment of nearby lakes and bays. The sediments often contain the methane-producing bacteria that slowly convert the mercury deposits to methyl mercury, which quickly enters the food chain. In these circumstances, the

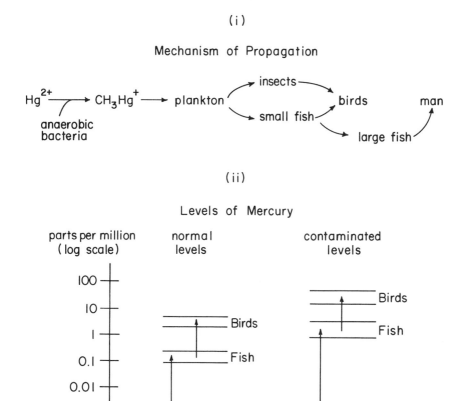

(i)

Mechanism of Propagation

(ii)

Levels of Mercury

Figure 4.24 Propagation of Mercury in Food Chain

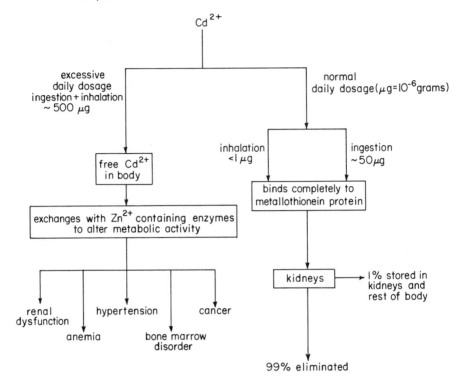

Figure 4.25   Metabolism of Cadmium

Source: Dose data abstracted from L. Friberg, M. Piscator, and G. Nordberg, *Cadmium in the Environment* (Cleveland: CRC Press, 1971), pp. **25, 26.**

Table 4.9   Effect of Effluents from Zinc Mines and Smelting Works on the Concentration of Cadmium in Vegetables (Sasu River Basin, Japan)

Type of Vegetable	Mean Cadmium Concentration (ppm)	
	Control Area	Sasu-Shiine Basin
Rice	0.08	0.37
Bean paste	0.04	0.27
Mushroom	0.1	0.37
Carrot	0.15	0.44
Eggplant	0.1	0.3
Spinach	0.4	0.85
Potato	0.08	0.14
Onion	0.1	0.15

Source: L. Friberg, M. Pisacator, and G. Nordberg, *Cadmium in the Environment* (Cleveland: CRC Press, 1971), pp. 129–32.

fish in the area can have mercury concentrations higher than 20 ppm in their tissues. The victims of the Minamata disease had diets consisting mainly of fish taken from the polluted bay. These fish were subsequently found to have mercury concentrations of 27-102 ppm. Soon after the Minamata disaster, it was discovered that many fish in the Great Lakes had high levels of mercury, and important commercial fisheries had to be closed as a result. Since then new technology has been introduced in almost all mercury-using plants, and this has eliminated most of the mercury in their effluents. However, in many localities the damage has already been done, since the large amounts of mercury already dumped in sediments will continue to be a source of methyl mercury for many years to come. No effective way of cleaning up these sediments has yet been found.

Cadmium

A third heavy metal of current environmental concern is cadmium. At elevated levels, cadmium is known to cause kidney problems, anemia, and bone marrow disorders, and it has been implicated as a cause of hypertension and possibly cancer. Again, cadmium is a natural part of our environment. Indeed, the body seems to have a natural defense against cadmium in the form of a small protein called *metallothionein,* which is found in the kidneys and binds cadmium quite effectively. Most cadmium that is ingested is, therefore, trapped in the kidney and eliminated, as shown in Figure 4.25. A small fraction of the cadmium normally ingested is stored in the body, however, and gradually accumulates with increasing age. In its chemical properties, cadmium is similar to zinc, which is an essential element found at the active sites of many enzymes. It seems likely that when an excessive amount of cadmium is ingested so that the metallothionein-binding capacity is exceeded, cadmium then competes with zinc at key enzymatic sites.

Because of its chemical similarity, cadmium occurs naturally in association with zinc minerals. Zinc mining and smelting operations disperse a substantial amount of cadmium into the environment. Growing plants have a requirement for zinc, and many of them take up and concentrate cadmium with the same biochemical apparatus. The only known outbreak of environmental cadmium poisoning also occurred in Japan, in the Sasu River Basin. Many people in the area developed a painful condition called the "itai itai," or "ouch ouch," disease, in which their bones became fragile and subject to numerous fractures. As shown in Table 4.9, it was found that the crops in the area had greatly elevated levels of cadmium as a result of irrigation with river water that contained effluents from a variety of mining and smelting operations. While no other outbreaks of this type have been observed elsewhere, with the increasing use of zinc and cadmium in industry, the levels of cadmium in the environment have been increasing and are a cause for concern.

6 | Cancer

While there are numerous toxic effects, both acute and long-term, associated with different chemicals, the most dreaded is cancer. This disease is now responsible for almost one-fifth of all deaths in the United States. Only heart disease takes more lives. Moreover, there is a strong likelihood that most cancers have environmental causes. The most striking evidence for this comes from the patterns of the incidence of cancer in different parts of the body in different countries. Figure 4.26 shows that Japanese people have much higher death rates from

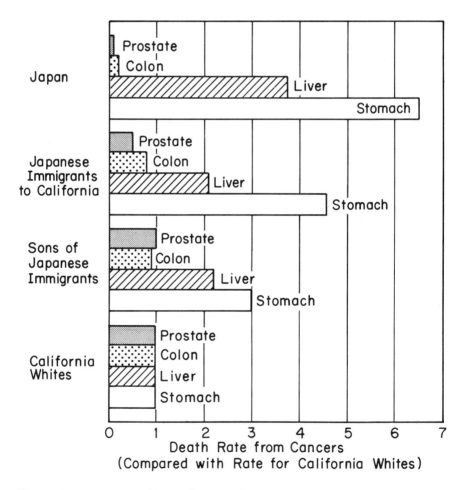

Figure 4.26 Change in Incidence of Various Cancers with Migration from Japan to the United States

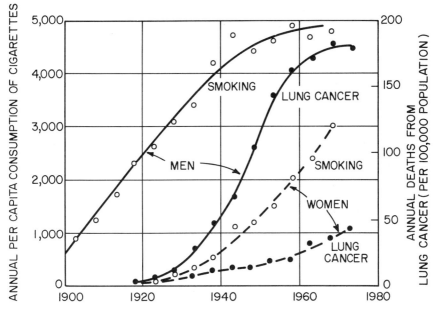

Figure 4.27 Cigarette Smoking and Lung Cancer

stomach and liver cancer and lower rates from colon and prostate cancer than do white residents of California. These differences are much less pronounced in Japanese immigrants to California, while their children show a pattern still closer to that of native Californians. Since genetic factors are the same for Japanese immigrants to California and for Japanese people who remain in Japan, these differences clearly indicate an environmental origin. One presumes that there are some factors in the living arrangements, possibly in the diet or the drinking water or the atmosphere, that are different in Japan than in California and account for the observed changes. At the moment, we have no idea what these factors are.

We do know the most probable cause of lung cancer, which is currently the most common form of cancer and accounts for one-fifth of all cancer deaths. Figure 4.27 shows the marked correlation between the increase in cigarette smoking among men early in the century and the incidence of lung cancer some 20 years later. A similar correlation is now emerging among women who started smoking later and whose incidence of lung cancer is now on the rise. The time delay is a characteristic of cancer and is one of its most insidious properties. It often takes 20 years or longer for a cancer to develop, making it difficult to trace the cause. This also means that if we are exposing ourselves to a new cancer-causing agent, we might not know about it for more than 20 years.

Many chemicals are capable of causing cancer. Laboratory tests show wide differences in the carcinogenicity of various chemical agents when applied to

Table 4.10 Chemicals Recognized as Human Carcinogens

Chemical Mixtures	Site of Cancers
Soots, tars, oils	Skin, lungs
Cigarette smoke	Lungs
Industrial chemicals	
2-Naphthylamine	Urinary bladder
Benzidine	Urinary bladder
4-Aminobiphenyl	Urinary bladder
Chloromethyl methyl ether	Lungs
Nickel compounds	Lungs, nasal sinuses
Chromium compounds	Lungs
Asbestos	Lungs
Arsenic compounds	Skin, lungs
Vinyl chloride	Liver
Drugs	
N,N-bis(2-chloroethyl)-2-naphthylamine	Urinary bladder
Bis(2-chloroethyl)sulfide (mustard gas)	Lungs
Diethylstilbestrol	Vagina
Phenacetin	Renal pelvis
Naturally occurring compounds	
Betel nuts	Buccal mucosa
Aflatoxins	Liver
Potent carinogens in animals to which human populations are exposed	
Cyclamates	Bladder
Sterigmatocystis	Liver
Cycasin	Liver
Safrole	Liver
Pyrrolizidine alkaloids	Liver
Nitroso compounds	Esophagus, liver, kidney, stomach

Source: C. Heidelberger, "Chemical Carcinogenesis," *Annu. Rev. Biochem.* 44 (1975): 81.

animal species such as mice and rats. Similar patterns probably apply to humans, although extrapolations from laboratory studies to predictions about human beings is one of the most troublesome questions in cancer research. In other cases we know that chemicals can cause cancer in humans from tragic experience. Epidemiologic studies can implicate chemicals as cancer-causing agents either because of a high incidence of cancer observed in an occupationally exposed group, or because the chemical causes a specific and rare type of cancer that can be traced back to the source of exposure. Table 4.10 gives a list of chemical carcinogens along with the types of cancer they produce. The chemicals cover a wide range of types, with a few obvious similarities. Some are industrial chemicals, some are drugs, and others occur naturally. For example, the aflatoxins which are found naturally in peanuts that are infested with certain molds, are highly carcinogenic.

We do not know in detail how chemical carcinogens produce cancer, but as shown in Figure 4.28, it is likely that they attack the genetic material in the nuclei

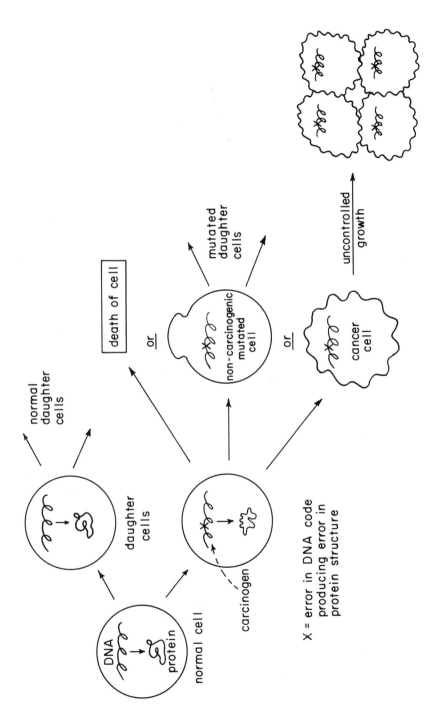

Figure 4.28 Effect of a Chemical Carcinogen on Cell Growth

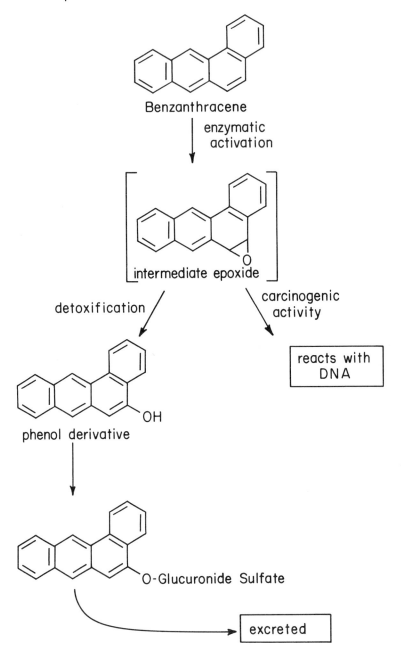

Figure 4.29   Activation of Polycyclic Aromatic Hydrocarbons

Source: C. Heidelberger, "Chemical Carcinogenesis," *Annu. Rev. Biochem.* **44** (1975):87.

of cells, the DNA molecules. The DNA contains the genetic code, which specifies the chemical sequence of proteins as well as other DNA molecules. Cells reproduce by duplicating their DNA and then dividing in two. Damage to the DNA can result in a mistake in the genetic code. Most often this results in the death of the cell, but if the cell survives, the mistake can be passed on to the daughter cells when the DNA is copied. This is called a *mutation*. If a mutation occurs in a germ cell that gives rise to an offspring of the organism, all the progeny will carry the same coding error, which may be expressed as an alteration in some functions of the organism.

Cancer is a condition in which a cell grows and divides uncontrollably, invading normal body tissues. The mechanisms that control its growth are evidently impaired, and this is thought to result from damage to the DNA. It is known from laboratory studies on insects and bacteria that chemicals that are known to induce cancer usually are effective at producing mutations as well. In fact, tests for mutagenicity in bacteria are coming to play an important role in screening chemicals as potential carcinogens.

Most cancer-producing chemicals have to be activated in the organism to express their carcinogenic properties. This is illustrated in Figure 4.29 for the

Figure 4.30 Activation of Dimethylnitrosamine in the Body

compound benzanthracene. This is a member of the class of polycyclic aromatic hydrocarbon compounds that are found in tars and on fossil fuel soot and are known to be highly effective in producing cancers. Yet benzanthracene by itself is not particularly effective at inducing mutations in bacteria. It becomes mutagenic, however, if it is activated by enzymes from animals. Apparently the chemical must first be oxidized, probably to the epoxide intermediate shown in brackets in the figure. This intermediate can react through two different pathways. It may react with DNA to induce mutations or cancer. Alternatively, the epoxide may react to form the phenol product shown, which has an oxygen atom bonded to the aromatic ring. This oxygen atom is the point of attachment for making another derivative called a *glucuronide sulfate,* which the body is able to excrete. This biochemical reaction scheme represents an enzymatic detoxification mechanism for benzanthracene and for many other foreign organic compounds as well. Such compounds are not soluble in water and are stored in the fat until they can be activated in this manner to produce a water-soluble derivative that can be excreted. It is one of nature's ironies that the same activation mechanism can produce cancer if the activated molecule first reacts with DNA.

The upper part of Figure 4.30 shows a similar activation scheme for dimethylnitrosamine. Again, reaction with oxygen produces an intermediate, which in this case can transfer a positively charged methyl group, called a *methyl cation,* to the DNA. Nitrosamines are powerful carcinogens and are of increasing concern because of the possibility that they can be formed in the stomach from common constituents of the diet. The lower part of Figure 4.30 shows that sodium nitrite can react with dimethylamine and hydrochloric acid to produce dimethylnitrosamine. Dimethylamine and other similar amines are present in meats and fish, and hydrochloric acid is a natural constituent of gastric juice. Sodium nitrite is a widely used preservative, particularly in bacon, hot dogs, and other cured meats. While no direct link has been established between these products and cancer, there is clearly cause for concern; and the use of sodium nitrite is currently under review.

7 | Conclusion

We have seen that the biosphere too has its natural balances, which can be upset by human intervention. World agricultural production has become precariously tied to fossil fuel energy, and it needs to be weaned away from this dependence through less energy-intensive practices and alternate energy forms. The widespread application of chemical pesticides has produced ecological imbalances, and the need for more selective methods of pest control is increasingly recognized. The human organism is a marvelously balanced biochemical system that can maintain itself in the face of substantial environmental fluctuations. Over the long term, however, it does require a nutritionally balanced diet, and it is endangered by the buildup of toxic substances, by-products of industrial activity, which threaten to overwhelm its defenses. A particularly insidious danger is the loss of control of cellular division, leading to the growth of cancerous tissue. We need to know much more about how chemicals induce cancer in order to arrive at preventive measures.

This brings us to the end of the book, although we have certainly not exhausted the subject. Much more could be written and much more needs to be learned about all the environmental issues we have touched on. We hope we have given some concept of the scope of these issues and of the many interrelationships among them in the setting provided by the chemistry of the natural world that we inhabit.

Problem Set

Problems 1 and 2 refer to the following table:

Grams of Proteins of Corn and Beans Required to
Give Daily Requirement of Essential Amino Acids

	Corn	Beans
Tryptophan	70.0	47.9
Lysine	72.2	33.0
Threonine	37.5	44.3
Leucine	27.4	44.8
Isoleucine	49.0	39.3
Valine	38.8	44.9
Phenylalanine	35.0	39.3
Methionine	33.3	56.4

1. Given that corn consists of 7.8% protein and only 60% of it is absorbed by the digestive tract, calculate the number of grams of corn that must be ingested for an adequate protein intake. There are 368 kilocalories in 100 g of corn. How many calories must be consumed daily in order to get adequate protein? Given that the average American consumes 2,000–3,000 kcal daily, can an all-corn diet supply the proper balance of protein and energy?

2. Given that beans are 24% protein and 78% of the protein is absorbed by the digestive tract, calculate the number of grams of corn and beans that must be consumed to supply adequate protein for a person whose diet is half corn and half beans. If there are 338 kcal in 100 g of beans, calculate the number of calories consumed in this diet. (see problem 1 for additional data for corn.)

3. In 1970 a total of about 2.9 million kilocalories were consumed by farmers to raise an acre of corn (equivalent to 80 gallons of gasoline). This amount includes energy for labor, fuel, seeds, and chemicals. If the average solar flux during the growing season (100 days) is 245 w/m^2, how much solar energy reaches an acre of corn during this time? About 1.26% of this is converted into corn and about 0.4% into corn grain (at 100 bushels per acre). What is the total amount of energy stored in the corn? If half the energy of the corn residue is retrieved by biogasification, is there enough energy for the farmer to raise the crop?

4. a) In 1975 the United States produced 27.1 million metric tons (1 metric ton = 1,000 kg) of vegetable protein suitable for human use. Of this, 91% was fed to livestock to produce 5.3 million metric tons of animal protein. Calculate the efficiency of conversion of vegetable protein to animal protein.

   b) Assuming that humans need 60 g of protein per day, how many people could have been fed in 1975 on the surplus vegetable protein, if Americans decreased their meat consumption by 10%.

5. By planting legumes between corn rows in late August and plowing this "green manure" under in early spring, 133 pounds of nitrogen per acre can be added to the soil. The total energy cost for legume seeds and fuel requirements is 90,000 kcal/acre. Calculate the saving in energy relative to the amount of inorganic nitrogen fertilizer applied if the Haber process requires 8,000 kcal/pound of fixed nitrogen. The total amount of energy needed to grow an acre of corn, excluding the 133-pound nitrogen requirement, is 2×10^6 kcal. What percentage of the total energy budget can be conserved by using legumes rather than inorganic nitrogen?

6. a) Consider a *para*-substituted phenyldiethylphosphate insecticide of the following form:

$$X-\langle\underline{}\rangle-O-\overset{\overset{\textstyle O}{\|}}{P}(OC_2H_5)_2$$

   Why does the toxicity of the insecticide increase as the electron-withdrawing capacity of X increases?

   b) The electronegativity value of P is 2.1, that of S is 2.5, and for O it is 3.5. Using these facts, explain why phosphorothionate insecticides (containing phosphorus-sulfur double bonds rather than phosphorus-oxygen double bonds) are unreactive with cholinesterase but are activated in the insect's body by oxidizing enzymes. What advantage is there to using sulfur-containing insecticides?

7. Suppose a fruit fly is being killed with an insecticide. However, one out of a million fruit flies possesses an enzyme that breaks down the insecticide into nontoxic metabolic products. Assume that as the normal fruit flies quickly die off, the population of the resistant flies increases geometrically (i.e., 1, 2, 4, 8, . . .). If a new generation occurs every 23.5 days, in how many days will the fruit fly population be restored?

8. Ample evidence indicates that cancer is largely an environmental disease. However, the body is not a passive partner in the induction of the disease. Using benzanthracene and dimethylnitrosamine as examples (Figures 4.29 and 4.30), explain how the body actively participates in its own destruction.

9. Relate how mercury accumulation in the food chain led to the Minimata disaster. Why is the conversion to methyl mercury the key step in mercury toxicity?

10. Summarize the biochemical mechanism whereby chlorinated dioxins and PCBs can upset hormone function in animals. Why are the geometric dimensions of the molecule so important?

11. The chemistry of cadmium is quite homologous to that of zinc, and it replaces zinc with great facility in enzymes. However, the activity of cadmium-substituted enzymes differs greatly from that of the normal zinc-containing ones. To illustrate this, data are presented below for cadmium substitution in the zinc-containing enzyme, carboxypeptidase. This digestive enzyme catalyzes two different hydrolysis reactions as shown:

peptide bond hydrolysis

$$\sim N - \underset{\underset{H}{|}}{\overset{\overset{H}{|}}{C}} - \underset{R_1}{\overset{\parallel}{C}} - N - \underset{\underset{H}{|}}{\overset{\overset{H}{|}}{C}} - \underset{R_2}{\overset{\parallel}{C}} - O^{\ominus} + H_2O \longrightarrow \sim N - \underset{\underset{H}{|}}{\overset{\overset{H}{|}}{C}} - C\overset{\nearrow O}{\underset{O^{\ominus}}{}} + {}^{\oplus}H_3N - \underset{R_2}{\overset{\overset{H}{|}}{C}} - C\overset{\nearrow O}{\underset{O^{\ominus}}{}}$$

ester bond hydrolysis

$$R_1 - \overset{O}{\overset{\parallel}{C}} - OR_2 + H_2O \longrightarrow R_1 - C\overset{\nearrow O}{\underset{O^{\ominus}}{}} + HO - R_2 + H^{\oplus}$$

Plot the data for the two reactions given in the following table. Graph both plots on the same axes. Label the y-axis "% Cd substituted." Use the x-axis twice, once to plot peptidase activity and once to plot esterase activity. Draw the best straight line through the points.

% Cd Substituted	Relative Peptidase Activity	% Cd Substituted	Relative Esterase Activity
0	7.5	0	1.1
50	3.2	50	1.4
75	1.9	75	1.6
90	0.8	100	1.7
97	0.2		

Data taken from J. E. Coleman and B. L. Vallee, *J. Biol. Chem.* 236 (1961): 2244.

Suggestions for Further Reading

Nitrogen Cycle

Delwiche, C. C. "The Nitrogen Cycle." *Sci. Am.* 223 (September 1970):136.
Skinner, K. J. "Nitrogen Fixation." *Chem. Eng. News,* October 4, 1976, p. 22.
Brill, W. J. "Biological Nitrogen Fixation." *Sci. Am.* 236 (March 1977):68.
Brill, W. J. "Nitrogen Fixation: Basic to Applied."*Am. Sci.* 67 (July–August 1979):458.
Eady, R. R., and Postgate, J. R. "Nitrogenase." *Nature* 249 (1974):805.
Hardy, R., Burns, R., and Parshall, G. "Bioinorganic Chemistry of Dinitrogen Fixation." In *Inorganic Biochemistry,* vol. 2, edited by G. L. Eichhorn. New York: Elsevier Science, 1973.

Aleem, M. "Oxidation of Inorganic Nitrogen Compounds." *Annu. Rev. Plant Physiol.* 21 (1970):67.

Payne, W. J. "Reduction of Nitrogenous Oxides by Microorganisms." *Bacteriol. Rev.* 37 (1973):409.

Miyata, M., and Mori, T. "Studies on Denitrification." *J. Biochem.* 60 (1969):463.

Delwiche, C. C., and Bryan, B. A. "Denitrification." *Annu. Rev. Microbiol.* 30 (1976):241.

Nutrition and Food Production

Deathrage, F. E. *Food for Life.* New York: Plenum Press, 1975.

Sanders, H. J. "Nutrition and Health." *Chem. Eng. News,* March 26, 1979, p. 27.

Zelitch, I. "Photosynthesis and Plant Productivity." *Chem. Eng. News,* February 5, 1979, p. 28.

Miller, K. R. "The Photosynthetic Membrane." *Sci. Am.* 241 (October 1979):102.

Food and agriculture issue of *Scientific American* 235 (September 1976).

Food issue of *Science* 188 (May 9, 1975). Also published along with other articles in Abelson, P. H., ed. *Food: Politics, Economics, Nutrition and Research,* Science Compendium. Washington, D.C.: American Association for the Advancement of Science, 1975.

Steinhart, J., and Steinhart, C. "Energy Use in the U.S. Food System." *Science* 184 (1974):307.

Pimentel, D., et al. "Food Production and the Energy Crisis." *Science* 182 (1973):443.

Pimentel, D., Dritschilo, W., Krummel, J., and Kurtzman, J. "Energy and Land Constraints in Food Protein Production." *Science* 190 (1975):754.

Johnson, W. A., Stolzfus, V., and Craumer, P. "Energy Conservation in Amish Agriculture." *Science* 198 (1977):373.

Wortman, S. "Agriculture in China." *Sci. Am.* 232 (June 1975):13.

Revelle, R. "Energy Use in Rural India." *Science* 192 (1976):969.

Brink, R. A., Densmore, J., and Hill, G. A. "Soil Deterioration and the Growing World Demand for Food." *Science* 197 (1977):625.

Eckholm, E. P. *Losing Ground; Environmental Stress and World Food Prospects.* New York: W. W. Norton Co., Inc., 1976.

Lerza, C., and Jacobsen, M., eds. *Food for People, Not for Profit.* New York: Ballantine Books, Inc., 1975.

Lappé, F. M., and Collins, J. *Food First.* New York: Ballantine Books, Inc., 1978.

Insecticides and Neurochemistry

White-Stevens, R., ed. *Pesticides in the Environment,* vol. 1, parts I and II. New York: Marcel Dekker, Inc., 1971.

Eto, M. *Organophosphorus Pesticides: Organic and Biological Chemistry.* Cleveland: CRC Press, 1974.

Casida, J. "Insecticide Biochemistry." *Annu. Rev. Biochem.* 42 (1973):259.

Matsumura, F., Boush, G., and Misato, T. *Environmental Toxicology of Pesticides.* New York: Academic Press, 1972.

Kupfer, D. "Effects of Pesticides and Related Compounds on Steroid Metabolism and Function," *CRC Crit. Rev. Toxicol.* 4, no. 1 (1975):83.

Street, J. C. "Organochlorine Insecticides and the Stimulation of Liver Microsome Enzymes." *Ann. NY Acad. Sci.* 160 (1969):274.

Peakall, D. B. "Pesticides and the Reproduction of Birds." *Sci. Am.* 222 (April 1970):72.

Kaiser, K. "Pesticide Report: The Rise and Fall of Mirex." *Environ. Sci. Technol.* 12 (May 1978):520.

Weber, J. "The Pesticide Scorecard." *Environ. Sci. Technol.* 11 (August 1977):756.

Edwards, C. A. *Persistent Pesticides in the Environment,* 2nd ed. Cleveland: CRC Press, 1973.

Crosby, D. G. "The Fate of Pesticides in the Environment." *Annu. Rev. Plant Physiol.* 24 (1973):467.

Williams, P. P. "Metabolism of Synthetic Organic Pesticides by Anaerobic Microorganisms," *Residue Rev.* 66 (1977):63.

Stevens, C. F. "The Neuron," *Sci. Am.* 241 (September 1979):54.

Keynes, R. D. "Ion Channels in the Nerve-Cell Membrane," *Sci. Am.* 240 (March 1979):126.

Lester, H. A. "The Response to Acetylcholine," *Sci. Am.* 236 (February 1977):106.

Snyder, S. H. "Opiate Receptors and Internal Opiates," *Sci. Am.* 236 (March 1977):44.

Snyder, S. H. "The Brain's Own Opiates," *Chem. Eng. Bews,* November 28, 1977, p. 26.

Organic and Inorganic Toxic Chemicals

Kimbrough, R. D. "The Toxicity of Polychlorinated Compounds and Related Chemicals," *CRC Crit. Rev. Toxicol.* 2, no. 4 (1974):445.

Nisbet, I. C. T. "Criteria Document for PCB's," Environmental Protection Agency, 440/76-021, 1976.

"Subcommittee on the Health Effects of PCB's and PBB's, Final Report," Washington, D.C.: Department of Health, Education and Welfare, 1976.

Rawls, R. "Italy Seeks Answers Following Toxic Release," *Chem. Eng. News,* August 23, 1976, p. 27.

Walsh, J. "Seveso: The Questions Persist Where Dioxin Created a Wasteland," *Science* 197 (1977):1064.

Thomasson, W. A. "Deadly Legacy: Dioxin and the Vietnam Veteran," *Bull. Atom. Sci.* 35 (May 1979):15.

Vallee, B. L., and Ulmer, D. D. "Biochemical Effects of Mercury, Cadmium, and Lead," *Annu. Rev. Biochem.* 41 (1972):91.

Clarkson, T. W. "Recent Advances in the Toxicology of Mercury with Emphasis on the Alkylmercurials." *CRC Crit. Rev. Toxicol.* 1 (1972):203.

Chisholm, J. J. "Lead Poisoning." *Sci. Am.* 224 (February 1971):15.

Wessel, M., and Dominski, A. "Our Children's Daily Lead." *Am. Sci.* 65 (May–June 1977):294.

Fox, J. L. "Research Solving Body's Detoxifying System." *Chem. Eng. News,* June 4, 1979, p. 24.

Gillette, J. R., Davis, D. C., and Sasame, H. A. "Cytochrome P450 and Its Role in Drug Metabolism." *Annu. Rev. Pharmacol.* 12 (1972):57.

Ridley, W. P., Dizikes, L. J., and Wood, J. M. "Biomethylation of Toxic Elements in the Environment." *Science* 197 (1977):329.

Wood, J. M. "Biological Cycles for Toxic Elements in the Environment." *Science* 183 (1974):1049.

Poland, A., and Kende, A. "2,3,7,8-Tetrachlorodibenzo-*p*-dioxin: Environmental Contaminant and Molecular Probe." *Fed. Proc.* 35 (1976):2404.

Suess, M. J. "The Environmental Load and Cycle of Polycyclic Aromatic Hydrocarbons." *The Science of the Total Environment* 6 (1976):239.

Carter, L. "Chemical Plants Leave Unexpected Legacy to Two Virginia Rivers." *Science* 198 (1977):1015.

Hartung, R., and Dinman, B., eds. *Environmental Mercury Contamination.* Ann Arbor, Mich.: Ann Arbor Science Publications, 1972.

Friberg, L., Piscator, M., and Nordberg, G. *Cadmium in the Environment.* Cleveland: CRC Press, 1971.

Goldwater, L. J. "Mercury in the Environment." *Sci. Am.* 224 (May 1971):15.

"Airborne Lead in Perspective." Washington, D.C.: National Academy of Sciences, 1972.

Murray, C. "EPA Criticized for Chemical Wastes Handling." *Chem. Eng. News,* November 13, 1978, p. 18.

Pojasek, R. B. "Disposing of Hazardous Chemical Wastes." *Environ. Sci. Technol.* 13 (July 1979):810.

Murray, C. "Chemical Waste Disposal, A Costly Problem." *Chem. Eng. News,* March 12, 1979, p. 12.

Maugh, T. "Toxic Waste Disposal, A Growing Problem." *Science* 204 (1979):819.

Maugh, T. "Hazardous Wastes Technology Is Available." *Science* 204 (1979):930.

Maugh, T. "Incineration, Deep Wells Gain New Importance." *Science* 204 (1979):1188.

Maugh, T. "Burial Is Last Resort for Hazardous Wastes." *Science* 204 (1979):1295.

Cancer

Cairns, J. "The Cancer Problem." *Sci. Am.* 233 (November 1975):64.

Miller, E. C., and Miller, J. A. *Molecular Biology of Cancer,* edited by H. Busch. New York: Academic Press, 1974.

Croce, C., and Koprowski, H. "The Genetics of Human Cancer." *Sci. Am.* 238 (February 1978):117.

Setlow, R. B. "Repair Deficient Human Disorders and Cancer." *Nature* 271 (February 23, 1978):713.

Nicolson, G. L. "Cancer Metastasis." *Sci. Am.* 240 (March 1979):66.

Heidelberger, C. "Chemical Carcinogenesis." *Annu. Rev. Biochem.* 44 (1975):81.

Epstein, S. "Cancer and the Environment." *Bull. Atom. Sci.* 33 (March 1977):22.

Weisburger, E. K. "Natural Carcinogenic Products." *Environ. Sci. Technol.* 13 (March 179):278.

Maugh, T. "Chemical Carcinogens: How Dangerous Are Low Doses?" *Science* 202 (1978):137.

Maugh, T., "Chemical Carcinogens: The Scientific Basis for Regulation." *Science* 201 (1978):1200.

"Public Policy: Chemicals and Cancer." *Chem. Eng. News,* January 16, 1978, p. 34.

"News Forum: Should the Delaney Clause Be Changed?" *Chem. Eng. News,* June 27, 1977, p. 24.

Devoret, R. "Bacterial Tests for Potential Carcinogens." *Sci. Am.* 241 (August 1979):40.

McCann, J., and Ames, B. N. "A Simple Method for Detecting Environmental Carcinogens as Mutagens." *Ann. NY Acad. Sci.* 271 (1976):5.

Fox, J. L. "Ames Test Success Paves Way for Short-Term Cancer Testing." *Chem. Eng. News,* December 12, 1977, p. 34.

Ames, B. N. "Identifying Environmental Chemicals Causing Mutations and Cancer." *Science* 204 (1979):587.

APPENDIX

Units of Energy and Radiation

1. Forms and units of energy.
    a) Heat and work are interconvertible forms of energy.
        (1) *Heat* is energy that flows from one body to another because of a difference in their temperatures. Common units of heat energy are:
            (i) One calorie* is the heat needed to raise the temperature of 1 g of water 1° C (specifically, from 14.5 to 15.5° C, since the heat capacity of water varies somewhat with temperature).
            (ii) One British thermal unit (Btu) is the heat needed to raise the temperature of 1 lb of water 1° F (from 63 to 64° F).
        (2) *Work* is energy that is transmitted when a force acts against a resistance to produce motion. Work = force × distance, and force = mass × acceleration. Common units of work energy are:
            (i) One erg is the work done by a force that accelerates a 1-g mass at 1.0 cm/sec² for a distance of 1 cm.
            (ii) One joule is the work done by a force that accelerates a 1-kg mass at 1.0 m/sec² for a distance of 1 m.
            (iii) One foot-pound (ft-lb) is the work done by a force of 1 lb (a 453.59-g mass accelerated at 32.1740 ft/sec²) over a distance of 1 ft.
    b) Kinetic and potential energy; Power.
        (1) Kinetic energy (K) is the work that a body can do by virtue of its motion:

$$K = \frac{1}{2} \text{(mass)} \times \text{(velocity)}^2$$

        (2) Potential energy is the work that a system of bodies is capable of doing by virtue of the relative position of its parts, that is, by virtue of its configuration (e.g., water falling from a height or chemicals reacting in a battery).

*Nutritionists use the Calorie (capital C), which equals 1,000 calories, or 1 kilocalorie (kcal).

223

(3) *Power* is the rate at which work is done. Power = work/time. Common units of power are:

    (i) 1 watt (w) = 1 joule/second

    (ii) 1 horsepower = 33,000 ft-lb/minute

(Note: power × time = work; hence, watts × seconds = joules; watts × hours = 3,600 joules; and 1 kilowatt-hour (kwh) = 3.6×10^6 joules.)

c) Radiant energy. Energy is also caused by light waves. The photons of electromagnetic radiation have no rest mass and travel with a constant velocity, depending only on the medium (air, water, glass, etc.). In a vacuum (empty space), the velocity of light is $c = 3 \times 10^{10}$ cm/second. The oscillations of the light wave are measured by the wavelength, λ (in meters or subunits of meters), or by the frequency, $\nu = c/\lambda$ (in cycles per second, cps or hertz). The energy of a light wave is directly proportional to its frequency, $E = h\nu$, where h is Planck's constant, 6.626×10^{-27} erg·second. Often the frequency is expressed in wave numbers, $\bar{\nu} = 1/\lambda$, leaving out the velocity of light.

The electromagnetic spectrum covers a wide range of wavelengths, from radiowaves (λ in meters) through microwaves (centimeters), infrared waves (micrometers), ultraviolet waves (tenths of micrometers), x-rays (angstroms, i.e., atomic dimensions), and γ rays (thousandths of angstroms, i.e., nuclear dimensions). The visible region of the spectrum, to which the human eye responds, is quite narrow, from about 0.4 μ (blue light) to about 0.7 μ (red light). This is also the region of maximum sunlight intensity.

d) Some useful units and conversion factors:

    (1) Length: meters (m)

        1 meter = 10^{-3} kilometer (km) = 10^2 centimeter (cm) = 10^3 millimeter (mm) = 10^6 micrometer (μm or μ) = 10^9 nanometer (nm) = 10^{10} angstrom (Å)

    (2) Mass: grams (g)

        1 gram = 10^{-3} kilogram (kg) = 10^3 milligram (mg) = 10^6 microgram (μg) = 10^9 nanogram (ng) = 10^{12} picogram (pg)

    (3) Temperature: Degrees Kelvin or absolute (°K) = degrees centigrade (°C) + 273. Degrees Farenheit (°F) = (9/5)°C + 32

    (4) Energy: As we have seen, there are many units of energy, relating to the different forms that energy can take:

        calorie: This is the basic unit of heat energy. Chemists are accustomed to using calories or kilocalories (kcal). Nutritionists use Calories, which are actually kilocalories.

British thermal unit (Btu): This unit of heat energy is used in engineering practice.

$$1 \text{ Btu} = 252 \text{ calories}$$

joule: This is the basic unit of work and has been adopted as the fundamental unit of energy of the International System of Units.

$$1 \text{ calorie} = 4.184 \text{ joules}$$

kilowatt-hour (kwh): This unit is used in measuring electrical energy production or consumption.

$$1 \text{ kwh} = 3.6 \times 10^6 \text{ joule} = 860.4 \text{ kcal}$$

cm^{-1}: The energy of light waves is proportional to their frequency, which is usually expressed as the wave number ($\bar{\nu} = 1/\lambda$) in cm^{-1}. For example, green light with 500-nm wavelength has a wave number, or "energy," of $(500 \times 10^{-7} \text{ cm})^{-1} = 20,000 \text{ cm}^{-1}$. It is possible to relate the wave number to the equivalent quantity of heat, or chemical energy per mole of photons; thus

$$1 \text{ kcal/mol} = 349.8 \text{ cm}^{-1}$$

electron volts (ev): This unit is commonly used by physicists in describing radiation and elementary particles. It is the amount of energy acquired by any charged particle that carries unit electronic charge when it falls through a potential difference of 1 v. It can be related to the equivalent wave number of electromagnetic radiation:

$$1 \text{ ev} = 8,064.9 \text{ cm}^{-1}$$

A multiple of this unit that is commonly used is the megaelectron volt $= \text{Mev} = 10^6 \text{ ev}$.

2. Units of radiation. Radiation is measured in different ways, depending on the purpose of the measurement. The *curie* is a unit of radiation *rate:* One curie corresponds to 3.7×10^{10} radioactive disintegrations per second.

The *roentgen* is a unit of radiation exposure that specifies what radiation *would do:* One roentgen is the intensity of radiation that, on passing through 1 cm^3 of dry air (at 0° C and 1 atm pressure), would create 1 electrostatic unit (esu)* of positively charged ions and 1 esu of negatively charged ions.

The *rad* is a unit of absorbed dose. It describes what radiation *has done:* One rad is the amount of radiation that deposits 100 ergs of energy per gram of tissue. (It happens that 1 roentgen of radiation deposits about 100 ergs of

---

*1 esu = 2.08×10^9 times the charge of a single electron.

energy in 1 g of biological tissue, so exposure to 1 roentgen is equivalent to a 1-rad dose.)

The *rem* (roentgen-equivalent-man) is a unit of biological dose, based on the rad, multiplied by a modifying factor to allow for the biological effectiveness of different kinds of radiation:

$$1 \text{ rem} = 1 \text{ rad} \times M$$

M is taken to be unity for β and γ rays, but is assigned a value of 10–20 for α rays, depending on their energy, to allow for the higher density of damage.

Index

Absorption of solar radiation, by ozone, 81, 83
Acetylcholine, 184-85, 188
Acid mine drainage, 131, 133
Acid rain: composition of, 129-31; effect of on fish, 130, 132; increased mineral leaching from, 131; from tall smokestacks, 113-14
Acids, definition of, 127-28
Action spectrum, 84
Activated carbon: in industrial wastewater treatment, 154-55; in tertiary sewage treatment, 151, 152; in treatment of drinking water, 159
Activated charcoal. *See* Activated carbon
Activated sludge. *See* Sewage sludge
Activation barrier: for carbon , 93-95; for NO oxidation, oxidation, 96-97
Aflatoxin, 210
Agriculture in poor countries, 171-75; water pollution from, 159-161
Air, composition of, 71-72
Airplanes, energy efficiency of, 53, 54
Albedo, 1-2; effect of human activities on, 69-70
Aldrin, 183, 185
Algae, in lake productivity, 138, 139
Alpha rays: damage to biological tissue from, 28-29; definition of, 19, 20
Alum (aluminum sulfate): in drinking water treatment, 158; in phosphate removal, 144
Aluminosilicate clays: as builder, 136, 137; in neutralization of rain, 129-30; in oil spills, 147
Aluminum, recycling of, 56, 57
Amino acids: essential amino acids, 177, 178; frequency; of 178
Ammonia: from catalytic converter, 110; from nitrogenase enzyme, 167-68
Ammonia stripping, 151, 152; energy requirements for, 152
Ammonium nitrate. *See* Fertilizer

Animal, wastes of. *See* Cattle feedlots
Anion exchangers, synthetic, 155
Anthracite coal, 16, 17
Aquifer: depletion of by coal industry, 18-19; pollution of by fertilizer, 161; U.S. reserves of, 125, 127
Aromatic hydrocarbons, as lead substitute in gasoline, 110
Asbestos, health effects of, 176
Atmosphere: density profile of, 80, 82; lapse rates in, 80-81, 82; temperature profile of, 80-81, 82; *See* also Troposphere; Stratosphere
Atmospheric window, 72-73; and CFM spectra, 76, 77
Automobile emissions: air to fuel ratio in, 107, 108; chemical composition of, 107, 108; control of, 108-113; from diesel engines, 118; relation of carbon monoxide to, 98, 99; relation of to smog, 107-8
Avogrado's number, 127

Base: definition of, 127-28. *See* also pH
Benzanthracene, as carcinogen, 212, 213-14
Benzo(a)pyrene, as constituent of soot, 118
Beta rays: damage to biological tissue from, 29-30; definition of, 19
Bicarbonate ion. *See* H_2CO_3, Calcium carbonate
Binding energy curve, 19, 20
Biochemical energy, 95
Biochemical oxidation, 95
Biogasification, 45, 46; in Third World agriculture, 174
Biomass as sink for CO_2, 74, 76
Birds, DDT contamination of, 182, 183
Bituminous coal: geographical distribution of, 16-17; sulfur content of, 16-17; pyrites in, 18; grinding of, 18
Black body radiation. *See* Hot body radiation

227

Black lung disease, 18, 117
BOD (biological oxygen demand): of domestic sewage, 148, 149; of feedlots, 161; of manufacturing, 148, 149; of secondary effluent, 149
Breeder reactions, 24-25
Breeder reactor: components of, 24-26; with thorium, 28
Builders, 136, 137
Buried plant matter: atmospheric oxygen from, 3; fossil fuels from, 3
Buzzard's Bay, Massachusetts, 147

$CaCO_3$. *See* Calcium carbonate
Cadmium: effect of on fish, 146; toxicity of, 206-7
Calcite. *See* Calcium carbonate
Calcium, causing water hardness, 133
Calcium carbonate, in neutralization of rainwater, 129, 130
Cancer: from benzo(a)pyrene, 118; body's role in formation of, 212, 213-14; from chemicals, 209-10; as environmental disease, 208-9; of lungs from asbestos, 118; from nitrosamines, 213, 214; of skin, from UV radiation, 83-85; from smoking, 209. *See also* Carcinogenic chemicals; Mutations
Carbamates: decomposition of, 184, 187; insect resistance to, 185, 188; mechanism of action of, 184, 188; toxicity of, 184-85
Carbohydrate: as body nutrient, 175, 176; energy stored in, 3, 175
Carbon, as lake nutrient, 140, 141. *See also* Activated carbon
Carbon dioxide: acidity of rain from, 128-29; barrier to formation of, 93-95; biomass as sink for, 74, 76; greenhouse effect from, 72-76, 79, 80; increase of from burning fossil fuel, 3, 74, 75; oceans as sink for, 74, 76; sources of, 74, 76; stability of relative to CO, 96, 97. *See also* greenhouse effect
Carbonic acid. *See* H_2CO_3
Carbon monoxide: annual emission of in U.S., 97-98; from automobile emissions, 97-99, 107-8; control of in catalytic converters, 108-10; health effects of, 98, 100, 101; oxidation of, 96, 97; reaction of with hemoglobin, 98, 100; stability of at high temperature, 96, 97
Carcinogenic chemicals, listing of, 210
Catalytic converter, 108-10
Catalysts: in Haber process, 169; in water-splitting reaction, 43, 45, 46

Cation exchangers, synthetic, 155
Cattle feedlots: methane from, 45; pollution from. 161
Cesium-137: as health problem, 29, 30
CFMs (chlorofluoromethanes): ban of, 92-93; in ozone destruction, 90-92; as cause of greenhouse effect, 76-77
CH_4, scavenger of chlorine atoms, 92. *See* also Methane; Natural gas
Chain reaction, 23, 24
Chelating agents: as antidote for lead poisoning, 199-200; in builders 136, 137
Chemical energy: from photosynthesis, 3; from electricity, 43, 44
Chemical scrubbers for SO_2 removal, 114, 116
Chesapeake Bay, kepone contamination of, 190-091
China, petroleum reserves, 9
Chloracne, 193
Chloralkali plants, mercury contamination from, 205
Chlorinated hydrocarbons: dioxin-like, 192-95; in drinking water, 159; effect of on fish, 146; at Love Canal, 191; removal of from water, 155, 159. *See* also Organochlorinic pesticides; TCDD
Chlorination; of drinking water, 158-59; in sewage treatment, 152
Chlorine atom: from CFMs, 91, 92; in ozone destruction, 90-92; removal of by methane, 92
Chloroform, removal of from drinking water, 159
Cigarette smoking, lung cancer from, 209
Clays. *See* Aluminosilicate clays
Climate, human impacts on, 79
CO. *See* Carbon monoxide
CO_2. *See* Carbon dioxide
Coal: geographic distribution of, 16, 17; heating values of, 16; sulfur content of, 16, 17; types of, 16; U.S. reserves of, 11,12; worldwide reserves of, 13, 14
Coal conversion. *See* Coal gasification; Coal liquefaction
Coal-fired plants, efficiency of, 48
Coal gasification: hydrogen demand in, 14, 18; sulfur removal in, 14-15; water demand in, 14, 18
Coal liquefaction: direct catalytic hydrogenation, 15, 16; Fischer-Tropsch chemistry, 15, 16; methanol synthesis, 15, 16
Coal mining: acid mine drainage from, 131, 133; hazards from, 18
Combustion, 94, 95

Commercial heating. *See* Home and commercial heating
Conservation of energy. *See* Energy conservation
Consumption of petroleum, by four largest consumers, 8-9, 10
Control rods, 24, 25, 26
Coolant: in pressurized light water reactor, 24; in breeder reactor, 26
Cooling towers, 49, 50
Cooling water: effect on aquatic life, 49; use of in U.S., 125, 126
Copper: as essential nutrient, 198; as oxidation catalyst, 94, 95
Core meltdown of nuclear reactor, 31
Corn, yields of with fertilizer use, 169-71
Cosmic rays, radioactivity from, 30
Crop rotation, 169, 170
Crude oil: refining of, 6,7

DDT: accumulation of in environment, 182; hazards of, 182; insect resistance to, 183, 184, 185, 188; mode of action of, 181-82
Deforestation, 174
Denitrifying bacteria: in nitrogen cycle, 168-69; in sewage treatment, 153; as source of N_2O, 88
Depletable energy resources in the United States, 10-13
Depletion allowances for primary ores, 57
Detergent, 134-36; as source of phosphate 141, 143, 144
Deuterium-deuterium fusion reactions, 34, 35
Deuterium-tritium fusion reaction, 34, 35
Developing countries, agriculture in, 171-75
Dibenzofurans, chlorinated, 192, 195
Dieldrin, 183, 185
Diesel engine, particulates from, 118
Diet: protein balance of, 179, 180
Dioxin, 192, 194. *See* also TCDD
DNA, damage to from cancer, 210-14
D_2O: as fusion fuel, 34
Domestic sewage treatment, 148-50; sludge disposal from, 149; tertiary treatment, 149, 151, 152-54
Drinking water: effect of nitrate pollution on, 161; treatment of, 158-159
Dry cooling tower, 49, 50
Dump sites for toxic wastes, 191

Earth, radiation from. *See* Terrestrial radiation
Efficiency. *See* Energy efficiency

Eggshell fragility from DDT, 182
Electrical transmission, problem of, 43
Electricity: efficiency of, 48-49, 52, 53; from hydrogen, 43, 44; from nuclear energy, 23, 24-26; from ocean thermal gradients, 42; from solar energy, 38, 40-41; sources and flow of through U.S. economy, 52, 53, 54; use of waste heat from generation of, 54-56; from wind, 41-42
Electrodialysis, 156-57, 158
Electrolysis of water, 43, 44, 45, 46
Electrostatic precipitators, 118
Emphysema, 117
Energy: consumption of and standard of living, 51, 53; sources and flow of through U.S. economy, 52, 53. *See* also Coal Fusion reactors; Nuclear power; Petroleum; Solar energy
Energy balance of earth. *See* heat balance of earth
Energy conservation: with heat pump use, 54, 55; with industrial process heat use, 56; by recycling, 56-58; with use of waste heat from electricity generation, 54-56. *See* also Energy efficiencies
Energy efficiencies: electricity production, 48-49, 53; electric resistance heating, 54; heat pumps 54, 55; household and commercial heating, 53, 54; recycling, 56; total energy use in U.S., 52, 53; transportation, 53, 54. *See* also First law efficiency; Second law efficiency
Energy fluxes on earth's surface, 1-2
Energy growth curves: for U.S. and world consumption, 4-5; for U.S. petroleum production, 7-8; for worldwide petroleum production, 8-9
Energy in manufacturing, 56, 57
Energy reserves in the United States, 10-13
Enzymes: acetylchlorinesterase, 184, 188; carcinogenic activation by, 212, 214; DDT-ase, 183, 184; nitrogenase, 168, 169; replacement of zinc in, by cadmium, 207
Equilibrium constant, for water ionization, 127, 128
Erosion: from agriculture, 159-60; in developing world, 174
Essential amino acids, 177, 178
Essential elements, dose-response for, 197-98
Euphotic zone, 138
Eutrophication, 137-44
Evolution of atmospheric oxygen, 3
Exponential growth, doubling periods of, 4, 50

Famine, 173
Fats: nutritional need for, 175, 176; storage of DDT in, 182
Ferric chloride, for phosphate removal, 144
Fertilizer: high cost of, 170; increased yields from, 169-72; increase in N_2O from, 168-69; industrial production of, 168-69; role of in Green Revolution, 171-74; sewage sludge as source of, 149; water pollution from, 159-61
Filtration in water purification, 154, 155, 159
Fischer-Tropsch reaction, 15-16
Fish: contamination of by kepone, 190-91; effect of acid rain on, 130, 132; effect of ocean dumping on, 144-47; effect of power plants on, 49
Fission: induced, 23, 26; spontaneous, 19, 21. See also Chain reaction; Nuclear power; Nuclear weapons
Fission products: disposal of, 33; radioactivity from, 29-30
Fixed nitrogen. See Nitrogen fixation
Food chain: DDT accumulation in, 182, 183; methyl mercury accumulation in, 204-205
Food consumption, 4
Food production: in the developing world, 171-75; effect of fertilizer on, 169-71; effect of nuclear war on, 90; effect of temperature change on, 79; role of nitrogen cycle in, 167-69
Fossil fuels: causing increase in atmospheric CO_2, 3, 74, 75; consumption of in 1975, 4. See also Coal; Petroleum; Natural gas; Shale oil
Free radicals: as cause of engine knocking, 110-11; as hydrocarbons in smog formation, 104-7. See also Hydroxyl radicals
Freight, energy efficiency of, 53, 54
Freight rates: for modes of transport, 53, 54; for recyclable materials, 57, 58
Fuel cell, 43, 44
Fuel rods, 23, 24, 25
Fusion energy, reserves of in the U.S., 12, 34
Fusion reactions, 34, 35
Fusion reactors: environmental hazards of, 37; laser implosion, 36, 37; magnetic containment, 34, 36

Gamma rays: damage to biological tissue from, 29-31; defitinition of, 19
Gas centrifuge isotope seperation, 26
Gaseous diffusion isotope separation, 26

Gasoline: from Fischer-Tropsch reaction, 15-16; lead pollution from, 202-3; from oil refining, 6, 7
Geothermal energy: global flux of, 2; U.S. reserves of, 11, 12
Grain: high yielding varieties, 172-73; traditional varieties, 172-73
Great Lakes, mercury pollution in, 207
Greenhouse effect: absorption of terrestrial radiation due to, 72-73, 74; from CFMs, 76-77; projected trend in, 79, 80. See also Carbon dioxide
Green Revolution, 171-73
Gross national product, relation of to energy consumption, 51, 53
Groundwater: use of in irrigation, 161; U.S. reserves of, 125, 127. See also Aquifer
Growth curves. See Energy growth curves

Haber process, 168, 169
Half-life: of fission products, 29-30; of plutonium, 19, 21, 22; of tritium, 34
Hard coal. See Anthracite coal
Hardness of water, 130, 133; in precipitation of soap, 135, 136
H_2CO_3, in natural acidity of rain, 128-29. See also Calcium carbonate
Heat balance of earth: effect of atmospheric particles on, 70-71; effect of change in albedo, 69-70; effect of energy use on, 49-50, 69
Heating energy. See Home and commercial heating; Industrial process heat
Heat pump, efficiency of, 54, 55
Heavy water. See D_2O
Hemoglobin: effect of carbon monoxide on, 98, 100; effect of lead on, 198-99
HNO_2. See Nitrous acid
HNO_3. See Nitric acid
HO2. See Hydroperoxyl radical
H_2O: greenhouse effect of, 72-73, 74, 76. See also Water
Home and commercial heating: efficiency of, 52, 53-54, 55; with heat pumps, 54, 55; by solar energy, 38, 39; from waste heat of electricity generation, 54, 55, 56
Hormone: effect of DDT on, 182; TCDD interference with, 193-94, 196; use of in pest control, 189-90
Hot body radiation: peak wavelength of, 67-68; rate of, 67-68
Hunger, 173
Hydrocarbons. See Unburned hydrocarbons
Hydroelectric power, U.S. reserves of, 12, 13

Hydrogen: bubble at Three Mile Island, 31; directly from sunlight, 43, 44; in fertilizer production, 169, 170; need for in coal conversion, 14-15, 18; for storing energy, 43-45; from thermochemical cycle, 56
Hydrogenation of coal: to methane, 13-15; to liquid fuels, 15-16
Hydrogen economy, 43, 45
Hydrogen sulfide,. See H₂S
Hydrologic cycle, energy of, 2
Hydrolysis, of nonpersistent pesticides, 184, 187
Hydroperoxyl radical, in smog formation, 105, 107
Hydrophilic character: of carbohydrates, 175; in detergents, 135

Hydrophobic character, in detergents, 135
Hydropower, U.S. reserves of, 12, 13
Hydroxyl radical: formation of in stratosphere, 88, 89; reaction with nitrogen oxides, 88, 89; in smog formation, 107

Ice Ages, 78-79
Ice caps, melting of, 50, 70
Incineration: dioxins from, 196; of sludge, 149
India: DDT levels in, 182; plutonium bomb of, 27
Induced fission, 23, 24, 25
Industrial wastes, dumping of, 191, 192, 193
Industrial process heat, combined with electricity generation, 56
Industrial wastewater treatment, 155-58
Industry: energy use in U.S., 52, 53, 56; water use in U.S., 125, 126
Infrared radiation: absorbed by carbon dioxide and water, 72-73, 74; absorbed by CFMs, 76-77; emitted by earth's surface, 67-68
Insecticides, water pollution from, 159-60. See also Carbamates; DDT; Kepone contamination; Organochlorine pesticides; Organophosphate pesticides
Iodine-131, radioactivity from, 29-30
Ion exchange resins, synthetic, 155
Ionizing radiation. See Radioactivity
Iraq, mercury poisoning in, 204
Iron: as biochemical oxidation catalyst, 95; as essential element, 198
Irrigation: cadmium contamination from, 207; pollution from, 161; use of in U.S., 125, 126

Isotopes: definition of, 19; enrichment of, 26. See also Gas centrifuge; Gaseous diffusion isotope separation; Lasers, isotope enrichment of

Juvenile hormones, 189-190

K⁺, blocking of flow of, by DDT, 181
Kepone contamination, 190-91
Knocking in gasoline engines, 110

Lakes: effect on fishlife from acid rain, 130, 132; effects of phosphates on, 140-44; limiting nutrient in, 141, 142, 143, 144; U.S. reserves of, 125, 127
Lake Tahoe, 152
Landfills: for sludge disposal, 149. See also Dump sites for toxic wastes
Lapse rate, profile of in atmosphere, 80-81, 82
Lasers: as fusion reactors, 36, 37; in isotope enrichment, 27
Latent heat of water, 2
Lead: antidote for, 199-200; effect of on fishlife, 146; exposure to, 200-202; from gasoline, 110, 202, 203; physiological effects of, 198, 199, 201
Legumes: as cover crop, 159; fixed nitrogen from, 169
Lignite coal, 16, 17
Lime, for removing phosphates, 144, 151, 152
Limestone scrubbers in SO₂ removal, 114, 116
Limiting nutrient in lakes, 141, 142, 143, 144
Limits to energy growth, 4-5, 50
Little Ice Age, 78
Liquefaction. See Coal liquefaction
Lithium: in fusion reactions, 34, 35; in fusion reactors, 34, 36, 37
Los Angeles smog, 81, 101, 102, 107
Love Canal, 191, 192, 193
Lung cancer; from asbestos, 118; from cigarette smoking, 20
Lysine, deficiency of in cereals, 180

Magnesium: causing water hardness, 130, 133
Magnetic containment reactor, 34, 36
Malaria, control of with DDT, 181, 182
Malathion, 185, 186
Manchester, England, lead in city dust of, 200

Manure: as fertilizer, 169, 170-71, 174; methane from, 45, 46. *See* also Cattle feedlots
Mass transit, efficiency of, 53, 54
Meat, protein content of, 178; as waste of biological energy, 180
Mediterranean fruit fly, control of, 190
Meltdown, of nuclear reactor core 31
Melting of polar ice caps, 50, 70
Membrane techniques in wastewater treatment, 155-58
Mercury: in lake sediments, 205, 207; Minamata disaster due to, 204, 205, 207; poisoning from organomercurial fungicides, 203-4; sources of pollution from, 205-7; toxic forms of, 203, 204
Metabolism, 175
Metallothionein, 207
Metals, as oxidation catalysts, 113, 114. *See* also Iron
Methane: from biological gasification, 45, 46, 149, 161; production of in poor countries, 174; use of in fertilizer production, 168, 169. *See* also CH_4; Coal gasification; Natural gas
Methanol: from coal, 15, 16; from urban wastes, 47
Methionine, deficiency of in beans, 179, 180
Methoxychlor, 181
Methyl mercury. *See* Mercury
Mexico, petroleum reserves in, 9, 10
Micelles, 134, 135
Middle East, petroleum reserves in, 9, 10
Minamata, Japan, 204, 207
Mitochondrion, in respiration, 94, 95
Moderator, 24
Molina, M.J., 92
Moonshine whiskey, lead poisoning from, 200
Müller, Paul, 181
Municipal sewage, effect of kepone on, 190-91. *See* also Domestic sewage
Municipal water supplies, U.S. use of, 125, 126. *See* also Drinking water
Mutations, in carcinogenesis, 211, 213

N_2. *See* Nitrogen
Na+, blocking flow of by DDT, 181
Natural gas, reserves of in U.S., 11, 12. *See* also Coal gasification; Methane
Neptunium-239 in breeder reactor, 25
Nerve gas, 184
Nervous system, effect of pesticides on, 181, 184, 188
Net primary productivity, 3
Neurotransmitter, 184

Neutrons: damage to fusion reactors from, 37; role of in fission reactors, 23, 24, 25, 26; ratio of, to protons, 19, 22
New England, acid rain in, 129-30, 131
New York Bight, 146
NH_3. *See* Ammonia; Fertilizer
Nitrate: as lake nutrient, 141; water pollution by, 160, 161
Nitric acid, as sink for NO_2, 88
Nitric oxide. *See* NO
Nitrifying bacteria, in sewage treatment, 153
Nitrogen: as lake nutrient, 140, 141, 142; resistance to oxidation, 93
Nitrogenase 168, 169
Nitrogen cycle, 167, 168
Nitrogen dioxide. *See* NO_2
Nitrogen fixation: by bacteria and algae, 167, 168; by Haber process, 168, 169
Nitrogen oxides. *See* NO, NO_2, N_2O
Nitrosamines, 161, 213, 214
Nitrous acid: as sink for NO, 88,89
Nitrous oxide. *See* N_2O
NO: in atomobile emissions, 107, 108; high temperature formation of, 95-97; from nuclear explosions, 90; in ozone destruction, 87-88, 89; removal of in catalytic converter, 108-10; removal of from stratosphere 88, 89; in smog formation, 101-7, 108; sources of, 88, 89; from supersonic aircraft, 88-90; U.S. emissions of, 97, 98
NO_2: absorption of solar radiation by, 104, 105; in automobile emissions, 107, 108; formation of from NO, 96, 97; in ozone destruction, 87-88, 89; removal of from stratosphere, 88, 89; in smog formation, 101-7, 108
N_2O from increased fertilizer use 168-69; from microbial action, 88, 89, 168-169; as source of NO in stratosphere, 88, 89
Nonpersistent pesticides, 183-84; 187
Norway, acid rain in, 129, 130, 131, 132
NTA (nitrilotriacetate): as builder 136-37; hazards of, 136
n-type semiconductor, 38, 40 Nuclear chain reaction, 23, 24
Nuclear decay, 19, 21, 22
Nuclear power: accident from, 31; accident insurance for, 31-32; breeder reactor for, 24-26; fuel cycle in, 32-33; fuel reprocessing in, 33; fuel reserves for, in U.S., 11, 12; plant efficiency for, 49; pressurized lightwater reactor for, 23, 24; radioactivity from normal operation of, 30; waste disposals for, 33. *See* also

Fission; Isotopes; Plutonium;
Radioactivity; Uranium
Nuclear weapons, 23, 26–28; radioactivity
from, 29; reduction in ozone layer from,
90
Nucleons, 19–20
Nutrient cycle of lakes, 138, 139

O_2. See Oxygen
Ocean: chemical dumping in, 146; as CO_2
sink, 74, 76; effect of temperature
change on, 80; petroleum contamination
of, 146–47; primary productivity in,
144–46; for sludge disposal, 149
Ocean thermal gradients: amount of energy
available to U.S. from, 11, 12, 13;
electricity generation from, 42
Offshore oil drilling, effect of on oceans,
146–47
OH. See Hydroxyl radical
Oil. See Petroleum
Oil shale. See Shale oil
Oil spills, 146–47
Oligotrophic lake, 138
Organic farming, 170–71
Organic wastes: as energy source in U.S.,
12, 13; methanol from, 47
Organochlorine pesticides, 183, 185;
removal of from wastewater, 154, 155.
See also Chlorininated hydrocarbons;
DDT
Organophosphate pesticides: degradation
of, 184, 187; insect resistance to, 185,
188–89; mechanism of action of, 184,
188; toxicity of, 184–85
Oxidation. See Combustion; Free radicals;
Oxygen; Respiration
Oxygen, reactivity of, 93–97
Ozone: absorption of ultraviolet light by,
83; depletion of from CFMs, 90–93;
depletion of from fertilizer use, 169;
depletion of from nuclear weapons, 90;
depletion of from supersonic transport,
88–90; destruction of by nitrogen
oxides, 87–90; in drinking water
treatment, 158; formation reactions of in
stratosphere, 85–87; heating of stratosphere
by, 81; relation of to skin cancer, 83–85;
in smog formation, 104, 105, 106

PAH. See Polycyclic aromatic
hydrocarbons
PAN (peroxyacetylnitrate), 101, 103, 106,
107
Paper, recycling of, 56, 57

Paper mills, as source of mercury pollution,
205
Particles: climatic effects due to 70–71,
77–78; control of, 118; from diesels,
118; from human activity, 70; light
scattering from, 70–71; from natural
sources, 70; respiratory problems from,
113, 115, 117–18; as sulfuric acid
aerosol, 113, 114; toxic chemicals from,
117–18; U.S. emissions of, 97–98
PCBs, 192–93, 195. See also Chlorinated
hydrocarbons
Persistent chemicals: DDT 182; other
organochlorines, 183
Pesticides, water pollution from 159, 160.
See also Carbamates DDT; Kepone
contamination; Organochlorine
pesticides; Organophosphate pesticides
Petroleum: contamination of oceans by,
146–47; overreliance of Third World
agriculture on, 173–74; refining of, 6, 7;
U.S. reserves of, 6–8, 10. See also Fossil
fuels
pH: of acid rain, 129–30, 131; definition of,
127, 128; of lakes, 129, 130, 132; of
oceans, 129; of rain, 128–29
Phenols, toxic by-products from
chlorinated derivatives of 192, 194
Pheromones, 189–90
Phillippines, agricultural research institute
in, 172
Phosphates: as cause of eutrophication,
141–43, 144; in detergents, 136, 137,
143; mobilization of from lake
sediments, 143–44; removal of, 144, 151,
152
Photochemical energy: in electrolysis, 43,
45, 46; in photosynthesis, 3, 45–47
Photosynthesis: as energy source for U.S.,
12, 13; response of to increase in CO_2,
76; response of to ozone depletion, 90;
in origin of atmospheric oxygen, 3;
stored energy in, 3. See also Chlorophyll
Photovoltaic cell, 38, 40, 41
Photovoltaic effect, 38
Phytoplankton in lake productivity, 138,
139
Pipelines, efficiency of, 53, 54
Platinum in catalytic converters, 109, 110
Plutonium: in breeder, 25–26; cancer from,
29; disposal of, 33; half-life of 19, 21,
22; radioactivity from, 29; in weapons,
26–27
Polar ice caps, melting of, 50, 70
Polycyclic aromatic hydrocarbons,
carcinogenic activation of, 212, 214. See
also Benzo(a)pyrene

Potassium ion. *See* K⁺
Pottery, lead poisoning from, 200–201
Precipitation. *See* Rainfall
Pressurized light water reactor, 23, 24
Price-Anderson Act, 32
Primary production: in lakes, 140, 141; in oceans, 144–46; in plants, 3
Proteins: amino acids in, 177–80; complementarity of, 179, 180; nitrogen cycle in production of, 167, 168; in nutrition, 175–80; structure of, 175, 176, 177; wasteage of in meat production, 180
p-type semiconductors, 38, 40
Pyrites in coal, 18

Radiating body. *See* Hot body radiation
Radiation balance of earth. *See* Heat balance of earth
Radicals. *See* Free radicals
Radioactivity: background level of, 30; decay of, 33; health hazards from, 28–30; of reactors, 30–31; from reprocessing, 33; from uranium mining, 32; from waste disposal, 32
Radium: cancer from 32; in uranium mining, 32
Radon: cancer from, 32; in uranium mining, 32
Railroads, efficiency of, 53, 54
Rainfall: distribution of, 125, 126; effect of greenhouse effect on 76; energy of, 2; acidity of, 128–29. *See also* Acid rain
Recycling, energy saved from, 56, 57
Refining petroleum, 6, 7
Renewable energy resources in the U.S., 10–13
Reprocessing nuclear fuel, 33
Residential heating. *See* Home and commercial heating
Respiration, in carbon cycle, 3
Reverse omosis, 156
Rice, in Green Revolution, 172–73
Roland, F.S., 92
Runoff: from acid rain, 131; in contamination of ocean, 146; of nitrates, 161; in sewage treatment, 154

Salt domes for nuclear waste disposal, 33
Sasu River Basin, Japan, cadmium poisoning in, 206, 207
Secondary treatment of sewage, 148–50
Second law of thermodynamics, power plant efficiency due to, 48

Sediments: mercury in, 205, 207; mobilization of phosphates from, in lakes, 143–44; role of in ocean spills, 147
Selenium, human need for, 198
Semiconductors: amorphous type, 41; n-type, 38, 40; p-type, 38, 40; silicon, 38, 40, 41
Seveso, Italy, TCDD poisoning in, 191
Sewage sludge, 149
Sewage treatment. *See* Domestic sewage treatment; Industrial wastewater treatment
Shale oil, reserves of in the U.S., 11, 12
Sillicate clays. *See* Aluminosilicate clays
Silicon solar cells, 38, 40, 41
Skin cancer, 83–85
Sludge. *See* Sewage sludge
Smog: chemistry of, 101–7; control of, 107–13
SO₂. *See* sulfur dioxide
Soap, 133–36. *See also* Detergent
Sodium carbonate as builder 136, 137
Sodium ion. *See* Na⁺
Sodium nitrate, formation of nitrosamines from, 213, 214
Sodium silicate as builder, 136, 137
Soft coal. *See* Bituminous coal
Soil:as filter in sewage treatment, 153–54; reactions of with rainwater, 129, 130
Solar cell. *See* Semiconductors; silicon solar cell
Solar energy: to avert thermal pollution, 50; for electricity generation, 38, 40–42; flux of, on earth, 1–2, 67, 68; for home heating, 38, 39; indirect forms of, 41–42; for photochemical energy storage, 3; for photogeneration of hydrogen, 43, 45, 46; use of in Third World agriculture, 174–75; U.S. supply of, 10, 11, 12, 37–38
Solar radiation: absorption of by NO₂, 102, 104, 105; absorption of by ozone, 83; effect of particles on, 70–71; relation to earth's temperature, 77–78; spectral distribution of, 67–68
Solar stoves 174–75
Soot: as catalyst for SO₂ oxidation, 113, 114; as source of polycyclic aromatic hydrocarbons, 117, 118, 214; toxic substances in, 117–18
Spontaneous fission, 19, 21
Standard of living and energy consumption, 51, 53
Steel recycling, 56, 57
Stefan-Boltzmann law, 67–68
Sterilization, in insect control, 190

STP (sodium tripolyphosphate) 136, 137.
See also Phosphate
Stratified charge engine, 112
Stratosphere, 81-82
Streamflow, for cooling power plants, 49;
uses of in U.S., 125-27
Strip mining, 18
Strontium-90, 29
Strontium titanate electrolysis cell, 43, 45,
46
Subbituminous coal, 16, 17
Sulfur dioxide: acid rain from, 114; air
quality, standard for, 17; catalytic
oxidation of, 113-14; from coal
burning, 17-18; control of, 113, 114,
116; formation of sulfuric acid aerosol
from, 113, 114; health effects resulting
from, 113, 115; high temperature
stability of, 96, 97; U.S. emission of,
97, 98
Sulfuric acid: from acid mine drainage, 131,
133; atmospheric formation of aerosol,
113, 114; as by-product of coal
gasification, 14-15; cause of acid rain
by, 114, 129-30, 131
Sun. See Solar energy
Sunburn, 83-84
Supersonic aircraft, ozone depletion from,
88-90
Surface layer of ocean, in ocean thermal
gradients, 11, 42
Surfactants, as detergents, 134, 135
Sweden, energy consumption of compared
to U.S., 53; pH of rain in, 129-30, 131
Symbiosis between nitrogen-fixing bacteria
and plants, 169, 175
Synapse between nerve cells, 184
Synthetic resins, wastewater treatment by,
155

2,4,5-T (2,4,5-trichlorophenoxyacetate),
192, 194
TCDD (tetrachlorodibenzo-p-dioxin),
191-96
Temperature: effect of greenhouse effect
on, 76, 77, 79, 80; effect of particles on,
70-71, 77-78; natural fluctuations of
78-79
Temperature inversion, 81
Terrestrial radiation, 67-68; absorption of
by carbon dioxide and water, 72, 73;
absorption of by CFMs, 75, 77
Tertiary treatment of sewage, 149, 151-154;
energy for, 152-53; land use for, 153-54
Tetraethyl lead in gasoline, 110-11, 202,
203

Thermal pollution: effects of, 49-50, 69;
from electricity generation, 48-49
Thermal stratification, in lakes, 138, 139
Thermosphere, 81
Third World. See Developing countries,
agriculture in
Thorium: to avert nuclear proliferation, 28;
in breeder reactor, 28
Three Mile Island nuclear accident, 31
Tidal energy: natural flow of, 2; U.S.
supply of, 12, 13
Toxic metals: 197-207; on soot, 117-18
Toxic organic chemicals, 190-96. See also
Cancer; Carbamates; Chlorinated
hydrocarbons; DDT; Organochlorine
pesticides; Organophosphate pesticides
Toxic wastes, dump sites for, 191, 193
Transportation energy, efficiency of, 53, 54
Tritium: in fusion reactions, 34, 35; in
fusion reactors, 34, 36, 37; health
hazards of, 37
Tropopause, 81, 82
Troposphere 81
Trucks, efficiency of, 53, 54
Tryptophan, 178

Ultrafiltration, 156
Ultraviolet light: absorption of ozone by,
83; in ozone formation 85-87; plant
damage from, 90; reaction of with
CFMs, 91, 92; skin cancer from, 83-85
Unburned hydrocarbons: in automobile
exhaust, 107-8; control of from
automobile exhaust, 108-13; in smog
formation, 101-7; U.S. emissions of, 97,
98
United States; energy flow in, 52, 53;
energy resources of, 10-13; 1978
National Energy Act of, 58; recycling
policy of, 57-58; reserves of water in,
125-27
Uranium-235: energy concentrated in, 24;
enrichment of, 26; induced fission of,
23; in nuclear bomb, 26-27; in
pressurized light water reactor, 23, 24;
reprocessing of, 33; spontaneous fission
of, 19, 21; U.S. reserves of, 10, 11, 12
Uranium-238: in breeder reactor, 24-26;
reprocessing of, 33; U.S. reserves of, 10,
11, 12
Uranium mining, hazards of, 32, 33
Urban wastes. See Organic wastes

Visible light, spectrum of, 67, 68
Volcanoes, particles from, 70, 77-78

Waste disposal from nuclear power, 33
Waste electrical heat: as consequence of second law of thermodynamics, 48-49; thermal pollution from, 48-50; uses of, 54-56
Waste heat in U.S. energy use, 52, 53,
Water: acid, base solutions of, 127, 128; demand for in coal gasification, 14, 18; uses of, 125-127. U.S. reserves of 125, 127. See also Drinking water, Eutrophication; Hardness; H₂O; Lakes, Ocean; Rainfall
Water-splitting reaction: by electrolysis; 43, 44; by photoassisted electrolysis, 43, 45, 46; by thermochemical cycle, 56
Weapons proliferation. See nuclear weapons
Western U.S. coal deposits: environmental problems in exploitation of, 18, 19;

reserves of, 16, 17, 18; sulfur content of, 16, 17 18
Wet cooling tower, 49, 50
Wheat: amino acid content of, 178; complementarity of with beans, 179, 180; role of in Green Revolution, 172-73
Wien's law, 67, 68
Wind power, 41-42; U.S. energy potential of, 11, 12
Wood, misuse of in Third World, 174

X-rays, radioactivity from, 30

Zeolite, as builder, 136, 137
Zinc mining, cadmium contamination from, 207